Traded Options

Second Edition

Other titles in the *Millard on . . .* Series

Traded Options

Second Edition

Brian J. Millard

JOHN WILEY & SONS

Chichester • New York • Weinheim • Brisbane • Singapore • Toronto

First edition published as *Traded Options Simplified* by Qudos Publications, 1989

This edition copyright © 1997 by John Wiley & Sons Ltd,
Baffins Lane, Chichester,
West Sussex PO19 1UD, England

National   01243 779777
International   (+44) 1243 779777
e-mail (for orders and customer service enquiries):
cs-books@wiley.co.uk
Visit our Home Page http://www.wiley.co.uk
or http://www.wiley.com

Reprinted September 1997

Other Wiley Editorial Offices

John Wiley & Sons, Inc., 605 Third Avenue,
New York, NY 10158-0012, USA

VCH Verlagsgesellschaft mbH Pappelallee 3,
D-69469 Weinheim, Germany

Jacaranda Wiley Ltd, 33 Park Road, Milton,
Queensland 4064, Australia

John Wiley & Sons (Asia) Pte Ltd, 2 Clementi Loop #02-01,
Jin Xing Distripark, Singapore 129809

John Wiley & Sons (Canada) Ltd, 22 Worcester Road,
Rexdale, Ontario M9W 1L1, Canada

Library of Congress Cataloging-in-Publication Data

Millard, Brian J.
    Traded options / Brian J. Millard.
        p.   cm. — (The Millard on— series)
    Rev. ed. of: Traded options simplified. Bramhall, England : Qudos
Publications, c1989.
    Includes index.
    ISBN 0-471-96780-7
    1. Options (Finance)   2. Financial futures.   I. Millard, Brian J.
Traded options simplified.   II. Title.   III. Series: Millard, Brian
J. Millard on— series.
HG6024.A3M55   1997
332.63'228—dc21
                                                96–46656
                                                CIP

British Library Cataloguing in Publication Data

A catalogue record for this book is available from the British Library

ISBN 0-471-96780-7

Typeset in 10.5/12pt Times by Dorwyn Ltd, Rowlands Castle, Hants
Printed and bound in Great Britain by Redwood Books, Trowbridge, Wiltshire.
This book is printed on acid-free paper responsibly manufactured from sustainable forestation,
for which at least two trees are planted for each one used for paper production.

Contents

Preface

The first edition of *Traded Options Simplified* was published in 1989, when it was pointed out that the average private investor steered well clear of options, mainly because of a lack of understanding of the technicalities of this specialised market and a feeling that the risk involved in their use was totally unacceptable.

Since then there has been a rapid growth in the use of options and futures by the institutions and professional investors. The merger in 1992 of the London International Financial Futures Exchange and the London Traded Options Market to create the London International Financial Futures and Options Exchange (LIFFE) has provided extra stimulus to this growth. Now we are in the position that more and more private investors can see the attraction of traded options in providing a more balanced investment stance than simply investing in shares. Investment in traded options allows the investor to take a profitable position whatever the anticipated state of the market, be it rising, falling or trending sideways, whereas successful investment in shares is totally dependent on a rising market.

This book is intended to take the mystique out of traded options, as well as removing some major misconceptions. It is shown that far from being extremely risky, the proper application of logical methods can make traded options a safer vehicle for profit than a straightforward investment in shares, for example providing protection when the market falls. The same logical methods make the selection of the correct traded option for the particular investment circumstances hardly any more difficult than the selection of the correct share.

The early chapters in this book are devoted to ways in which the current trend in a share price or the FTSE100 Index can be determined. It is crucial to success in options that the investor should be correct more often than not in his view of the current direction of the trend in the underlying security and its probable target area. The reader is led via a consideration of moving averages to the powerful technique of channel analysis which enables the investor to determine probable turning points and future reversal levels in trends.

Brian J. Millard
Bramhall

1

Risk and the Stock Market

Prior to the crash of 1987, those investors taking part in the Government's privatisation of TSB, British Gas, Rolls-Royce, etc. might have thought that money could be made for the asking in the stock market. Gains of 10% or even 20% were common within a few days of initial dealings. Investors rushed to buy into each privatisation issue because they anticipated that they would achieve a better return on their capital by this method than by leaving their money on deposit. The weight of money washing around made these anticipated gains self-fulfilling prophecies. The fact that many investors were hurt in the crash of October 1987 did bring an air of realism to such investments, and investors now accept the fact that there is a higher degree of risk associated with investment in the stock market than there is with investment in say a bank deposit account or a building society. Since investors also appreciate that the potential for gain is much higher in the stock market, then consciously or otherwise, they have some understanding of the relationship between risk and return, which can be stated quite simply as "the higher the return, the higher the risk".

Outside the common factor that they wish to make a profit from their investments, investors are a very diverse set of people with many different ideas about how much profit can be achieved and how they can go about making this profit. Some will be perfectly satisfied if they do slightly better than if they had put their money into a building society, while others have very much higher expectations, say of perhaps doubling their money within a couple of years. Some investors will take the view that once made, an investment should be left to mature for a number of years, since the underlying trend of the stock market has been rising for nearly 20 years, albeit with the occasional blip, and therefore a profit becomes inevitable. Others prefer a more active approach, buying and selling at frequent intervals, taking advantage of short-term fluctuations in the market. A very large proportion of the investors who bought into the privatisation issues appear to fall into the first category of leaving their investments untouched for many years. However, they differ from the first category in one important respect—they have not taken a conscious decision about how their investments are to be managed, but have taken no decision at all, because they have no idea what to do. In other words, they did not set themselves any objective when they first made the investment. Such investors are always in danger of losing money, because they can be left holding on to their shares in a falling market.

MINIMISING THE RISK

As applied to the stock market, the concept of risk would appear to imply that there are "good" shares and "bad" shares, but one of the most successful amateur investors ever on the New York Exchange, Nicholas Darvas, restates this quite admirably: there are only rising shares and falling shares. Since a rising share will not rise for ever, and a falling share has a floor of zero, nothing is surer than that rising shares will turn into falling shares, while falling shares except for those thankfully rare cases where the company goes out of business, will turn into rising shares. This vision of the stock market now helps to clarify our ideas of risk as being dependent on how far along an existing upward or downward trend the particular share is at the point in time at which an investment in that share is contemplated. Risk should be minimal when a share begins to rise after a fall, and maximal when a share begins to fall following a rise. Quite obviously the major component of risk can be seen to be the timing of the investment. Buying in just after a downward trend has turned into an upward trend would be a low-risk exercise, while buying in just after an upward trend has turned into a downward trend would be a very high-risk exercise.

This view does help to emphasise the importance of timing, but is still a simplification, since the concept of "trend" needs to be examined rather more closely. A chart of the FTSE100 Index since the beginning of 1983 (Figure 1.1) will help the discussion by showing that the term "trend" needs a timescale attached to it. Quite clearly, since the position at the right-hand part of the chart (December 1995) is nearly four times higher than the position at the beginning of the chart (December 1982/January 1983), the FTSE100 Index can be said to have risen, with some adjustments on the way, during this period. If this had been a share which an investor had bought in January 1983 and forgot about until now, then that investor would say that the share had been in an upward trend during this 13-year period. If, however, we take another investor who bought in June 1987, and forgot about his purchase until November 1987, then this investor would say that the share had been in a downward trend during the five-month period. In other words, the 13-year trend has been upwards, while during this period a five-month trend has been downwards. These two investors have dissimilar views about the direction of the market because one has a longer-term view than the other even though these time periods overlap.

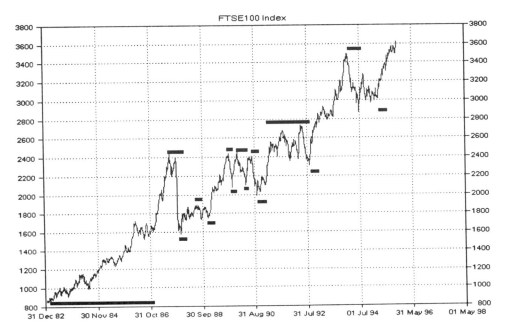

Figure 1.1 The FTSE100 Index illustrating the more obvious periods of high and low risk since the beginning of 1983. Periods of high risk are marked above the plot of the Index, while those of low risk are marked below the plot

A glance at the enlarged portion of this chart shown in Figure 1.2 will show a similar message for trends of a different timescale. In June 1991 the FTSE100 Index was just above 2500, whereas by October 1995 it was above 3500. Thus the four-year trend had been an upward trend. On the other hand, at the beginning of 1994 the Index was just below 3500, and by June 1994 it was down to just below 2900. Thus the six-month trend was downwards.

This concept of a share price history or Index history being a complex mixture of trends of widely differing timescales co-existing at the same time is an important one to grasp. We will see later that moving averages, for example, can be used to isolate trends of a particular timescale, so that the investor can focus on those trends that are appropriate to his style of investment. At this stage, it is not necessary to put exact lengths of time on trends, but at least to recognise that they can be sorted approximately into short-term, medium-term and long-term trends, where long-term means trends of longer than say two years' duration, medium-term refers to trends of about six months to two years' duration and short-term anything less than six months. By the time we come down to trends of a few days, we are entering the realms of unpredictable random movement.

Coming back to the view that the time just after a change in trend direction from falling to rising is a time of low risk, then it is also obvious

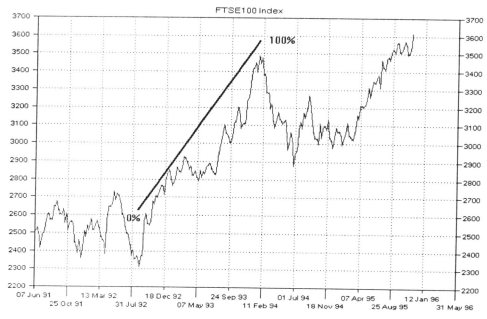

Figure 1.2 An enlarged section of the plot in Figure 1.1 showing the increase in risk from zero to 100% between August 1992 and February 1994

that the risk varies according to whether the trend in question is a short-term, medium-term or long-term trend. The risk is lowest for long-term trends and highest for short-term trends because by their very definitions, the unexpected end of a long-term trend is further away in time than that for shorter-term trends, and the overall rise in price or Index points caused by a long-term trend is larger than that caused by short-term trends. By the time a long-term upward trend is reaching its turning point, a consider-able profit will already be in the bag for those investors who got in at the beginning. Note that the risk involved in making a purchase increases as time goes by from the turning point.

One of these periods of changing risk is shown by the heavy sloping line in Figure 1.2, taking the period which starts in late August 1992 and extends to January 1994. At the beginning of the period the Index was at 2312.6 and at the end it had reached 3484.2, a rise of 1171.6 points, i.e. 50.7%. The risk built up from zero to 100% over this period of time.

Of course, all that we have been illustrating here is with the benefit of hindsight, a very valuable commodity. We were able to say that the risk was zero or the risk was 100% because we knew the subsequent move-ment of the Index. Naturally, the key to determining these periods of low and high risk at the time lies in developing good indicators of market turning points, and much effort has been expended by many analysts, including this author, on this problem. This aspect is discussed in a later chapter.

MAXIMISING THE RETURN

The return on an investment can be defined in a number of ways. We have to compare the value of the investment at some point with the original amount invested in that asset, in addition taking into account any dividends that may have been generated during the holding period. A simple definition, adequate for our purposes, would then be:

$$\text{Return} = \frac{\text{ending value} - \text{starting value} + \text{dividends}}{\text{starting value}} \times 100\%$$

With this definition, it is of course possible to have negative returns, so that in the case of a total loss and no dividend payments:

$$\text{Return} = \frac{0 - \text{starting value} - 0}{\text{starting value}} \times 100\% = -100\%$$

There is still something missing from this definition, and that is the length of time over which the return has been calculated. Without this time period, a share which doubles in value in six months would appear to give the same return as a share which took 10 years to do the same. Since this is patently not acceptable in terms of our investment philosophy, we should relate all returns to the same time period, in order that we will be able to compare the returns of two different investments.

We have a number of time periods to choose from, each of which can be defended as a logical choice depending upon one's personal investment characteristics. A one-year period has some logic because interest rates are quoted as "per annum". A six-month period has less logic although dividends are usually paid six-monthly. A quarterly period is more appropriate for US investors because dividends there tend to be paid quarterly. However, the maximum timespan of nine months available in the traded options market precludes these longer time periods, and many investments in options may be for much shorter periods of weeks and sometimes days. Because of this, the most sensible standard time period for computing return on an investment will be taken to be the week. We can now define a weekly return (WR) as being:

$$\text{WR} = \frac{\text{ending value} - \text{starting value} + \text{dividends}}{\text{ending value} \times \text{number of weeks invested}} \times 100\%$$

Note that in the case of traded options, there is no dividend payment unless the option has been exercised into the underlying security before the latter becomes ex-dividend.

Strictly speaking, the WR calculation should also take into account the costs involved in the transaction, but the difficulty in doing this is that costs may vary from one broker to another, and costs will also vary with the number of contracts taken (Chapter 2). Since we cannot therefore arrive at a consistent value, this will be left out of WR calculations, although where possible an indication of the costs involved will be given.

We can now see quite clearly from this definition of WR that high WRs are obtained either from a large increase in the value of the investment over some medium term, or from a smaller increase in the value over a shorter term. The highest WRs are obviously obtained by a fortuitous combination of a large increase over a short time period.

This rather lengthy preamble to the question of investment return is necessary to clear the way to the following important statement: *volatile shares give the highest weekly returns*. The simplest way of choosing volatile shares was discussed in the author's book *Stocks and Shares Simplified*, and amounted to selecting those shares with the highest ratio of high to low value in the yearly high/low column in those newspapers with a good coverage of daily share eprices. As far as the London Traded Options are concerned, volatility is one of the criteria used in selecting the growing number of shares for which traded options are available. It is of interest to state the other criteria used, since they involve the aspect of safety of the underlying shares. During the five years prior to the introduction of option trading, the company must not have defaulted on the payment of interest, dividend or sinking fund instalment, or committed any breach of borrowing limitation. The company should also have a substantial market capitalisation, and there must be at least 10 000 equity shareholders.

It is useful to compile for the shares for which traded options are available, a volatility table of the ratio of yearly high to low value. This is done in Table 1.1, the ratio being calculated at the end of October for each of the years 1993, 1994 and 1995. The table is useful from the point of view that the average change in the share price over each year is given as 1.577, 1.404 and 1.442. For shares which have risen from the yearly low to the yearly high during the year in question, this corresponds to price increases of 57.7%, 40.4% and 44.2% respectively. For shares which have fallen from a high to a low during the year, this corresponds to losses of 36.6%, 28.8% and 30.7% respectively. For those investors in shares, the gains represent the highest that could be made over the year by perfect timing of the buying point at the yearly low, and of the selling point at the yearly high. This of course excludes dealing costs which will account for a few percent of the overall gain. Note that perfect timing will only be achieved by pure chance; no technical system can spot the exact lows and highs as they occur. In reality, the soonest that any system based on daily data could detect lows and highs is the following day. This is because lows and highs are troughs and peaks, and therefore a low does not become a low

Table 1.1 High/low ratios during previous year for traded options shares in October 1993, 1994 and 1995

Share	1993	1994	1995	Share	1993	1994	1995
Allied Domecq	1.278	1.276	1.241	LASMO	1.5	1.567	1.343
Argyll	1.5	1.381	1.535	Lucas Industries	1.641	1.481	1.219
Asda	1.825	1.389	1.818	P&O	1.563	1.382	1.391
British Airways	1.556	1.438	1.359	Pilkington	2.263	1.437	1.506
Boots	1.345	1.212	1.295	Prudential	1.376	1.389	1.363
British Steel	2.806	1.489	1.304	RTZ	1.262	1.408	1.306
British Petroleum	1.577	1.38	1.262	Redland	1.696	1.412	1.428
Bass	1.477	1.307	1.404	Royal Insurance	1.535	1.474	1.626
Commercial Union	1.184	1.474	1.357	Tesco	1.406	1.418	1.444
Cable & Wireless	1.656	1.404	1.265	Grand Metropolitan	1.237	1.313	1.287
Courtaulds	1.287	1.366	1.264	Ladbroke	1.401	1.475	1.268
ICI	1.314	1.28	1.259	United Biscuits	1.342	1.312	1.358
Kingfisher	1.334	1.651	1.311	Rolls-Royce	1.777	1.338	1.307
Land Securities	1.829	1.355	1.183	Vodaphone	1.564	1.379	1.539
NatWest Bank	1.589	1.481	1.441	Williams	1.209	1.306	1.177
PowerGen	1.901	1.352	1.311	Abbey National	1.296	1.37	1.433
Sainsbury	1.471	1.381	1.229	Amstrad	2.266	2.137	2.301
Shell Transport	1.371	1.155	1.148	Barclays	1.697	1.29	1.631
Standard Chartered	2.181	1.562	2.109	Blue Circle	1.867	1.444	1.324
Storehouse	1.387	1.36	1.5	British Gas	1.306	1.422	1.338
Unilever	1.317	1.289	1.209	Dixons	1.468	1.717	2.27
Zeneca		1.284	1.437	Hillsdown	1.702	1.366	1.234
BAA	1.262	1.241	1.276	Lonrho	2.007	1.377	1.291
Thames Water	1.267	1.399	1.296	National Power	1.731	1.298	1.316
Glaxo	1.624	1.381	1.442	Scottish Power	2.08	1.495	1.219
HSBC		1.662	1.629	Sears	1.337	1.321	1.233
Reuters	1.406	1.363	1.454	Forte	1.569	1.35	1.22
British Aerospace	3.804	1.489	1.811	Tarmac	1.894	1.683	1.532
BAT Industries	1.228	1.518	1.35	Thorn EMI	1.322	1.291	1.613
BTR	1.394	1.327	1.257	TSB	1.675	1.459	1.716
British Telecom	1.269	1.376	1.131	Tomkins	1.317	1.389	1.268
Cadbury Schweppes	1.224	1.313	1.406	Marks and Spencer	1.307	1.21	1.22
Eastern Electricity	1.640	1.519	1.739	Trafalgar House	1.49	1.25	2.761
Guinness	1.409	1.321	1.313	Fisons	1.657	1.485	2.507
GEC	1.515	1.316	1.308	FTSE100 Index	1.203	1.223	1.22
Hanson	1.249	1.359	1.301	**Average ratio**	**1.577**	**1.404**	**1.442**

until the following day, when the price has risen from it. Similarly, a high does not become a high until the following day when the price has fallen from it.

One feature of this table is that there is a measure of consistency amongst involatile shares. Of the 20 least volatile shares in 1993, 16 remained in the bottom 20 for both of the years 1994 and 1995. Of the 30 least volatile shares in 1993, 23 remained in the bottom 30 for both of the years 1994 and 1995. As a rough rule of thumb, therefore, there is a good chance that a share which has exhibited low volatility in a particular year will continue to do so. This was also true for the period 1985 to 1987 covered in the first edition of this book. This can be useful as an aid to deciding between two possible options where in other respects of timing, etc., there appears to be little to choose between them. As for the opposite concept of high volatility, it was true that in the period 1985 to 1987 shares which were volatile in 1985 tended to remain so for the next two years, but this linkage is not so obvious for 1993 to 1995.

RISK AND RETURN

Although we have stated that volatile shares give the highest weekly returns, we should be quite clear that volatile shares can also give the highest losses, i.e. the lowest weekly returns. Therefore, in the absence of correct timing of the investment, there is a greater risk associated with investment in volatile shares than with their less volatile counterparts. The simplest starting point is to assume an investment made in an average share from all the shares available in the UK stock market, and made at some random point in time, i.e. with no reference to the high or low state of the market in general or the low or high state of the particular share price at the time of the investment. A graph of risk versus return may then look like that shown in Figure 1.3(a). Except for one point on this graph, no attempt is made to put any values on either of the axes. The object is simply to illustrate a few points which can then be carried forward through this analysis.

The first point to make is that the return may be either negative or positive, i.e. we may lose some capital or gain some capital. The most negative return would be –100%, which of course represents the point at which we lose all our money. There is no maximum value on the most positive return, since this may, in fortunate circumstances, rise to many thousands of percent.

The second point to make is that however small we would like it to be, there is still some chance of a total loss, so any stock market investment graph never starts from a point of zero risk, but from some small positive value.

Since Figure 1.3(a) typifies the risk/return relationship for an average share rather than a particularly volatile one, then we can compare this with two other cases—one where we have selected a volatile share and have achieved superior timing of the buying decision, and one in which the timing is disastrously wrong. Figures 1.3(b) and (c) show these two other situations. Where the timing is good, as in Figure 1.3(b), then the risk associated with a particular return is much lower than for the average case. It should be seen quite clearly from the figure that the risk of total loss (–100% return) or of zero gain is considerably less than in the average case (Figure 1.3(a)). Where the timing is bad, as in Figure 1.3(c), then the risk

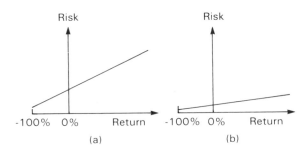

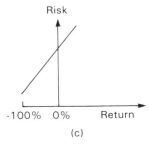

Figure 1.3 Risk–return relationships: (a) average case; (b) volatile case with good timing of investment; (c) volatile case with bad timing of investment

associated with a particular return is higher than in the average case, and very much higher than when the timing is good. This is also very obvious for the total loss and zero gain points on the graph. Clearly, investors are always looking for a situation in which the risk is minimised while the return is maximised, i.e. to approach the position shown in Figure 1.3(b), but naturally this state of affairs is difficult to achieve.

The main components of risk and return are the volatility of the particular share price and the timing of the investment. Readers of *Stocks and Shares Simplified* will be aware that this author's view is that investment should take place in volatile shares. We have already commented on the way in which involatile shares tend to stay involatile (Table 1.1). The investor should make a selection from the remaining shares in the list on the grounds that there is a higher probability that these will remain volatile. The main way in which risk can be decreased then lies in the selection of the correct buying and selling times. There will be periods during which buying shares will be highly risky, and periods when buying shares is less risky. This was shown for the FTSE100 Index in Figures 1.1 and 1.2.

The author's view of the market is that the most important decision an investor has to take is *When?* The *What?* decision, although important, is of secondary importance. The market itself dictates when to buy and when to sell at levels of acceptable risk. Investors who step out of synchronisation with the market do not increase their possibility of a high return. They simply increase the risk associated with that return. As long as this fact is realised, then it is perfectly acceptable for them to yield to pressure from brokers, bank managers, investment newsletters, etc., to make investments at times other than market lows and to sell at times other than market highs.

Chapters 3 and 4 of this book examine in some detail ways of deciding the best buying and selling points in the market. The use of moving averages as indicators of market turning points has already been covered extensively in *Stocks and Shares Simplified*. Readers of that book will also have seen that longer-term moving averages were used to try to predict the extent of future price movements. This approach has now been called "channel analysis", and is the subject of another book by this author (see Appendix). Channel analysis gives the investor the most powerful method ever devised for stock market prediction. The predictive technique is of vital importance in giving the investor not only a feeling for the direction which the market in a particular share is taking, i.e. upwards, downwards or sideways, but also some idea of the target area for which the market is headed. This last aspect will be essential in enabling the investor to categorise himself in terms of expectation, as discussed later.

WHY INVEST IN TRADED OPTIONS?

An investor who restricts his activities to the buying and selling of securities quoted on the major markets is operating under quite severe restraints. These can be summarised as:

• Profits are made only if the share price rises.
• Buying and selling is limited to certain periods in the overall price cycle if risk is to be minimised.
• Moving outside such periods increases risk without a compensating increase in the return from the investment.

Consideration of these restraints shows that an investor may have to spend months or even years out of the market if the latter is trending downwards. Typical returns from such investment average out somewhere in the range 10–50% on an annualised basis.

Of course, there have to be some positive aspects to this type of investment, some of which may be summarised as:

• A long-term policy of buy and forget is often successful, thus suiting investors with little time to spend on management of their portfolios.
• Decisions on what to buy and when to buy are relatively simple if general guidelines are followed.

The risk of total loss is quite small if an investor sticks with shares of say the top 100 companies. Generally speaking, the more time that is spent on studying the market, the greater will be the return.

The advantage of using traded options is that the investors achieve total flexibility in terms of timing, degree of risk and the return on the investment. The following points can be compared with those made above:

- Whatever the direction of the market, upwards, downwards, or sideways, a profitable stance can be taken.
- A position can be taken at any time during the overall market cycle.
- The investor can choose the amount of risk appropriate to his psychology. In general the higher the risk the higher the return to the investor.
- The return on an investment can range up to many thousands of percent.

However, not all aspects of traded options are positive, and there are some disadvantages:

- The longest timescale possible in the traded options market is nine months.
- There is a bewildering array of possibilities available, making decisions quite difficult to take.
- There is a substantial risk of total loss, even with options in giants such as ICI and British Telecom.

In view of these major advantages, we might ask why only a small proportion of those investors active in the stock market use traded options as part of their investment strategy. There are several reasons for this, one major reason being that traded options are perceived as being much riskier than normal investment in shares. Another reason is that traded options appear to be complicated to understand, requiring a great deal of specialised knowledge.

It is to be hoped that both of these difficulties will be rectified by this book. Certainly it will be seen that traded options, used correctly, can actually reduce the risk of investing in the stock market. Hopefully, this book will also aid the understanding of the subject so that investors will see that traded options form an invaluable part of the wider investment scene.

Finally, it is useful to show the trade-off between risk and return as exemplified by two investors. One of these invests in a share, while the other invests in a call option. Both investors, naturally, expect a useful rise in the price of the share itself. At 26th June 1995, the Argyll share price was 314p. The July 330 calls were selling at 2p, the October 330 calls at 12p and the January 330 calls at 19p. The "conservative" investor who bought shares saw them rise to 364p over the next two weeks. Therefore

$$\text{Percentage gain} = \frac{364 - 314}{314} \times 100\% = 15.9\%$$

Since the gain was made over two weeks,

Weekly return (WR) = 15.9/2 = 7.95%

Annualised percentage gain = 52 × WR = 52 × 7.95 = 413.4%

These are of course very impressive returns when expressed as annualised percentage gains or weekly returns. However, compare these with those made by the investor in the July call options at 2p. Within the two-week period these had increased in value to 33p. Therefore

$$\text{Percentage gain} = \frac{33-2}{2} \times 100\% = 1550\%$$

Since this gain of 1550% in the call option premiums was made over a period of two weeks, it follows that:

WR = 1550/2 = 775%

Annualised percentage gain = 52 × WR = 52 × 775 = 40300%

However, we must not forget that these returns from investing in options are only obtainable at the expense of a far greater risk than is the case with the shares. The options example with its enormous gain was deliberately chosen as an example of taking a high risk. The July call options had only some four or five weeks to run to expiry. The investor was putting his money on the probability of the share price rising by more than 16p in this time in order to bring the options into the profit zone. This represents a 5% gain over the period, and is at the high end of expectation for share price movement, bearing in mind our comments from Table 1.1 that the average yearly high to low ratio is of the order of 40–50%.

A lesser risk position could have been taken by the investor convinced that the share price was going to rise in the near future by going for the October options. This gives a timescale three months longer. The investor pays more for this additional time—the premium is 12p rather than 2p—but then allows himself more time for the share price to move up by 16p to bring the options into profit. This will make the profit considerably less as can be seen by the fact that these October options had moved to 44p within the two weeks. Therefore

$$\text{Percentage gain} = \frac{44-12}{12} \times 100\% = 266.7\%$$

WR = 266.7/2 = 133%

Annualised percentage gain = 52 × WR = 52 × 133 = 6933%

The risks involved when both investors have got it wrong, and the share price does not rise, can be shown by supposing, for example, that the Argyll share price had fallen slowly over the five weeks, i.e. to the expiry date of the July options. If the price was then, for the sake of argument, 290p, then the loss to the investor in the shares is:

Percentage loss = $\dfrac{290 - 314}{314} \times 100\% = -7.6\%$

Since this loss occurred over a period of five weeks,

WR = $-7.6/5 = -1.52\%$

Annualised percentage loss = $52 \times 1.52 = 79.04\%$

Compare this with the July 330 call option position, which now expires worthless, since the striking price of 330p is higher than the share price of 290p at the option expiry time:

Percentage loss = $\dfrac{0 - 2}{2} \times 100\% = -100\%$

Since this loss occurred over a period of five weeks,

WR = $-100/5 = -20\%$

Annualised percentage loss = $52 \times 20 = 1040\%$

This example clearly shows the trade-off between risk and return. Those investors who are seeking a higher return from their investment must of necessity tolerate a higher risk. Those investors who are uncomfortable with a high degree of risk can take a position where the risk is lower, but they will have to be satisfied with a lower return.

2

Technical Terms in the Traded Options Market

Before we can enter into any meaningful discussion on traded options, it is necessary to define the numerous technical terms used so that these can be clearly understood.

Equity option: in particular a traded option, just like an ordinary share, is a marketable item involving buyers and sellers. In traded options jargon a seller is also called a "writer" of the traded option. On opposite sides of a traded options deal, therefore, we have a buyer and a writer. Options are of two types: call options and put options.

Call options: the buyer of a call option has the right to buy shares from the writer at an agreed price, known as the exercise price or strike price, at any time up to and including the expiry date.

Put options: the buyer of a put option has the right to sell shares to the writer at an agreed exercise price at any time up to and including the expiry date.

Option class: all the various options available in the shares of a particular company, taking into account puts, calls, exercise prices and expiry dates.

Option series: all the options in a class which share the same exercise price and expiry date. Examples are Boots March 200 series, Shell July 1000 series, etc.

Exercise (strike) price: the agreed price at which shares will be bought by the buyer from the writer of a call option if the buyer exercises the option. Similarly it is the price at which the shares will be sold by the buyer of a put option to the writer if the buyer exercises the option.

Expiry date: the date on which the option expires. Options have a maximum life of nine months.

Index options: since the first edition of this book, a new type of option based on movements in the FTSE100 Index has been introduced. Options of this type are known as Index Options for obvious reasons.

Premium: the price which the buyer pays for the call or put option. This is the only aspect of the contract which can vary in price since it is subject to normal market forces.

Out-of-the-money: call options where the share price is below the strike price, and put options where the share price is above the strike price.

At-the-money: call options or put options where the share price is equal to the strike price.

In-the-money: call options where the share price is above the strike price, and put options where the share price is below the strike price.

Consideration: the cost of the option based on the premium and number of contracts, but excluding commissions, etc.

Contract: one contract is the minimum unit which can be traded. A contract usually refers to an option on 1000 shares in the underlying security. There are exceptions to this, however, and this unit can change as a result of rights issues, etc. When placing an order with a broker, do not mention the number of shares for which you are buying the option, but simply the number of contracts, from one contract upwards, i.e. for options on 5000 shares you would buy five contracts. Do not forget the mathematics, which in the case of five contracts for an option quoted as having a premium of, say, 20p would lead to a consideration of

$$1000 \times 20p \times 5 = £1000$$

i.e.

$$\text{usual no. of shares per contract} = 1000$$
$$\times \text{ premium } = 20p$$
$$\times \text{ no. of contracts } = 5$$

Of course, the dealing costs are omitted from this calculation, but examples will be given later.

In the case of options on the FTSE100 Index, the unit of trading is £10 per index point. Thus to purchase one contract when the quoted premium is, say, 85 points for a particular exercise price and expiry would mean a consideration of

$$£10 \times 85 = £850$$

This would have to be multiplied by the number of contracts if more than one contract is purchased.

EXPIRY DATES AND EXERCISE PRICES

When a new equity option class is created, its expiry dates are assigned permanently into one of three available cycles. The first cycle has expiry dates of January, April, July and October, the second cycle expiry dates of February, May, August and November, and the third cycle dates of March, June, September and December. The consequence of having such cycles is that for any option, there are always three different expiry dates available, with the maximum being nine months away from the date of introduction. The other two are then six months and three months in the future. As time passes, these dates obviously come nearer; but when, three months from the introduction of the option, the short-term option naturally expires, it is replaced by a new option once again nine months in the future. The actual day of expiry in the particular month is usually the third or fourth Wednesday in the month, except for those occasions when the Exchange is closed for a bank holiday such as Christmas or Boxing Day. The buyer of options must take great care to be aware at all times of the impending expiry of an option, since decisions have to be taken regarding the fate of the options. Forgetting about the expiry of an option could be expensive.

For Index options in the FTSE100 Index, the expiry months are different. The situation is slightly complicated by the fact that there are two types of exercise possible. The American-style exercise works just like equity options in that they can be exercised at any time up to and including the expiry day. The European-style options can only be exercised on the expiry day itself, and not before. In American style the expiry months of June and December are always available, plus additional months such that the nearest four calendar months are always available. For European style, the expiry months are March, June, September and December plus additional months so that the three nearest calendar months are always available.

Where you have purchased an option, there are three decisions available to you at all times during its lifetime:

1. **Sell the option** at any time prior to the expiry date.
2. **Exercise the option** by buying the underlying security at the exercise price (call option) or selling the underlying security at the exercise price (put option).
3. **Do nothing**. Eventually the option expires. Naturally this course should only be taken where there is no advantage in exercising the option, i.e. when it has become worthless.

Where you have written an option, i.e. taken a premium for it, then there are only two decisions available to you, a third decision being out of your hands. Thus:

1. **Do nothing.** There is no need to do anything if the option has become valueless to the purchaser, since he will not exercise against you in such circumstances.
2. **Close your position** by buying the identical option. You may have to pay more or less than the amount you received in the first place when writing the option. You do this if you anticipate circumstances approaching where it becomes attractive for the purchaser to exercise against you and you wish to remove this liability.
3. The buyer of this option may **exercise it against you**. You have no control over this.

Just as expiry dates are decided by the traded options market authorities (LIFFE), so are the exercise prices. These prices will depend totally upon the underlying security price at the time the option is created. At that time, two exercise prices are created, one below and one above the security price. The difference between these two prices is usually about 10% of the share price.

Exercise prices are taken from a predefined series, so that computer programs can easily determine the next highest or next lowest exercise price from any given one. Thus, exercise prices increase by 5p up to a value of 50p, then by 10p up to a value of 140p, then by 20p up to a value of 300p, then by 40p up to a value of 500p, then by 50p up to a value of 1000p, then by 100p, and so on.

The thinking behind traded options is to try to maintain the availability of exercise prices above and below the current security price. This means that as the price of the underlying security rises or falls outside the current range of exercise prices, new ones will be introduced to maintain this situation. These are introduced on the day after the underlying share price has exceeded the second highest or fallen below the second lowest available exercise price. Such security price rises or falls can mean that a particular exercise price disappears from your newspaper. If this happens before the expiry date, it does not mean that the series ceases to exist, but that the newspaper does not wish to use too much space in its traded options listings. Of course a price movement the wrong way means that the option has become worthless, but a favourable price movement can convert your option into a pot of gold.

You will sometimes see exercise prices that do not conform to the predetermined series. This happens because the shares of the underlying security have been split via a scrip issue, rights issue, etc. When this occurs, LIFFE will carry out an adjustment, the underlying principle being that neither the option buyer nor the option writer should benefit from the change, i.e. it should be neutral. The share price will move down in line with the arithmetic of the scrip issue. Thus a 1 for 1 will cause the share price to halve. The exercise price will be moved proportionately in the same way, thus preserving its relationship to the share price. The number of shares per contract will also have to be adjusted so that the value of the shares underlying the option will remain as it was before the scrip or rights issue.

DEALING COSTS

The costs involved in dealing in traded options are comprised of two components: broker's commission, and a fee to the London Clearing House (LCH). Broker's commission is also subdivided into a fixed charge for the contract note plus an amount based on the level of option money involved. The fixed charge at present is £2.50 for the contract note. Broker's commission in the traded options market is subject to a minimum, but this differs from dealer to dealer. As a guide, the minimum commission is usually £20, although it may be possible to find brokers charging £15. There is often a different minimum for small deals, such as £10 for option money below £200. Commissions are based on bands, the rate being 2.5% for the first £5000 of option money, 1.5% for the next £5000 of option money, and finally 1% on the excess option money above this £10 000 level. Thus for brokers charging a £20 minimum, this minimum covers the two charge bands up to £10 000. The LCH fee is £2.50 per option contract.

It is vital to understand how these dealing costs can eat into the profit margin, and normally an investor should be investing not less than £750 in order that these costs are kept down to a sensible level. This can be demonstrated from the following two examples.

Example 1

Buy one contract of Boots December 550 calls @ 41p:

	£
Option money = 1000 × 41p	410.00
Commission = 2.5% of £410	10.25
Since this is below minimum,	
Minimum charge applied	20.00
Contract note charge	5.00
LCH clearing fee	2.50
Total charges	27.50
Total to pay	**437.50**

When the option is sold, provided the gain is not so enormous as to take the option money from the sale to above £10 000, then the individual charges will be the same again. The total charges will therefore again be £27.50. Based on one contract, where the option money is £410, a gain of more than 6.7% must be achieved in order to cover these buying charges. Since the charges in closing the position may be similar, a gain of nearly 14% will be needed to clear both sets of charges.

Example 2

Buy five contracts of Boots December 550 calls @ 41p:

	£
Option money = 5 × 1000 × 41p	2050.00
Commission = 2.5% of £2050	51.25
Contract note charge	5.00
LCH clearing fee	2.50
Total charges	58.75
Total to pay	**2108.75**

In this example, where the amount of money being applied is greater, it will only be necessary to make a gain of just over 2.8% in order to cover the buying charges and just over 5.7% to cover the eventual probable closing charges. Because of the minimum charge, therefore, it is only above about £700–750 of option money that the charges come down to a tolerable level.

PAYMENT FOR TRADED OPTIONS

Note that unlike the buying and selling of normal shares, where all payments are made at the end of the rolling five-day settlement, option payments have to be made by 10 a.m. on the business day following the buying or selling of the option. Since this may be physically difficult in certain circumstances, the broker will probably ask for money to be paid into an account before you can start dealings. You cannot exercise an option on the same day as you purchase it because, under the above payment rule, you will not have paid for it until the next day.

INSTRUCTING YOUR BROKER

Nowhere on the investment scene is there such an opportunity for confusion when instructing your broker than in the traded options market. It is absolutely vital that the correct form of words is used to convey your requirements. After all, in normal investment, you simply tell your broker whether you wish to buy or sell a certain share, and how many shares are involved. You may also wish to put a limit on the price you are prepared to pay.

On the traded options scene, there are four types of transaction:

1. Buying an option by paying its premium so as to become its holder.
2. Selling (writing an option) which is not already held, i.e. taking its premium.
3. Selling an option which is already held via transaction 1.
4. Buying an option in order to cancel out the writing of an option via transaction 2.

In traded options dealings you have to show whether you are opening or closing a position, the number of contracts involved, and the particular series, i.e. Allied Domecq April 300 calls. Thus to buy an option contract (transaction type 1), you use the phrase "opening purchase" and when you sell that option at a later date (transaction type 3) you use the phrase "closing sale". One example would be "opening purchase of three contracts in Allied Domecq April 500 calls".

To write an option contract (transaction type 2) you would say "opening sale" and state the particulars of the option you wish to write. To close this position, use the phrase "closing purchase" for the circumstance where you wish to buy back the identical position, thus ending your liability as a writer.

As in any other market where prices are moving, it is important to get an indication of the price you will have to pay if you are a buyer, and the premium you can expect to receive if you are a writer. The broker will give you such an indicative price, but this may not be the price you will have to pay or receive. As with shares, you will be quoted a buying premium and a selling premium. The difference between these, known as the *spread*, should be, according to LIFFE rules, between certain limits. As examples, with premiums over 100p the spread should not exceed 10p. With premiums of up to 9.5p the spread will be not more than 2p. Buyers of options will have to pay the higher of the two quoted prices, while writers will receive the lower of the two prices.

The broker is obtaining the indicative prices from the screen, but the sequence of events if you execute a deal is as follows.

Your broker contacts a broker on the LIFFE floor, who then visits the "pit" where that particular option is traded to obtain the best bid and offer prices for the series in which you wish to deal. If the prices are in line with those that you have indicated to your broker, the deal is done. The floor brokers will confirm to your broker that the deal has been arranged and the price or prices at which the deal has been done.

It is important, because of the sometimes rapid movements in the market, that you arrange for your broker to call you back to inform you of the details of the bargain which has been struck on your behalf. All deals which you have carried out will result in your receiving a contract note the next day or the day after that. Treat these with care and try to keep them in a binder in chronological order. Make sure that you are aware of all your positions at all times.

New traders may worry about what might happen if they are holding a position at expiry and some unforeseen circumstance such as an accident prevents them instructing their broker to exercise it. Although they accept no liability, brokers will try to protect you by exercising any options you may be holding if they are of any value. It is not fair to your broker to put him in such a position, so keep a careful eye on the expiry dates of your options.

3

Technical Indicators 1. Moving Averages

This chapter will deal with the moving average method of determining the turning points in share prices. Readers of *Stocks and Shares Simplified* will of course be reasonably familiar with the concept of moving averages as indicators of buying and selling points, but will benefit from the somewhat different treatment that follows.

WEEKLY AVERAGES

Medium- and Long-term Averages

It can be seen by referring again to Figure 1.1 in Chapter 1, that the market, as indicated by the FTSE100 Index, tends to move in waves over the course of time. These waves are not constant in either their distance apart (wavelength) or their height (amplitude), but vary considerably. Moreover, there is present at any one time a confusing mixture of these waves. The object of the moving average approach is to use a simple mathematical treatment to sort out, from the complex mixture, waves of a duration that will prove to be useful in deciding when to buy and sell in the market. It is possible to some extent to visualise various wavelengths that are present by looking at the chart with your eyes screwed up. By doing this the fine detail of the weekly prices start to disappear, and the underlying trends become more apparent. The moving average is much more flexible, since by changing the number of weeks of the moving average calculation, waves of different wavelengths can be seen.

Without going into the mathematics deeply, the function of moving averages can be presented fairly clearly. Any average is of course calculated by adding together the items being averaged, and then dividing by the number of items involved. Thus a five-week average is obtained by adding five consecutive weekly prices and dividing by five. The term "moving" is applied simply because this process of averaging is continued every week until there are no more weekly prices left, so the averaging process is moved along the weekly prices from the starting point, which may be years back in time, until the most recent price has been used. Since the first five weekly values are used to calculate the first value of the five-week average, which can be tabulated, as shown shortly, against the fifth week, it follows that we will end up with four fewer moving average values than we have number of weeks of prices. The number of weeks used in the average, such as five in the case just discussed, is known as the span of the average. If we choose some other span for the average, say 15 weeks instead of five, then the first average is tabulated against week 15, and we will end up with 14 fewer average values than the number of weekly prices, and so on.

As an example relevant to traded options, a calculation of such a moving average is shown for BTR in Table 3.1. The first 15 weeks' prices from 6th January 1995 to 14th April 1995, inclusively, add up to 4745.5, which is put in the 15-week total column. Dividing this by 15 gives 316.3667, which is the 15-week average entered in the last column. Although this process could be repeated by starting at the value for 13th January and adding the 15 values to 21st April 1995, inclusively, this is not the simplest way to continue the calculation. It is far easier to take the current 15-week total, add in the next value, i.e. in the present example 332.5 on 21st April, and then subtract the value 16 weeks back from the new total, i.e. 301.5 for 6th January, thus giving the new 15-week total. By this method, you only have to add one number and subtract one number from the running total each week. It is useful to mark off with a tick in another column the week whose value has been subtracted. This is demonstrated in the example.

For users with a computer and spreadsheet software, the process is quite simple if the first column is kept for the date, and the next column for the share closing prices. The third column can be used to keep the average. Most spreadsheets have an average function, but in the absence of this, the average can be calculated from the sum of each consecutive price over the 15-week period, divided by 15. Traded options and share analysis software such as Options Genius and Microvest (see Appendix) carry out multiple average calculations and display the results graphically as shown in the figures in this book.

The effect of applying a moving average to any data is to remove, although not terribly efficiently, fluctuations with a periodicity equal to or shorter than the span of the average. In the case of stock market data, applying a 15-week average, for example, will reduce the contribution of all those waves or movements which have a periodicity, i.e. the time between successive peaks of 15 weeks or less. By the same token a 53-week average would only allow through much longer wavelengths, of greater than one year between successive peaks. Quite obviously, by careful selection of various spans of moving averages, the investor can focus on waves

Table 3.1 Calculation of a 15-week moving average of BTR share prices

Date	Price	Subtract	15-week total	15-week average
06 01 95	301.5	×		
13 01 95	305.5	×		
20 01 95	307	×		
27 01 95	304.5	×		
03 02 95	304	×		
10 02 95	321	×		
17 02 95	311	×		
24 02 95	316			
03 03 95	314.5			
10 03 95	316			
17 03 95	321.5			
24 03 95	326			
31 03 95	328			
07 04 95	332			
14 04 95	337		4745.5	316.3667
21 04 95	332.5		4776.5	318.4333
28 04 95	329		4800.0	320
05 05 95	332.5		4825.5	321.7
12 05 95	337.5		4858.5	323.9
19 05 95	339		4893.5	326.2333
26 05 95	338.5		4911.0	327.4
02 06 95	341.5		4941.5	329.4333
09 06 95	338		4963.5	330.9

which (if they happen to be present) are appropriate to his frequency of buying and selling.

Some shares show far fewer dominant waves than others, and hence are useful for the purposes of illustrating what can be achieved by the use of moving averages. Since there are many thousands of shares available, it is sensible to select shares from those that fall into this similar category. BTR is such a share, and so for much of this chapter the BTR share price is used to illustrate the effect of various moving averages.

In Figures 3.1 to 3.4 are shown the share price of BTR since 1983, and the effect of various moving averages, of five-week, 15-week and 53-week spans. These are not magic numbers, but are used purely to illustrate various points. It will become obvious, as the discussion proceeds, how to select the span of the average best suited to the particular investment circumstances.

The share price itself (Figure 3.1) shows several major peaks and troughs as well as the small ripples superimposed on these major waves. Thus there are peaks in mid-1986 and mid-1987, at the end of 1989, and in the middle of 1993. There are corresponding troughs towards the end of 1986 and the end of 1987, in the middle of 1990 and at the end of 1994. By screwing up your eyes, these major waves, four in number, can be seen

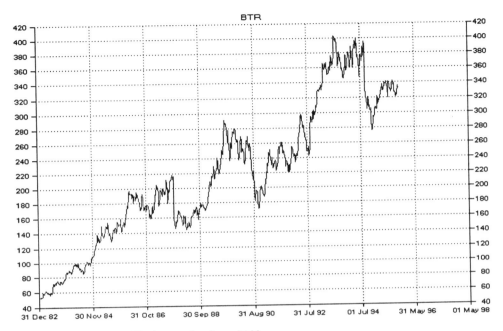

Figure 3.1   The BTR share price from 1983

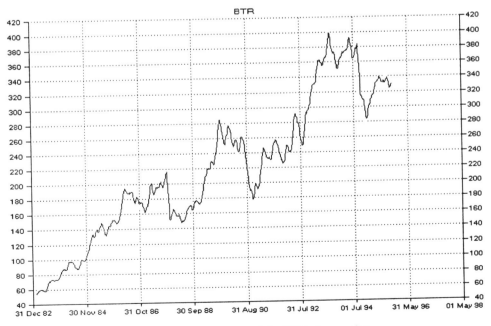

Figure 3.2   The five-week moving average of the BTR share price

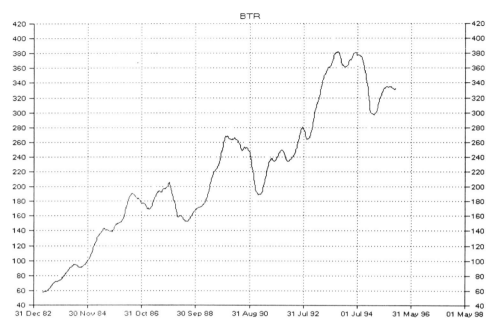

Figure 3.3   The 15-week moving average of the BTR share price

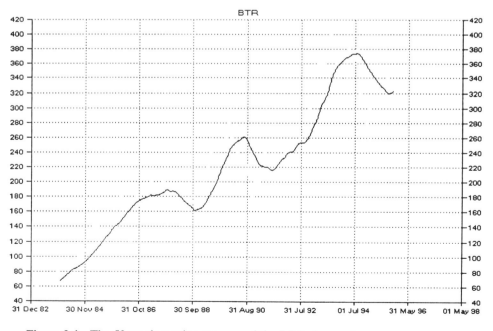

Figure 3.4   The 53-week moving average of the BTR share price

more clearly. A rough estimate shows the gap between the first and second wave tops to be about one year, and the gap between the third and fourth wave tops to be about four years. Further inspection shows the periodicity of waves or ripples of lesser duration to be very much shorter than these major waves, mostly being between say one week and 20 weeks.

Bearing in mind what we have said about the periodicities allowed through by various moving averages, we can therefore expect, before actually carrying out the calculation, that a five-week average would still show these minor ripples, a 15-week average would have lost most of the minor ripples, and a longer term such as 53 weeks will show only the major waves. Note that in a case such as this, it is necessary to move to 53-week or longer-term averages to highlight the waves of greater periodicity than 53 weeks. When any substantial wavelets of between 20 weeks and 53 weeks are not present, then an average of shorter span than 53 weeks can be used. There is a very good reason for trying to get away with the smallest span possible, and that is because the gain in fidelity of longer averages is offset by the loss of data points as exemplified by the calculation of the 15-week average in which 16 data points were lost. This also leads to unacceptable time lags before an average changes direction. These points are brought out in the discussion of the figures.

Figure 3.2 shows the five-week moving average of the BTR share price, and as expected, we retain a number of ripples superimposed upon the underlying waves. These ripples are, however, very minor in amplitude. It must be pointed out again that although share prices can move in common with each other, they also show a great deal of individuality. This is discussed later in the chapter.

Figure 3.3 shows the 15-week moving average of the BTR share price, and now the ripples with a periodicity of less than 15 weeks have been almost totally removed, giving a clear impression of the four large waves, even though the second and fourth have rather pointed tops. By applying a 53-week moving average, as shown in Figure 3.4, the waves now appear much more rounded. Not only that, but the first pair of waves which were separated by about one year now appear as one broader wave. This is of course because a 53-week average will remove fluctuations of periodicity less than or equal to one year, and the gap between the first and second waves is slightly less than one year.

Although the applications of various moving averages, as shown in these figures, is extremely valuable in highlighting the various waveforms present in share prices, we have not shown how they can be used as an aid to buying or selling of either shares or options. The simplest way in which they can be used is to determine turning points in the share prices. This is best illustrated by superimposing, say, the 53-week average upon the BTR share price, so that the relationship between these two can be more readily seen. This is done in Figure 3.5 for the same historical period that we have been discussing. The way in which the average is presented on this chart

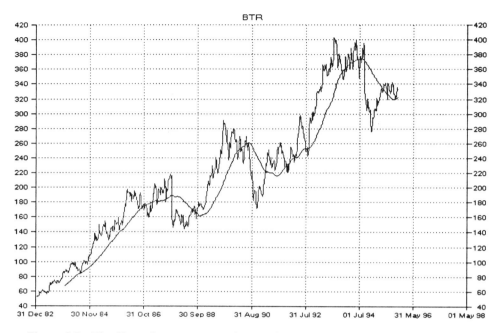

Figure 3.5   The 53-week average superimposed on the BTR share price

shows that there is a time lag between the jagged top of one of the major peaks in the share price and the corresponding top of the moving average peak. It will be shown shortly when the calculated data are given that this lag is usually one week less than one-half of the span of the moving average, i.e. seven weeks in the case of a 15-week average and two weeks in the case of a five-week average.

It becomes obvious that we can use the fact that an average has just passed its peak as an indication that the share price itself has already passed its peak, and therefore as a signal that the share should be sold. Conversely, when the average has just passed a trough we can use that fact as a signal that it is time to buy the particular share. Naturally this spotting of a peak or trough in the share price cannot be carried out on the share price itself because of the intermediate ripples in the price. Thus between early 1984 and the crash in October 1987, for example, there were five or six points at which the price appeared to have reached a peak, whereas the underlying trend was still upwards. Quite clearly, therefore, a moving average is a fairly good indicator of the peaks and troughs in a share price, but as we can see from the example in Figure 3.5, there is a major disadvantage, and that is that the signal is given, in the case of a 53-week average, up to 26 weeks after the price has peaked. We are faced with a dilemma here that we can reduce this time lag by shortening the span of the average, but, as can be seen from the five-week average chart in Figure 3.2, we reach a stage where a number of false signals are given. Therefore we have to reach a compromise between the value of the average as an indicator and the delay in giving the signal. Obviously, with a long delay, the price has moved so far that there is no point in buying or selling, since most of the opportunity has been lost.

   The effect of these delays can be seen for the area of the chart around the low point in the middle of 1990 in Figure 3.6 where the 15-week and 53-week averages are plotted together. The low point of the share price itself, 171p, occurred on 2nd November 1990. If the 15-week average had been used as the indicator of the turning point in the share price, then this bottomed out on 21st December, but of course this would not have become apparent until 28th December, when the average had risen from its low point of the previous week. The delay in this case is therefore eight weeks, and the share price then was 196p, i.e. a rise of 14.6% from its low point. If the 53-week average were taken as an indicator, then this bottomed out on 19th July 1991, which would not have become apparent until 26th July. The delay in that case would have been 38 weeks, and the share price then was 250p, i.e. a rise of 46.2%. The penalty in this case for using a much longer average is therefore 54p, or about a further 31% rise in the

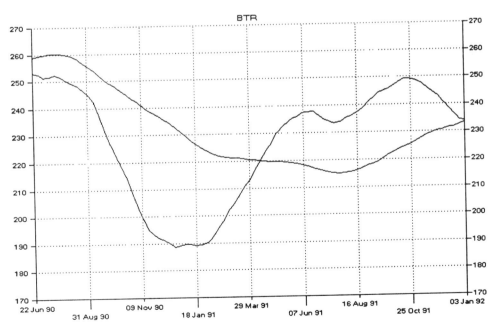

Figure 3.6   The 15-week and 53-week averages for BTR. The major bottom in the 15-week average occurs some 30 weeks before that in the 53-week average

share price. Naturally, if we had used a shorter average than 15-week, say nine-week, then the delay would have been shorter at three weeks, and the average would have given its signal on 23rd November, when the share price was 196p.

It becomes obvious that we have to strike a balance. The shorter the span of the average, the sooner does it react to a change in share price direction, and therefore we would normally be able to get in or out of the share at a more favourable price than is the case if we use a longer-term average. On the other hand, since shorter-term averages are showing up shorter-term trends, we could find ourselves buying into what is a short-term trend rather than the long-term trend that we were hoping to buy into and then finding it coming to an end before we have started to make a profit. We could also find ourselves selling as a result of a short-term downward trend which comes to a rapid end leaving the share price travelling upwards without us. Thus the balance is to accept lower gains from our investments in exchange for a greater certainty that we are entering into a longer-term trend.

It should be noted here that there is a difference in emphasis between someone who is investing in shares and someone who is investing in traded options. The investor in shares should be aiming to minimise risk at all times, even though this of necessity means that the profit in the buying and selling operation is reduced because the price has already moved some way in the direction of the trend before averages such as 13-week or 15-week indicate a turn. On the other hand, except when using special strategies, the investor in traded options is operating at higher risk, and, more importantly, is relatively comfortable with this degree of risk. As well as this, the traded options investor operates on a much shorter trading cycle. Such an investor can therefore utilise averages of much shorter spans in order to reap the benefit of the increased gearing. The effect of the delays for moving averages over five, nine, 15 and 21 weeks on both the BTR share price and the May 300 calls is shown in Table 3.2 for the reversal of the price fall seen in late 1994. The plot of the actual share price movement at this time is shown in Figure 3.7.

Table 3.2 illustrates two points quite clearly. Firstly, options can move very quickly in the few weeks following the actual peak or trough in share

Table 3.2 BTR share prices and premiums for May 300 calls at dates when moving averages turned up

Signal	Date	Share price	May 300 calls
Actual price peak	2 Dec 94	275.5	2
5-week average	30 Dec 94	293.5	8
9-week average	27 Jan 95	304.5	15
15-week average	10 Feb 95	321.0	25
25-week average	17 May 95	321.5	22

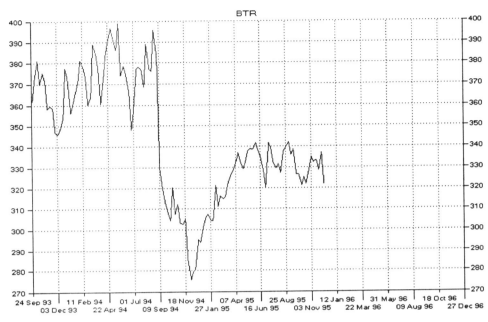

Figure 3.7   The recent price movement of BTR shares (to December 1995)

price. In this example, the value of the call option has more than doubled between 2nd December 1994 and 30th December 1994, when the five-week moving average gave its signal. Secondly, the delay between the signals from the five-week average and the 15-week average saw the share price rise by over 9%, but the put option became more than three times as expensive. This shows how vital early timing is in the traded options market. In many cases it is necessary to collect daily prices and calculate very short-term moving averages on them, for example 10-day and 20-day, but always bearing in mind that the shorter the average that is being used, the greater is the risk that the signal is false, so that one must be prepared to get out of a position very quickly if an adverse trend develops.

The minimum length of average which can be used while still retaining a situation where there would have been no false signals historically (a reasonable guide to lack of false signals in future) varies from share to share, and therefore has to be found by trial and error. One should always take the view that where a share price gives a disappointing result on a historical basis, one can always find another one which behaves more properly.

There is a further point about the waves present in share prices which is relevant to the selection of a particular span for a moving average, and that is that the amplitude of a wave increases as its wavelength increases. This means that, in the case of the BTR share price, the ripples of less than

Table 3.3 Calculation of a 15-week moving average difference for BTR

Date	Price	Subtract	15-week average	Difference
06 01 95	301.5	×		
13 01 95	305.5	×		
20 01 95	307	×		
27 01 95	304.5	×		
03 02 95	304	×		
10 02 95	321	×		
17 02 95	311	×		
24 02 95	316	×	316.3667	−0.366 667
03 03 95	314.5	×	318.4333	−3.933 333
10 03 95	316	×	320	−4
17 03 95	321.5	×	321.7	−0.2
24 03 95	326	×	323.9	2.1
31 03 95	328	×	326.2333	1.766 667
07 04 95	332	×	327.4	4.6
14 04 95	337	×	329.4333	7.566 667
21 04 95	332.5		330.9	1.6
28 04 95	329		332.2667	−3.266 667
05 05 95	332.5		333.0667	−0.566 667
12 05 95	337.5		332.9333	4.566 667
19 05 95	339		333.9667	5.033 333
26 05 95	338.5		334.7	3.8
02 06 95	341.5		334.7	6.8
09 06 95	338		334.2	3.8
16 06 95	335			
23 06 95	328			
30 06 95	319.5			
07 07 95	341.5			
14 07 95	339			
21 07 95	332			
28 07 95	329.5			

say 15 weeks duration have an amplitude of about 20p, while the major waves of more than a year's duration have amplitudes of between 50 and 100p. Therefore, if you can spot a share which has such a clear long-term wave pattern as BTR, it is advantageous to use the longer-term moving average which is necessary to highlight such a long wavelength and accept the greater time lag which this entails. There is one major proviso to this, and that is, as has been pointed out in Chapter 1, that the maximum life of a traded option is nine months. This means that the optimum wavelength which can be used would be that in which the time from the trough to the peak is nine months, i.e. a wavelength of 18 months, since wavelengths are defined as the distance from one peak to the next.

Short-term Price Movements

Moving averages as discussed above have, as explained, the property that they allow through the waves of longer periodicity than the span of the average, while waves of the same or shorter periodicity are attenuated. Because of this, we can only view short-term movements as wavelets superimposed upon longer-term waves. This can be seen from Figure 3.2 where the five-week average of BTR was presented. However, there is a way, involving an extra calculation, in which these short-term movements can be isolated. Without going into the mathematics to any great extent, it is possible to attenuate the longer-term variations and retain the short-term movements. In other words we will be able to view the data that were removed by the moving average smoothing process. This is done simply by subtracting the moving average from the original price data.

Before doing this, there is one important consideration, and that is that the data and the appropriate moving average are correctly aligned before subtraction is carried out. This requires a further explanation: mathematically, the average of a number of weekly prices has to be associated with the *central* week of the number of weeks taken. Virtually all books on the chartist approach to investment ignore this point and, just as we have done so far in this chapter, plot the average data as if they were associated with the last weekly price of the number of weeks taken. This is fine as long as only the fact that a moving average has changed direction is used as an indicator. How it is plotted is immaterial, since it is the latest numerical value that is being observed for a change in direction.

We have used this approach so far to avoid having to explain why the data would have been plotted half of their span back in time. However, the mathematical fact is that an average should be associated with the weekly value at a point one week less than half of the span back in time. Thus, in Table 3.1, the very first calculated point for the 15-week average should have been tabulated opposite week 7, i.e. seven weeks back opposite 17th February 1995 rather than opposite 14th April 1995. When such an average is plotted in this way, obviously the last plotted moving average point finishes this half of a span back in time, i.e. seven weeks back for a 15-week average. This point will not be laboured here for plotting of moving averages, since the object of this chapter has been to show how the various waves can be highlighted, and how the change in direction of the average signals a turning point for a particular wave. It will be important in the next chapter when the relationship between moving averages and share prices will be explored in much more detail. For the present, it is vital that the average is tabulated the correct half-span back in time before the subtraction is carried out.

As an example, we can take the data in Table 3.1, where the 15-week average was calculated, and use it to give numerical data which can then be plotted to highlight those movements of a shorter periodicity than 15 weeks. The 30 prices have produced 16 moving average values, and hence 16 values for the difference. In order to see the short-term movements in the BTR price, it is necessary to calculate a large number of these differences, as in Table 3.3, and then plot them. Note that unlike moving

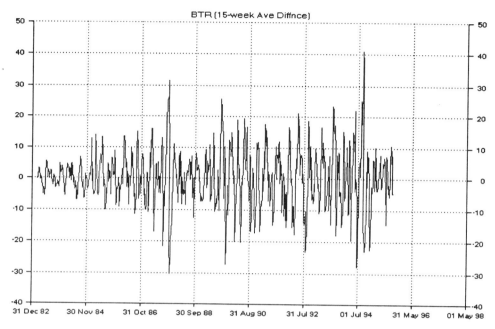

Figure 3.8 Differences between the BTR share price and the centred 15-week average

averages, which are always positive, the differences will fluctuate between positive and negative values. A plot of these differences from the 15-week moving average for BTR is shown in Figure 3.8.

The first impression is that there is some regularity in the plot although there are a few large swings in price, for example in late 1987 (due to the crash) and in mid-1994. A plot of the 15-week average differences for Fisons as shown in Figure 3.9 shows a quite different picture, especially around the centre section of the plot where the fluctuations are very irregular.

In order to see more detail, it is necessary to enlarge a section, and this is done for BTR in Figure 3.10. Besides what appears to be some four and a half complete waves, we find that a considerable number of very short-term fluctuations are superimposed. These very short-term fluctuations are totally unpredictable, but we can make some sense out of the four and a half complete waves.

The wavelength can be taken to be the distance in weeks from a point where the difference crosses zero the next point where it crosses zero going in the same direction, but ignoring any minor crossings of the zero line. The successive wavelengths (the first one starts at week 424) are 22, 24, 14 and 21. The average value of these is 20 weeks, and therefore we can state that, at least during the sections displayed in the figure, there was

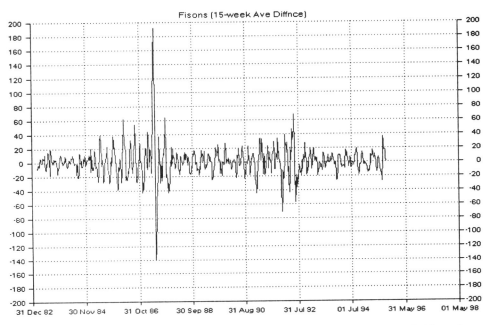

Figure 3.9 Differences between the Fisons share price and the centred 15-week average

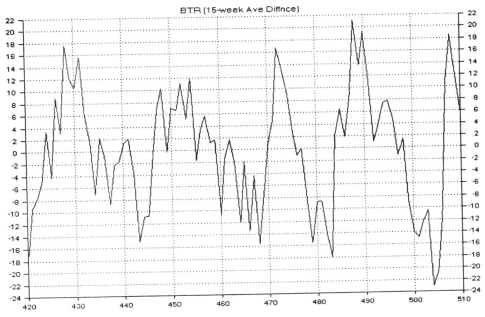

Figure 3.10 An enlarged section of the BTR 15-week average difference

present a short-term fluctuation in the BTR share price with a duration of about 20 weeks. The amplitude of this fluctuation (trough to next peak) varied from about 40p down to about 25p. At this point, because the topic will be covered in depth in the next chapter, we will just hint at the prospect held out by knowing the short-term cyclicality of a share. This is that we can predict with an accuracy of a week or two, when such a cycle is starting on its upward or downward track. Provided that longer-term waves are headed in the same direction, and this proviso cannot be stressed too highly, then there is a major opportunity to profit from an investment in the correct traded option. The direction of the longer-term waves is of course obvious from the charts of the longer-term averages, as shown earlier, but the investor should be careful that such a longer-term wave is not already too far along its cycle so that a reversal of direction is imminent.

DAILY AVERAGES

Obviously, weekly averages impose a limitation on the shortest movements that we can study. A three-week average probably represents the shortest practical value for a weekly average, and in many circumstances there are fluctuations which are well defined and have shorter periodicity. In such cases, quite obviously it is necessary to turn to daily data and daily averages in order to study these short-term effects. Taking Commercial Union as an example, a daily plot and weekly plot over a fairly short time period can be used to illustrate the differences that can be seen from these two approaches.

Figure 3.11(a) and (b) show the weekly data and daily data respectively from early 1992. The immediate impression is that the weekly plot is rather smoother than the daily plot. The extremes of movement are slightly different, since if a maximum is reached on a day other than Friday, this maximum would not be the same in the weekly plot. Thus the highest point reached by Commercial Union in the weekly chart is 696p, whereas in the daily chart it is 706p. The lack of smoothness in the daily chart is because of the presence of very short-term movements. Since it takes a minimum of three points to establish either a peak or a trough, the shortest wavelengths present in daily data will be three-day ones, while the shortest present in weekly data will obviously be three-week ones. Thus the additional wavelengths which can be seen in the daily data but not in the weekly data will be all those from three days up to one day less than three weeks, i.e. 14 days. In the weekly data, while there are a few ripples of wavelength three weeks, there are more with a wavelength of about five to ten weeks' duration. The amplitude of these latter waves is such that it is questionable whether, in view of the time lag for their moving average signals, a profit could be made out of them by normal investment in CU shares. It is quite a different proposition as far as traded options are concerned, however, since the leverage gives quite respectable profit potential in both call and put options. In view of this, naturally the main

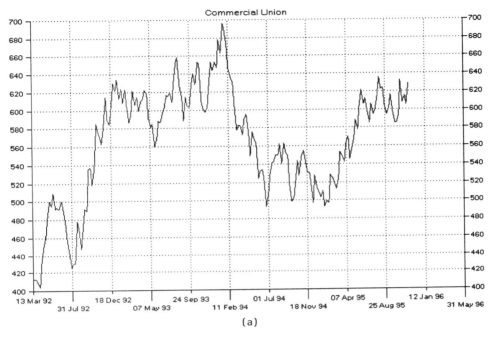

(a)

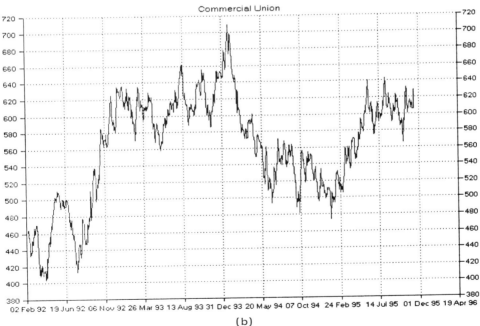

(b)

Figure 3.11 (a) Weekly data for Commercial Union; (b) daily data for Commercial Union over the same period

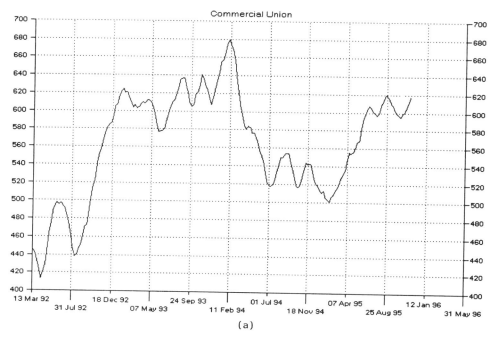

(a)

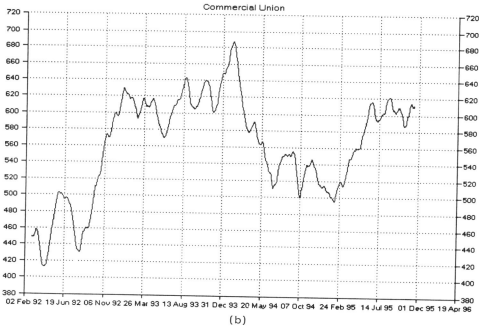

(b)

Figure 3.12 (a) Five-week average of weekly Commercial Union data; (b) 15-day average of daily Commercial Union data

concern is in how close to the peaks and troughs we can get with signals generated from the daily data and weekly data. As can be seen from Figure 3.12(a) and (b), the shortest-span moving averages which give smooth enough curves for Commercial Union data are the five-week average and the 15-day average. The actual time lags for the peak and trough signals in the weekly data are given in Table 3.4. In the case of the daily data, there are of course a few additional minor peaks and troughs observable compared with the weekly data, but to keep the comparison meaningful, only those peaks and troughs corresponding, to within a few days, of those shown in Table 3.4 are shown in Table 3.5.

The time lags in the daily data are of course business days, not calendar days, i.e. there are five business days to a stock market week. The advantages of using daily data and a daily moving average are immediately apparent from a comparison of these two tables. The minimum time lag in the case of the daily data is five days and the maximum is 13 days. For the weekly data the minimum is three weeks (i.e. 15 days) and the maximum is four weeks (i.e. 20 days). Not only that, but the troughs found in the daily data are lower in price than those in the weekly data, while the peaks in the daily data are higher in price than those in the weekly data. Thus an investor using daily data will be given an action signal closer to a trough which is lower in value than in the weekly case, and an action signal closer to a peak which is higher in value than in the weekly case.

It is important to understand the link between the action signal being given, and when action can be taken. In *Stocks and Shares Simplified*, the emphasis was on using weekly closing prices. Thus the buying or selling

Table 3.4 Some peaks and troughs in weekly data for Commercial Union, with the signals given by a five-week moving average

Date	Price	Signal given	Lag	Price	Comment
20 Jan 95	493	10 Feb 95	3	528	trough
2 Jun 95	621	30 Jun 95	4	585	peak
30 Jun 95	652	28 Jul 95	4	612	trough
4 Aug 95	635	1 Sep 95	4	594	peak
29 Sep 95	585	20 Oct 95	3	632	trough

Table 3.5 Some peaks and troughs in daily data for Commercial Union, with the signals given by a 15-day moving average

Date	Price	Signal given	Lag	Price	Comment
23 Jan 95	473.5	8 Feb 95	12	500	trough
6 Jun 95	640	20 Jun 95	10	605	peak
28 Jun 95	575	11 Jul 95	9	614	trough
8 Aug 95	643	22 Aug 95	10	618	peak
10 Oct 95	565	17 Oct 95	5	598	trough
20 Oct 95	632	8 Nov 95	13	615	peak

Table 3.6 Monday prices for Commercial Union obtained from the signals given for weekly data in Table 3.4

Date	Price	Action taken	Price	Advantage
20 Jan 95	493	13 Feb 95	527	+1
2 Jun 95	621	3 Jul 95	584	−1
30 Jun 95	652	31 Jul 95	615	−3
4 Aug 95	635	4 Sep 95	600	+6
29 Sep 95	585	23 Oct 95	622	+10

signal would be given on Friday evening, when that week's closing price became available. The investor could then buy or sell when the market opened on Monday morning. For simplicity, all calculations regarding rises and falls from when a signal was given assumed the investor obtained the Friday closing price. For a reason which is not obvious, the investor operating on weekly signals will more often than not get a better price on Monday morning than the closing price the previous Friday, i.e. in the long run will do better than is suggested by the Friday pricing. This can be demonstrated by the Monday prices shown in Table 3.6. Taking the five signals in total, there is a 13p advantage compared with the Friday closings. In mathematical terms, since the delay in taking action, being one business day, is only one-fifth of the frequency of the data (i.e. five days) used in the calculation, the difference can be ignored.

For daily data, this is not the case. In mathematical terms, the delay of one day before action is taken cannot be ignored, since it is the same as the frequency of the data. By and large, the investor gets a poorer price the following day compared with the closing price when the signal is given. This is demonstrated by the data in Table 3.7. Here there is a total loss of 62p from the six signals compared with the prices obtaining at the close on the day the signal is given. While occasionally a better price is obtained the next day, overall the message given in Table 3.7 is correct. This means that the investor operating on daily signals must take a different course of action compared with the investor working with daily data. Probably the best option is to obtain the price on the share that you think may give a signal that day say an hour before the close, either from the teletext services on TV, or from a data feed to your computer if you have one, or by calling your broker. You can then decide if using this price as the temporary closing price would give a signal and take your buying or selling action just before the market closes.

Although, because of the shorter gap from a better price we saw when comparing Tables 3.4 and 3.5, the action signal will usually be given at a better price in the case of daily data than is the case with weekly data, this is not always true, since occasionally a very short-term fluctuation may operate to the disadvantage of the investor on the very day a daily signal is given. This might not happen on the Monday following the occurrence of a

Table 3.7 Next-day prices for Commercial Union obtained from the signals given for daily data in Table 3.5

Date	Price	Signal given	Price	Comment
23 Jan 95	473.5	9 Feb 95	518	−18
6 Jun 95	640	21 Jun 95	590	−15
28 Jun 95	575	12 Jul 95	614	0
8 Aug 95	643	23 Aug 95	613	−3
10 Oct 95	565	18 Oct 95	624	−26
20 Oct 95	632	9 Nov 95	615	0

Table 3.8 Price rises and falls obtainable by using the signals from five-week and 15-day moving averages for Commercial Union

Comment	Differences	
	5-week average	15-day average
Trough 1 to peak 1	57	105
Peak 1 to trough 2	−31	9
Trough 2 to peak 2	−15	4
Peak 2 to trough 3	−22	20
Trough 3 to peak 3	no signal	17

weekly signal. As we saw from Table 3.6, there might even be an advantageous Monday movement.

In traded options we can of course profit from falls as well as rises, so an important measure of the usefulness of an indicator is the difference between successive peaks and troughs and successive troughs and peaks in terms of the price of the share at the time of the signal. The data in the tables give three such differences, since there are three peaks and two troughs. The comparison between the weekly and daily differences taken from Tables 3.6 and 3.4, i.e. using Monday prices for weekly data and same-day prices for daily data, is shown in Table 3.8.

Note that in the sense we wish to use them, all the differences should be positive, not negative numbers. A negative number implies that the price prevailing when a peak is indicated is less than the price prevailing when the corresponding succeeding trough is signalled. Conversely it also means that the price prevailing for a trough is more than the price prevailing for the succeeding peak. Quite obviously these are situations where we would lose money. Table 3.8 shows clearly that except for the first trough-to-peak rise, the other three situations where the five-week average is used would result in losses. Thus in the type of market typified by this section of the Commercial Union share price, i.e. one of only relatively gentle rises, a five-week average is more than useless as an indicator for short-term fluctuations; it is positively dangerous, whether used for share purchase or in traded options investment. On the other hand, the 15-day average gives positive results for all those fluctuations. It almost doubles the gain achieved from the first trough-to-peak rise and gives respectable movements for the fall from the second peak to the next trough, and for the rise from the second trough to the third peak. Note that at the time of writing, the five-week moving average had not given a signal for the third peak.

The question which arises now is whether such short-term fluctuations, which obviously require moving averages of very short spans, are of any use in normal investment in shares as opposed to traded options, and the answer has to be a qualified *No*! Investment in shares depends upon a rise between a trough and the following peak, and in this example the first trough-to-peak rise was 105p, the second trough-to-peak rise was 4p and the third was 17p. Based on a share price of around 600p, the first rise would have been quite profitable, the second rise would have seen a loss and the third would have been essentially neutral. The message must be that, with a few exceptions, short-term movements with a periodicity of less than about six months are of no use to the investor in shares. The use of such short-term variations in traded option investment is a quite different story, and can best be illustrated by the premiums on the various Commercial Union call and put options prevailing at the times the signals were given. These are listed in Table 3.9.

Table 3.9 Behaviour of Commercial Union call option premiums during three share price rises

Date	Share price	Option	July	October
8 Feb 95	500	550	9	11
20 Jun 95	605	550	59	65
Gain	**21.0%**		**555%**	**490%**

Date	Share price	Option	October	January
11 Jul 95	614	550	70	81
22 Aug 95	618	550	75	88
Gain	**0.7%**		**7.1%**	**8.6%**

Date	Share price	Option	January	April
17 Oct 95	598	550	48	64
8 Nov 95	615	550	68	77
Gain	**2.8%**		**41.7%**	**20.3%**
17 Oct 95	598	600	4	30
8 Nov 95	615	600	32	44
Gain	**2.8%**		**700%**	**31.8%**
17 Oct 95	598	650	1	11
8 Nov 95	615	650	13	20
Gain	**2.8%**		**1200%**	**81.8%**

The large movement between 8th February and 20th June 1995, with a rise from 500p to 605p, i.e. 21%, gave considerable leverage in the call option with the actual gain depending upon which option had been selected. Thus the July 550s gained 555% and the October 550s 490%, an enormous gain compared with that in the share price. The small movement between 11th July and 22nd August, which saw the share price rise by only 0.7%, resulted in ten times as high a rise in the option premiums, being 7.1% for the October 550s and 8.6% for the January 550s.

The influence of both exercise price and expiry date can be seen in the changes in options premiums during the modest rise of 2.8% in share price between 17th October and 8th November 1995. The nearest expiry date, i.e. the January options, produced gains much higher than the next expiry of April. As to be expected, the out-of-the-money options produced spectacular gains, being 1200% for the January 650s!

Naturally, gains of this magnitude of thousands or many hundreds of percent are not commonplace, but gains of a few hundred percent are. Such gains result from correct timing of market movements, using the techniques in this chapter and the next, plus the choice of the correct options, using the principles discussed in later chapters in this book.

It should be noted that the behaviour of options is not always so positively linked to the change in share price. This aspect is discussed in the next chapter, but the position with put options during the fall from 22nd August to 17th October 1995 as shown in Table 3.10 illustrates this clearly. Here the share price fell by 3.2%, so it would have been expected that most of the put options available would have seen an increase in the value of their premiums over this period of time. Only the January 650 puts showed a gain, of fairly modest proportions (15.5%), between the two dates. All of the others showed losses, ranging from 3.5% to 85%. Thus the correlation between put premiums and the change in share price in the case of Commercial Union during this period was a negative one, while the correlation between call premiums and the change in share prices as shown in Table 3.9 was a positive one.

Table 3.10 Behaviour of Commercial Union put option premiums during a share price fall

Date	Share price	Option	January	April
22 Aug 95	618	550	7	14
17 Oct 95	598	550	1	6
Gain	**– 3.2%**		**–85%**	**–57.1%**
22 Aug 95	618	600	20	31
17 Oct 95	598	600	5	22
Gain	**–3.2%**		**–75%**	**–29%**
22 Aug 95	618	650	45	57
17 Oct 95	598	650	52	55
Gain	**–3.2%**		**15.5%**	**–3.5%**

4

Technical Indicators 2.
Channel Analysis

Moving averages used in the way discussed in the last chapter are extremely valuable indicators of a change in the direction of an underlying trend in share prices. Of course, knowing that the trend has changed direction is only of value if the assumption is made that the share price will continue in its new direction for a long enough period to enable a profit to be made. This knowledge is gained from a study of the past history of the moving average of the particular span that one is interested in. Simple experiments with short-, medium- and long-term averages can give an idea of the typical time for which trends continue. It will be noted of course that the longer the span of the average, the longer does that particular trend continue before changing direction, since the trends of lesser duration will have been filtered out (see Chapter 3). Viewing a moving average graphically tells us a great deal about how large or how small these trends are, and it is this that helps to put a brake on any euphoria we may have when a change in the direction of a trend is signalled. We are not able to tell with any great certainty just how long the trend will continue in its new direction.

The use of a moving average in isolation from the share price itself misses completely the valuable information that is available when a moving average and the share price are plotted on a chart at the same time. By this statement, we do not mean the widely used but mathematically incorrect practice of plotting the average with no time lag, and attaching great significance to those times where the price rises up through, or falls down below, the moving average in question. We mean the powerful technique of channel analysis, which without question is the most accurate indicator of future price movements available to us.

BASIS OF CHANNEL ANALYSIS

When used properly, channel analysis will enable us to forecast points in the immediate future at which a trend is expected to change direction.

Since our attention is focused upon that point, even when we take into account the unavoidable uncertainties in stock market predictions, we will be able to recognise that the change in direction has occurred only a very short time after the event, unlike the time lags which we have to accept with a more simplified use of moving averages. This in itself makes channel analysis the most important technical indicator available. However, it has additional properties that make it particularly appropriate for use in traded options investment—subject once again to a degree of uncertainty, it can tell us the target area into which the price will move, and how long it will take to get there.

The basis of the method of channel analysis is the observation that, when correctly plotted, share prices oscillate about a moving average, and the oscillations can be contained within boundaries above and below the moving average. These boundaries constitute a channel. Thus share prices move within a channel, and moreover, it will be seen from the examples in the rest of this chapter that the channel is of constant depth. This channel can be constructed by eye on a chart of the share price, or it can be constructed about the moving average plotted on the chart. In the latter case, of course, a computer is of great value in carrying out both the moving average calculation and the plotting function.

The increasing information which can be obtained from moving averages as we use them in different ways can be seen in Figure 4.1. Here we show the 15-week moving average for Allied Domecq plotted with the share prices themselves in the manner beloved of most technical analysts, i.e. with the moving average plotted up to date rather than half a span back in time. In Figure 4.2 we show the average plotted in the mathematically correct manner, half of a span back in time, i.e. with a lag of seven weeks. In Figure 4.3 we show the upper and lower boundaries adding to the moving average, these boundaries being of such a width as to enclose most of the extremities of the price movements, while Figure 4.4 shows the channels with the central moving average removed.

The only information that can be obtained from Figure 4.1 is that the 15-week average has changed direction more than 30 times during the period covered by the chart. The longest leg of one of the trends is about nine months, the shortest just three weeks, and the average usually turns upwards or downwards about nine weeks after a trough or peak. As an indicator, therefore, we can expect that a change in direction of the average signifies a new trend which started about nine weeks previously and which ought to last at least another nine weeks.

In the middle chart, the fact that the average is plotted half a span back in time now illustrates quite clearly the relationship between the price and the average. The price meanders about the average, but at points where the average is at a peak, the price has reached an even higher peak, and where the average has reached a trough, the price has reached an even lower level. These high or low points in the prices now coincide with high

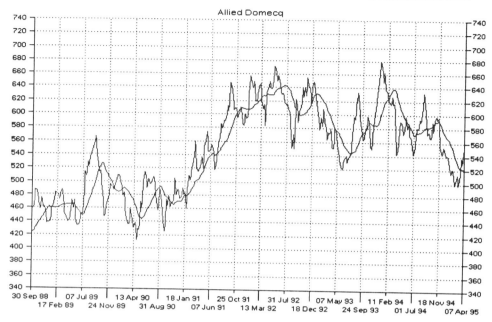

Figure 4.1 The share price of Allied Domecq with the unlagged 15-week average superimposed

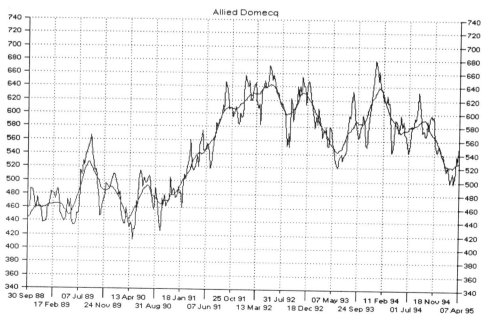

Figure 4.2 The share price of Allied Domecq with the centred 15-week average superimposed

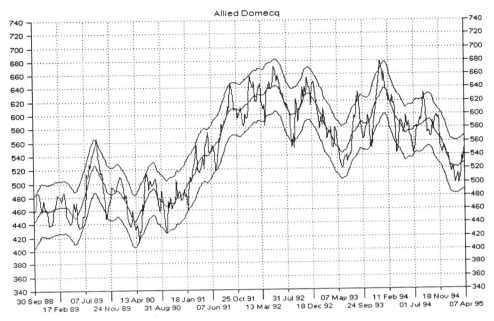

Figure 4.3   The share price of Allied Domecq with channels added to the centred 15-week average. Note how the upper and lower boundaries are equidistant vertically from the average

and low points in the average. The moving average now represents a "better" picture of the share price and where it is going, since the noise due to the short-term variations is eliminated. Since we have a "better" picture of the way the share price is behaving, we can much more readily predict where it will go in the future.

   Now if you examine more closely the way in which the price values themselves wander about the 15-week average, you will see that they never move too far away, and that it is easy to draw in the boundaries within which the price moves. This is done in Figure 4.3, with the restriction that the upper and lower boundaries are equidistant in a vertical sense from the central average. In Figure 4.4 the central average is removed so that the boundaries can be seen more clearly. The vertical depth of the channel is the same throughout the chart; this is an absolute necessity for channel analysis to be effective. Computer programs that draw boundaries a constant percentage away from the centre are not drawing channels of this type. Constant-depth boundaries as shown in Figure 4.4 should now bring home quite clearly the value of this approach of channel analysis. In its simplest use, we can say that we can project the channel forward into the near future by drawing smooth continuations of the existing channel lines. Then when a price starts to draw close to either the higher or the

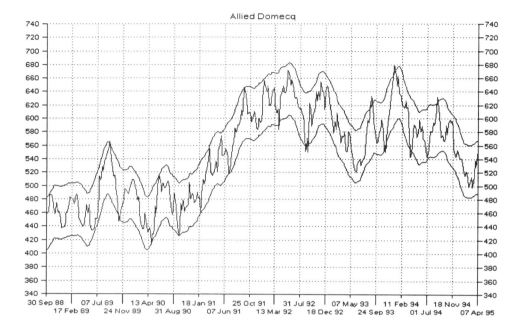

Figure 4.4   The centred average has now been removed so that the channels can be seen more clearly

lower boundary, we should watch it carefully, since once it has touched or passed slightly through this level, a reversal of direction is expected. Note that although in this example we produced the channel by calculating the 15-week average, plotting it and drawing in the boundaries, it is perfectly easy and straightforward to do this without any calculation by drawing the *smoothest two lines that will enclose most of the price movements, making sure that the vertical distance between the two lines is kept constant.*

You can take a photocopy of Figure 4.2 and try for yourself, or practise on any other chart that you have. It is useful to use either a flexible curve or the various curved stencils that are available from any good-quality stationers in order to enable the smoothest channels to be drawn. In this simplest way, therefore, channel analysis will enable us to improve our timing of a change in direction quite markedly. We can extrapolate this process until we run out of channels.

When carried out by computer, as are all of the charts in this book, the channels are drawn so that only a small, specified percentage (e.g. 2.5%) of price points lie outside the channels. Thus a small number of overshoots is tolerable, and even desirable if the maximum number of peaks and troughs are to lie close to the channel boundaries.

CHANNELS WITHIN CHANNELS

So far we have discussed the drawing of just one channel, whether this is done by eye or by calculation of an average. As can be seen from the chart in Figure 4.4, this highlights waves with periodicities up to two years. We know, however, from calculating much longer-term averages on stock market data that there are waves of much longer periodicity than this, and these can be highlighted, providing we have data over a long enough period of time, by drawing the appropriate channel to encompass the channel we have already drawn. Again, just as with the first channel, we can either adopt the approach of calculating a longer-term average, or simply draw in this second channel by eye. This channel is produced in Figure 4.5 from a calculation of a 53-week moving average, with the boundaries being drawn a constant amount above and below the average. For the sake of clarity, the average itself has been omitted, although naturally it will run down the exact centre of this channel. If we have enough data, we can continue in this way to draw further even longer-term channels to enclose the existing ones, although normally a short-term channel and a long-term channel will be sufficient. Sometimes we can even omit the short-term channel. In general, a channel based on a 53-week average is useful for highlighting trends of longer than one year's duration. However, where the resulting channel is still "lumpy", i.e. shows the influence of shorter-term fluctuations, it may be necessary to move to a larger value for the average to generate a more smoothly curved channel. The smoother the channel, the easier it is to project it into the future past the latest actual price point. The advantage in the case of Allied Domecq in moving to a 75-week channel can be seen from Figure 4.6, where the now smooth channel can be compared with that shown in Figure 4.5.

You should be able to start to see now how these channels can be used to predict future price movements. When the share price approaches the inner channel boundary we expect it to reverse direction, and when the inner channel approaches the boundary of the next outer channel, again we expect the inner channel to reverse direction. The key to prediction in the near future is of course the smooth extrapolation of the various channels into the future. When the channels are drawn by eye, or with the aid of a stencil, then naturally this projection into the future is part of the drawing process. If, however, the channels are drawn around the various calculated moving averages, then since the averages terminate half a span back in time, so will the channels. In such a case there will be two parts to the extrapolation process, firstly to bring the channel up to the present time and secondly to project it into the future. Of course since the prices themselves continue to the present time, these serve as a useful guide in extending the channels to the present, from which point they can be extrapolated into the future.

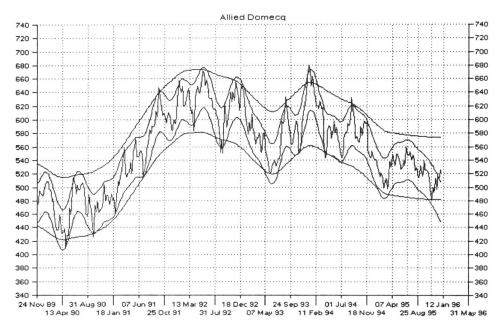

Figure 4.5   Allied Domecq: the 53-week channel enclosing the 15-week channel

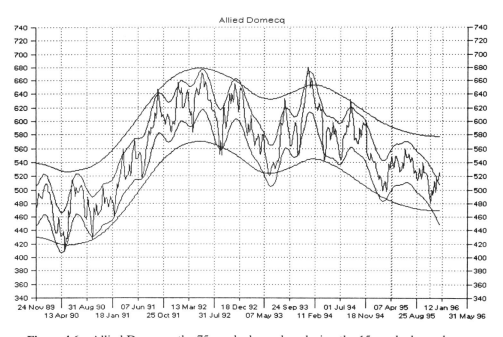

Figure 4.6   Allied Domecq: the 75-week channel enclosing the 15-week channel

It is useful to emphasise how we can determine various features as the share price history unfolds. For example, a minor trough in the weekly prices is only apparent a week after the event, i.e. when the price has moved up from the previous week's lower price. An intermediate trough is only apparent when the next minor trough to be seen does not descend as low. A major trough is only apparent when the next intermediate trough is at a higher level, and so on. These same arguments will apply to minor, intermediate and major peaks. Thus:

- **Minor troughs/peaks:** three successive weeks' (days') prices in the correct relationship.
- **Trough:** week (day) two lower than weeks (days) one and three.
- **Peak:** week (day) two higher than weeks (days) one and three.
- **Relevance to channels:** as many of these minor troughs/peaks as possible should touch boundaries of short-term channels.

- **Intermediate troughs/peaks:** three successive minor troughs/peaks in the correct relationship.
- **Trough:** minor trough two lower than minor troughs one and three.
- **Peak:** minor peak two higher than minor peaks one and three.
- **Relevance to channels:** as many of these intermediate troughs/peaks as possible should touch boundaries of intermediate-term channels.

- **Major troughs/peaks:** three successive intermediate troughs/peaks in the correct relationship.
- **Trough:** intermediate trough two lower than intermediate troughs one and three.
- **Peak:** intermediate peak two higher than intermediate peaks one and three.
- **Relevance to channels:** as many of these major troughs/peaks as possible should touch boundaries of long-term channels.

Naturally, what is meant by short-, intermediate- and long-term channels depends upon the characteristics of the particular share being studied. In the example we are using in this chapter, Allied Domecq, we shall be concerned only with intermediate and long-term channels when using weekly data for the analysis, and can in fact manage with just one channel. The short-term channels can only be defined with any degree of accuracy by using daily data, and these are discussed towards the end of this chapter.

EXAMPLES FROM THE ALLIED DOMECQ PRICE HISTORY

The way in which channel analysis is used to predict price movements is best illustrated by using the Allied Domecq chart as an example, taking several points at various times along the period covered by the chart. Although the channels in these examples have been drawn by the computer, any reader drawing channels on the charts of the Allied Domecq share price would end up with very similar positions for the boundaries, and would thus reach a similar conclusion in each case. In each example, the way the channels are drawn is explained as if the reader is doing this manually. The object of the analysis is to draw attention to the imminence of turning points, but of course since turning points occur relatively infrequently, most of the time the decision following from the analysis is that the price is expected to continue in the same direction. The first examples use weekly data, and it should be noted that there will be slightly more error involved in the determination of turning points using weekly data compared with daily data. Nevertheless, these examples serve to show the power of the method even when weekly data are used for the analysis.

19th February 1993 (price: 608p)

The chart from 24th November 1989 until 19th February 1993 for Allied Domecq is shown in Figure 4.7. It is possible to construct two channels over this time period, an inner channel and an outer channel. If drawing by hand, then the inner channel is constructed by drawing the upper

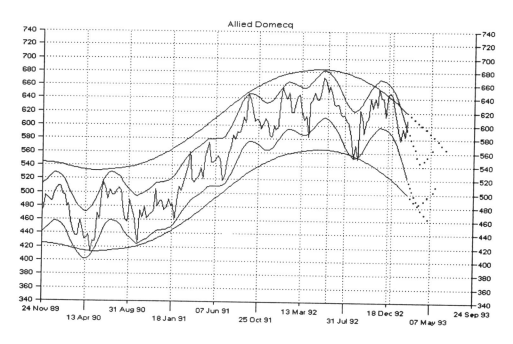

Figure 4.7   Allied Domecq: channel prediction on 19th February 1993

boundary so as to touch as many of the peaks as possible, bearing in mind the necessity to draw a smooth curve, and the same approach is used for the lower boundary. The width of the channel as measured vertically has to be kept constant, and in the present case is about 65p in vertical depth. This requirement to maintain a constant vertical depth may necessitate redrawing parts of the channel, the overriding aim being to enclose as much of the price movement as possible. Note that if the inclusion of one or two peaks or troughs of extreme movement would make the channel too wide, these should be allowed to overshoot or undershoot the channel to keep the width tighter.

As we progress along the chart, there will be occasions where the upper boundary will be better defined than the lower boundary, due to the closeness of successive peaks. On other occasions the lower boundary will be easier to draw. Adopt the approach of drawing the easiest boundary for each part of the price history and drawing the other boundary at the constant width above or below it as the case may be, the complete picture being then a much more realistic channel than if you try to draw it all in one go. By this means the inner channel should appear like that in Figure 4.7. Just as we drew the inner channel by drawing smooth curves to enclose most of the price movement, so we can draw an outer channel by drawing smooth curves to enclose the inner channel itself. This has also been done in Figure 4.7. Prediction of price movements in the immediate future is then done by extrapolating both the outer and inner channels with smooth lines forward in time as shown by the dotted lines in the figure. The price of 608p at the time the prediction is being made has been reached by a rise from a local low point of 578p which was reached on 29th January 1993. The immediate question is whether or not the price will continue this small upward movement to turn into a substantial price rise. Chartists would argue that since the trough at 578p represents a retreat of about two-thirds of the previous rise to 655p on 20th November from a previous low point of 550p on 11th September 1992, then the price is set for a rise to somewhere between 680p and 700p. An analysis of the channels gives a quite different forecast. The inner channel is headed downwards from its high point in late 1992, and the outer channel has also been falling since about April 1992. Thus we would expect the price to rebound downwards from the upper boundary of the inner channel where the price is currently standing if the channel is drawn manually. In the computer-drawn channel in Figure 4.7, the price is just above the channel boundary because of the 2.5% allowed tolerance for points lying outside the boundary, but for the purpose of the analysis can be considered to be at the boundary. Thus in the immediate near term we expect the price to fall from its present value of 608p.

In trying to establish a target area into which the price will fall, we now take note of where we expect the falling inner channel (which contains the price movement within it) to meet the lower boundary of the falling outer channel. This would appear to be in April 1993, and moreover, we can establish an approximate level for the lower boundary at that time as being just below 500p. To sum up, we have decided that the price is heading downwards and that it will continue to do so for about another two months, reaching perhaps 500p before reversing direction. As we can see from Figure 4.8, where the subsequent price movement is shown up to 9th July 1993, this was an excellent prediction. The price actually bottomed out in May at 520p. Thus we were a few weeks out in timing when the lowest point would be reached, and slightly out in predicting a fall of over 100p when the actual one was 88p. A fall such as this over such a relatively short period of two months would give enormous profits for those investors taking the correct position in options. Compare this with the chartists who would probably have predicted a price rise rather than a price fall!

9th July 1993 (price: 537p)

The chart relevant to a prediction at this point in time is shown in Figure 4.8. During our prediction based on the price data on 19th February, we expected the inner channel to be bouncing back upwards from the lower boundary of the outer channel some time towards the end of April. In Figure 4.8 we can see that the price has risen slightly from its low point of 520p on 4th June. The fact that the latest trough, formed at 530p on 2nd

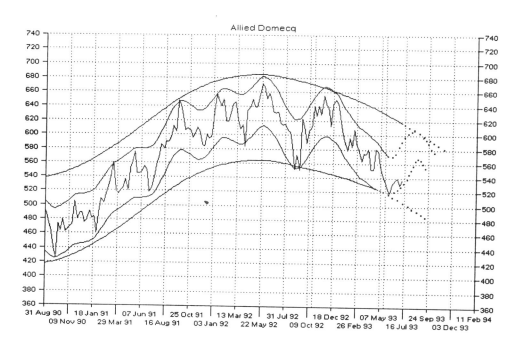

Figure 4.8 Allied Domecq: channel prediction on 9th July 1993

July, is higher than this previous trough of 520p suggests that the channel has now changed direction, i.e. is headed upwards, since of course the object is to place troughs on a channel boundary if this is possible without too much distortion of the curve of the channel. In other words, the trough position can define the current position of the channel. If we make the trough at 520p the lowest point of the channel, i.e. its turning point, then it does not require excessive bending upwards to make the boundary pass through the 530p trough as shown by the dotted extrapolation of the inner channel in Figure 4.8. This will also place this turning point of the inner channel on the boundary of the outer channel where it would be forced to bounce up. Since this extrapolation shows the inner channel to be rising, it will carry the price upwards with it. Thus our prediction is for a price rise from this point. If we continue the inner channel upwards until it meets the upper boundary of the outer channel, then this will give us some indication of the target area into which the price will rise. This level is shown in Figure 4.8 as being just over 600p, and probably occurring in mid-August.

The accuracy of this prediction is shown by the position on 13th August 1993 (Figure 4.9). The price had reached 597p the week before, and had then fallen back slightly to 593p. Thus the price is exactly in the target area on exactly the anticipated date!

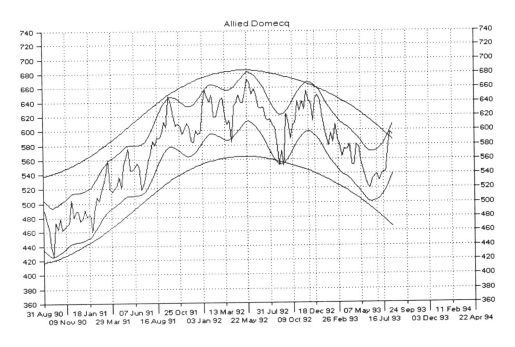

Figure 4.9 Allied Domecq: channel prediction on 13th August 1993 using weekly data. Channels are 75-week and 15-week

Since the price has risen to the target area, our attention is now focused on when we should sell, presuming we have bought the share, or close our position if we hold one in Allied Domecq options. We have to wait for the opposite situation to that obtaining in Figure 4.8, where the latest trough was higher than the previous one, heralding a rise in the inner channel. Now we have to wait for the next peak, and see if it is lower or higher than the previous one of 597p. If higher, then we can assume the inner channel is still rising, but if lower, that is the signal to get out. The following week the price rose to 615p, and the week after that to 633p. Since the price fell to 614p the week after that (3rd September), the peak formed by this is 633p and therefore higher than the previous one of 597p. By our previous criterion we should expect the channel to continue rising and therefore should stay with the share. However, there is one crucial observation to be made. The price has risen from the bottom of the outer channel to a point higher than the anticipated top in a matter of just over two months. This rate of gain is one that is not sustainable, and therefore we must expect a price reversal at any time. An inspection of any chart where a rapid price increase occurs (other than in a takeover situation where the subsequent price usually remains stable) shows that the fall from the peak is usually equally rapid. In the present case that is certainly true, since the price fell again on 10th September to 592p, i.e. a lower level than the point at which we started this analysis. The fall of 41p took place in just two weeks. It is impossible for investors, using weekly data, to protect against reactions of this rapidity. The investor would sell at 592p, which of course is in the original target area for the share price. The investor would be pleased to have achieved the target, but probably slightly aggrieved that an additional 20p or so had not been squeezed out of the situation. Even using a stop-loss of say 5% would have made no difference, since this would not have been triggered at 614p, being 19p or 3% down from the peak. The only way in which more profit might have been squeezed out would be by using daily data, as discussed in the following section.

IMPROVED ACCURACY USING DAILY DATA

We have already mentioned briefly that powerful though the technique of channel analysis is, there are still uncertainties in the prediction of stock market prices. The uncertainty lies in both the timing and the extent of a price trend. A channel can develop an extreme downward or upward hook which was not predictable. However, if the hook is preceded by indications that the price has reached a channel boundary, then this should mean that the investor, although unaware of the impending dramatic over-reaction, will have already taken action. Channel analysis will then have protected the investor against such drastic overshoots.

In the case of a trough or peak being several weeks too early or too late compared with the predicted time, the usual cause is the (unpredictable) increasing importance of short-term cycles. Since short-term cycles are most accurately described when daily data are used, then quite obviously it is imperative to use daily data when a predicted trough or peak is only a few weeks away in time.

3rd September 1993 (price: 614p)

Having illustrated the difficulty in dealing with rapid price movements at a channel boundary when weekly data are used, as in Figure 4.9, it is interesting to compare this with the position using daily data for the same period, as shown in Figure 4.10. Only the long-term channel has been drawn, and this is slightly different from the long-term channel in Figure 4.9 for two reasons. Firstly the data are slightly more recent in time, and the recent data have lifted the calculated channel. Secondly, the daily equivalent to a 75-week channel is a 385-day channel, but we are able to return to the equivalent of a 53-week (one-year) channel, i.e. a 265-day channel, because of the additional smoothness imparted by the daily data. The projection above the channel as drawn by the computer is within the tolerance allowed for overshoots and undershoots over the history of the share price.

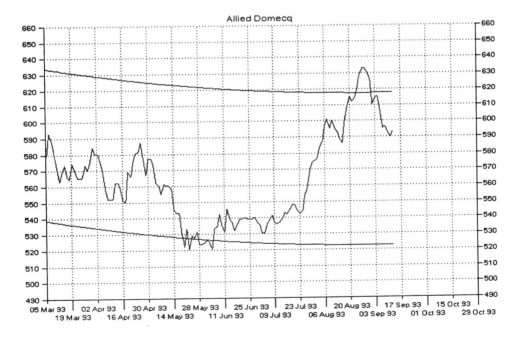

Figure 4.10 Allied Domecq: daily data around the time of the peak price in late August 1993 with long-term 256-day channel shown

Figure 4.10 shows quite clearly that the price at the first trough of 610p on 2nd September is some way below the upper channel boundary, having bounced down from it. This in itself is of course a danger signal, but when the price rises the following day (3rd September) to 614p, the negative aspect of the price movement is that the trough at 610p so formed is lower than the previous trough at 612p on 23rd August (this trough was prior to the peak price of 633p). We noted previously that this is a sign that the inner channel till turn down, and so we would sell at this point, i.e. at 614p, with an improvement of 22p over the weekly exit price of 592p.

31st December 1993 (price: 680p)

Figure 4.11 shows the position at the end of January 1994 with weekly data being used and the 75-week channel superimposed. The previous example showed the difficulty in getting out of a share which has shown a rapid rise and fall when weekly data are used. Figure 4.11 shows the difficulty in getting into a rapid rise when weekly data are used and the rise continues without pause for several weeks. The share price formed a trough at 550p on 12th November 1993, and it can be seen that this trough was at the lower boundary of the long-term channel. Thus a rise is expected from this point. The difficulty lies in the fact that rather than form a second trough a

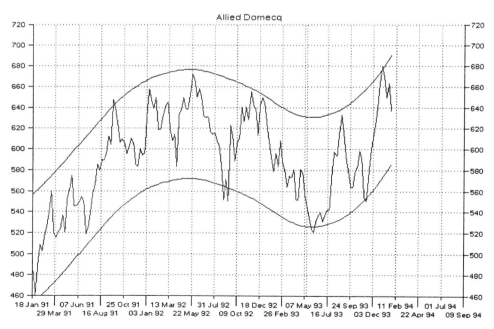

Figure 4.11   Allied Domecq: weekly data with 75-week channel as at December 1993/ January 1994

few weeks later at a higher level than the one at 550p, which would have enabled us to get into the share at a reasonable price, the price continued upwards without hesitation until the peak of 680p was reached. Thus the investor using weekly data would have been left behind.

When daily data are used, the picture is quite different, as shown in Figure 4.12. The lowest point was reached on 10th November 1993 at 546p. Allowing for the tolerance for a small overshoot, the price can be considered to be at the long-term channel boundary. Thus we expect the price to bounce upwards from this. We are now in the position of examining the troughs as they arrive to see if they are successively higher than each other. Following the initial one at the boundary, the next trough at 550p was formed two days later, but this is too close to the first in time to reach a decision that the price was on the way up. Another trough was formed at 550p on 16th November by virtue of the rise to 561p on the 17th. This trough is far enough away from the initial one that no distortion would be involved in bending an inner channel (not shown) to fit it. Thus the investor could be fairly comfortable that the price was now in an upward short-term trend. The price rapidly rose to over 680p, as shown by the price movement in Figure 4.13. Thus the investor using daily data would have captured a significant rise not available to the investor using weekly data.

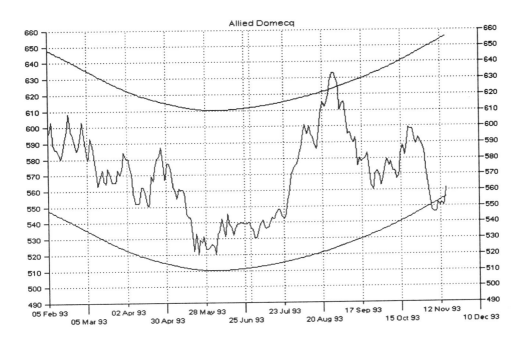

Figure 4.12 Allied Domecq: daily data with 265-day channel as at 17th November 1993

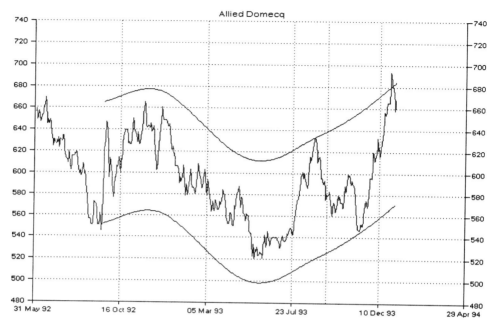

Figure 4.13   Allied Domecq: the substantial rise between mid-November and the end of December 1993

6th January 1993 (price: 668p)

Figure 4.14 shows the most recent portion of Figure 4.13 expanded so that daily movements can be seen. The long-term 265-day channel is superimposed. The latest price is 668p, the price having fallen from the peak of 693p. The channel depth is about 110p, and the price, having fallen by 25p from the upper boundary, is therefore a quarter of the way back to the lower boundary. Thus the outlook for a further rise is not good. Not only that, but the trough that has been formed by this rise to 668p from 558p is lower than the hesitation points of 680p on 31st December and 3rd January, and the one before the peak at 665p. Thus on our criterion of troughs being successively higher to maintain the upward impetus, the price is not going to move higher from this position. As far as future price movement is concerned, we would expect the inner channel to fall at approximately the same rate as it rose to the peak on 29th December. Thus it should meet the lower (rising) boundary around March 1994 at a target price of about 600p.

The position on 24th March 1994 is shown in Figure 4.15. The price is at 619p. The question here is whether this point is now a buying point. We note that the latest trough caused by the rise from 616p to 619p is higher than the previous dual troughs at 608p some weeks previously, and

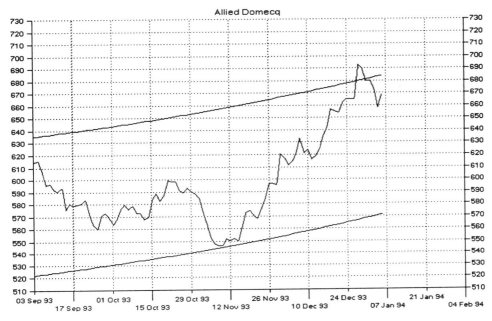

Figure 4.14 Allied Domecq: daily data with 265-week channel as at December 1993/ January 1994

therefore the present position would constitute a buying point *if this latest trough can be considered to be at the lower boundary*. The computer draws the boundary as shown, i.e. some way below the current price level. If we attempt to draw the channel by eye, then we would have to put a much tighter upward bend on it to force it to go through the trough on 23rd March. To do this would make the channel rise too steeply when compared with previous rising channels in this share. Thus on balance we would decide that the price has not just bounced up from the lower boundary but is still some way above it. Therefore we would not be considering buying into the share at this point but would wait to see when the price does reach the lower boundary. We would expect this to happen in another couple of months when the level will have risen to somewhere between 620 and 630p. The position a few weeks later on 13th April 1994 is shown in Figure 4.16. This shows that the price did not stop at the boundary but continued downwards, thus vindicating our decision to wait and see what happened after the decision point in March.

These examples using Allied Domecq serve to show quite clearly what can be achieved by using channel analysis compared with simple moving averages, and also the advantage that can be obtained by using daily data for the plots when approaching key predicted turning points. You should also begin to see that as we progress along the price history of a share, we

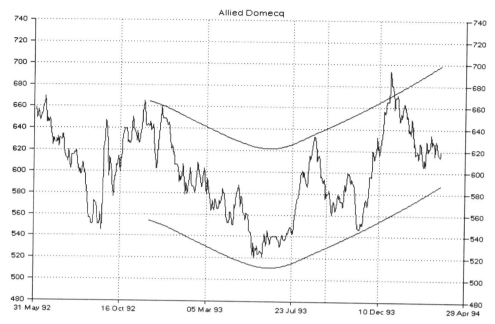

Figure 4.15   Allied Domecq: the position on 24th March 1994

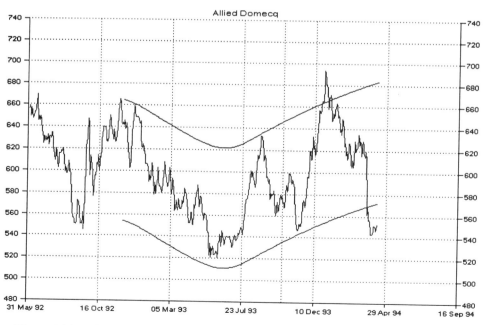

Figure 4.16   Allied Domecq: the position on 13th April 1994

will have greater or lesser degrees of certainty not so much about the direction of a trend, but about the target price for the trend. We should try to quantify this degree of certainty, because, as shown in the next chapter, it is crucial to understanding the amount of risk that we should take on board in our traded option strategy.

It must be pointed out that channel analysis, like any other mathematical technique applied to share price movement, is not infallible. It is certainly correct more often than decisions based on moving averages, but since the stock market and share prices are subject to random influences which might strike at any time, any prediction based on channels is subject to the same uncertainty. Just to put things into perspective, it is useful to show an example where this happened. Figure 4.17 shows the position with Allied Domecq on 18th October 1995. The long-term channel is only gently rising, having been falling earlier in the year. The channel seems to be well defined by the two troughs that lie on it. The latest trough on the boundary was at 506p on 10th October. The price of 517.5p on the 18th forms a trough at 515p on the 17th. Since this trough is higher than the one on the boundary (506p) the conclusion is that the share would be a good buy, and the expectation is for a rise to the upper boundary of nearly 100p.

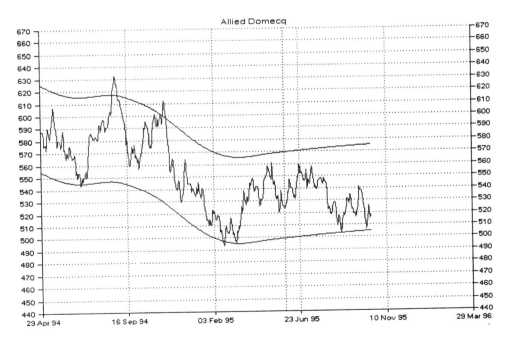

Figure 4.17   Allied Domecq: the position on 18th October 1995

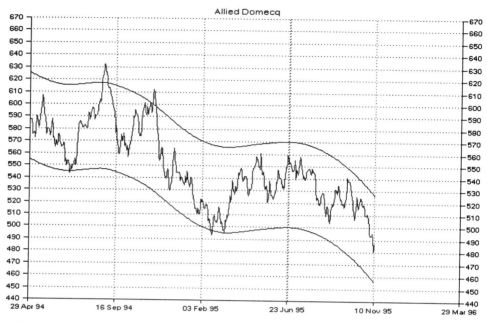

Figure 4.18   Allied Domecq: the subsequent price movement after mid-October 1995

Unfortunately, this is one of the cases where a random influence took over. The subsequent movement is shown in Figure 4.18. The price fell well below the estimated level of the lower boundary, down to 480.5p on 10th November, although it did recover later. The movement was so severe that it forced a change in direction of the long-term channel, which is now headed downwards after a period of virtually horizontal movement.

5

Relationship Between Share and Option Prices

Once an investor has come to a conclusion about the probable future course of a share price, and decides that he or she wishes to take advantage of the opportunities offered by investing in traded options, the investor is faced with a bewildering array of options from which to choose. There are call options and put options, various striking prices and various expiry dates, and the major difficulty is in deciding which of these is appropriate. However, behind the apparent chaos, there is a great deal of logic to the way in which options are priced. A careful consideration of the relationship between option prices and the underlying share prices will lead to a much better view of which is the correct option for a particular set of investment circumstances.

INTRINSIC VALUES AND TIME VALUES

The investor who has selected the share and taken a decision about the future movement of that share price has at this point simply reached an opinion. From now on his or her decision as to the exact option to buy will depend upon facts. These are only four in number:

1. The share price.
2. The option striking prices.
3. The option expiry dates.
4. The premiums for the various option series.

The interrelationship between these four facts is extremely subtle, but to ensure maximum profit at the degree of risk which the investor is prepared to accept requires a detailed attention to this relationship. As in any other stock market, there is no cut and dried formula which always works; it is possible, however, to arrive at a highly probable outcome. Those three items which have a numerical value, i.e. the share price, striking price and premium, can be used in a simple sense to calculate two further quantities, the intrinsic value and the time value for a particular series. For a call option, the intrinsic value increases as the share price rises, while for a put option the intrinsic value increases as the share price falls. In addition to the intrinsic value, options have a time value which decreases the closer the expiry date approaches, irrespective of whether they are call or put options.

Intrinsic Value of Call Options

Since an equity call option gives the holder the right to buy shares of the underlying security at a predetermined fixed price, then naturally this call option becomes more valuable as the share price rises. The intrinsic value of a call option is simply given by the relationship:

Intrinsic value = share price – strike price

The intrinsic value is normally in pence, since this is the unit that both share price and strike price are normally quoted in. Since option premiums are also quoted in the same unit, e.g. pence per share, then intrinsic values bear a direct relationship with the option premium, representing a part of it.

Where the strike price is equal to or greater than the share price, then obviously the intrinsic value is zero. Negative values of course have no meaning other than zero. It is only when the share price is greater than the strike price that there is an intrinsic value. Thus, taking as an example the three Barclays March calls of 700, 750 and 800, we find on 3rd January 1996 that the share price was 778p. By the above definition, we see that the 700 call has an intrinsic value of 78p, the 750 call an intrinsic value of 28p, and the 800 call no intrinsic value. This is of course perfectly logical, since on 3rd January we could exercise the March 700 option to buy Barclays shares at 700p or the March 750 option to buy Barclays at 750p when their market value is 78p and 28p higher respectively at 778p. Obviously we would not exercise the 800 option, since if we required Barclays shares we could buy them cheaper at the market price of 778p.

Just to make sure that intrinsic values are clearly understood, in Table 5.1 are shown a number of examples of share prices, strike prices and intrinsic values. Remembering our definitions of in-the-money, out-of-the-money and at-the-money call options given in Chapter 2, we can see that the intrinsic value of out-of-the-money options (strike price higher than share price) is zero in each case. Although there are no examples in the table, at-the-money options also have no intrinsic value. Only in-the-money call options (strike price below share price) have an intrinsic value. The concept of intrinsic value can be depicted graphically as in Figure 5.1. Here we have taken a call option with a strike price of 300p and show the effect of an increase in the share price on the intrinsic value. The intrinsic

Table 5.1 Intrinsic values for some call options on 3rd January 1996

Share	Share price	Strike price	Intrinsic value
Allied Domecq	549	500	49
		550	0
		600	0
British Aerospace	787	750	37
		800	0
		850	0
Barclays	778	700	78
		750	28
		800	0
FTSE100 Index	3715.6	3550	165.6
		3600	115.6
		3650	65.6
		3700	15.6
		3750	0
		3800	0
		3850	0

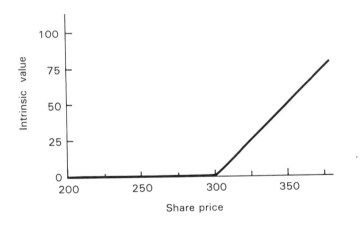

Figure 5.1 Intrinsic value of a 300-call option with increasing share price

value stays at zero until the share price reaches 300p. The line then rises at a slope of 45°, since every 1p excess of share price over 300p gives an equal increase in intrinsic value of 1p.

Table 5.1 also contains values for an index call option, i.e. those quoted for the FTSE100 Index. As mentioned previously, equity option premiums are quoted as pence per share, and since a contract is for 1000 shares, the consideration for a contract is therefore 1000 pence per penny of premium, i.e. £10 per penny of premium. FTSE100 Index options are quoted in index points. The cost of these is £10 per index point, thus premiums for equity options and for index options are directly comparable on a point-for-point basis as far as the final consideration per contract is concerned. Because of this, the relationship for intrinsic values of the FTSE100 Index options is the same, except that we use the FTSE100 Index itself instead of share price. Although the exercise level is in points rather than being a value in pence, and therefore is not strictly an exercise or strike price, the phrase is still used to describe it. Thus for call options in the FTSE100 Index:

Intrinsic value = FTSE100 Index – strike price

In order that the comparison between intrinsic values of equity and index options is perfectly clear, it is worth comparing the intrinsic value of Allied Domecq 500 calls with FTSE100 Index 3650 calls. The intrinsic value for the Allied Domecq calls is 49p, which represents £490 of intrinsic value per contract. The premium for the FTSE100 calls is 65.6 points, which represents £656 of intrinsic value per contract.

Time Value of Call Options

If an out-of-the-money option has no intrinsic value, one may well ask why it still commands a premium. The answer lies in the expectation that in the course of time, or rather in the course of the time remaining to the expiry date, the share price or FTSE100 Index will rise above the strike price, thereby turning the option into an in-the-money option which thus will have an intrinsic value. Thus the amount of time remaining to the expiry date has a value, which differs from one option to another, and which is called the time value. The time value can be defined as:

Time value = option premium – intrinsic value

For at-the-money and out-of-the money options, where the intrinsic values are zero, the relationship becomes:

Time value = option premium

From the relationship between premium, intrinsic value and time value, it can be seen that a higher intrinsic value (more in-the-money) will naturally lead to a higher premium. It should also be seen that the higher the time value, the higher the premium. The time value is a reflection of the amount of time remaining until an option expires. Therefore a July option in a particular share will have a higher time value than the equivalent April option. Similarly an April option will have a greater time value than an equivalent January option. This reflects the fact that where a considerable time is left to the expiry date, there is more chance that a price movement in the underlying share will occur in the anticipated direction. Quite obviously, the most expensive premiums are for the deepest in-the-money options with the longest time to expiry. Conversely, the least expensive options are those which are furthest out-of-the-money and with the shortest time to expiry.

In Table 5.2 are shown the premiums and intrinsic values and the time values calculated from these by difference for Allied Domecq, British Aerospace and Barclays for 3rd January 1996. While certain general conclusions can be drawn, and these are mostly in line with expectation, a more specific relationship between time values and share price cannot be deduced. One might expect that the difference in time values between short and long expiry options would be similar for the various strike prices. However, this is not the case with the data in Table 5.2. Thus, for Allied Domecq, the extra six months given by the July over the January option is worth an increase in time value of 17p, 26p and 16p respectively for the 500, 550 and 600 calls. This gives an average value of nearly 20p, i.e. 3.6% of the share price. Perversely, the additional time was worth much less for the 600 calls than for the 550 calls.

For British Aerospace the extra six months given by the August over the February option is worth an increase in time value of 33p, 36p and 32p

Table 5.2 Intrinsic values and time values for some equity call options on 3rd January 1996

Share (price)	Strike price	Expiry date	Premium	Intrinsic value	Time value
Allied Domecq (549)	500	January	51	49	2
		April	62	49	13
		July	68	49	19
	550	January	9	0	9
		April	27	0	27
		July	35	0	35
	600	January	1	0	1
		April	10	0	10
		July	17	0	17
British Aerospace (787)	750	February	56	37	19
		May	70	37	33
		August	89	37	52
	800	February	26	0	26
		May	44	0	44
		August	62	0	62
	850	February	10	0	10
		May	25	0	25
		August	42	0	42
Barclays (778)	700	March	88	78	10
		June	94	78	16
		September	102	78	24
	750	March	48	28	20
		June	60	28	32
		September	70	28	42
	800	March	21	0	21
		June	35	0	35
		September	46	0	46

respectively for the 750, 800 and 850 calls relative to the share price of 787p. These are much more in line with each other than was the case with Allied Domecq, and gives an average value of nearly 34p, and relative to the share price gives a value of 4.3%. Even though more in line, the additional time was worth a little less for the 850 calls than for the others.

For Barclays, the extra six months given by September over March options is worth 14p, 22p and 35p for the 700, 750 and 800 calls.

In Table 5.3 are shown similar data for various FTSE100 call options. There is now much more regularity in the time values. For any particular strike price, they increase with time, and no anomalous values from this respect can be seen in the table. Now that we have much more data, one interesting aspect is to be able to judge market sentiment. Thus, taking the

Table 5.3 Intrinsic values and time values for FTSE100 call options on 3rd January 1996

FTSE100 Index	Strike price	Expiry date	Premium	Intrinsic value	Time value
3715.6	3550	January	183	165.6	17.4
		February	202	165.6	36.4
		March	214	165.6	48.4
		April	220	165.6	54.4
3715.6	3600	January	137	115.6	21.4
		February	158	115.6	42.4
		March	173	115.6	57.4
		April	183	115.6	67.4
		September	216	115.6	100.4
3715.6	3650	January	89	65.6	23.4
		February	117	65.6	51.4
		March	135	65.6	69.4
		April	150	65.6	84.4
3715.6	3700	January	49	15.6	33.4
		February	82	15.6	66.4
		March	104	15.6	88.4
		April	119	15.6	103.4
		September	150	15.6	134.4
3715.6	3750	January	21	0	21
		February	53	0	53
		March	75	0	75
		April	92	0	92
3715.6	3800	January	6	0	6
		February	32	0	32
		March	53	0	53
		April	68	0	68
		September	100	0	100
3715.6	3850	January	1	0	1
		February	17	0	17
		March	35	0	35
		April	50	0	50

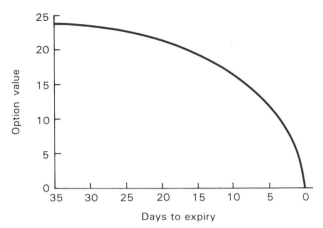

Figure 5.2 The decay of time value of call options as expiry day approaches. The share price is assumed to remain constant

April time values as a case in point, these increase steadily with increasing strike price from the 3550 calls to the 3700 calls with the FTSE100 Index at 3715.7. The time values then decrease steadily as the strike price moves on from 3700 to 3850. Since the highest value is for the 3700s, then the market believes that the April value of the Index will be around 3700, i.e. close to its beginning of January value.

Time values can be depicted graphically, as shown in Figure 5.2. For simplicity, we have assumed that the share price or FTSE100 Index value remains constant. Under this condition, time values decay in a fairly regular manner, becoming zero obviously at the expiry date. The value of a call option on expiry day will simply be its intrinsic value. If the option is out-of-the-money, then it will be worthless at that point.

For out-of-the-money options, the time value remains approximately constant until about six or eight weeks before expiry, when it then starts to fall rapidly, becoming, of course, zero at expiry date. The premiums for nine-month, six-month and three-month options for out-of-the-money options (i.e. those with no intrinsic value and whose premiums are solely due to time value) can be in a ratio as high as 3 to 2 to 1, while options which are more or less at-the-money will have a ratio of about 2 to 1.5 to 1 and in-the-money options closer than this in value. Although only a rough guide, this is very useful in helping to decide whether a particular premium is out of line with expectation.

There is one further aspect that we have yet to consider in this discussion of premiums, and that is the nature of the underlying share. If we take two shares which are standing at the same price and have similar option series, then we would be unlikely to find that each series has the same premium. In general, the more volatile the share, the higher will be the premium for a particular option series. However, since the intrinsic values for the option series of the respective shares are calculated only from the share price and the strike price, which are identical, then the intrinsic values will be the same. Because of this fact, the effect of the differing volatility of the shares is to be found incorporated into the time values.

Premium 1 = intrinsic value 1 + time value 1

Premium 2 = intrinsic value 2 + time value 2

If premium 1 is not equal to premium 2, then time value 1 is not equal to time value 2.

Since the timescales are identical, then time value 1 includes some value for volatility of share 1 and time value 2 includes some value for volatility of share 2. It is important, therefore, that some measure of volatility is kept for each security on the LIFFE Traded Options list. The simplest way of doing this is to calculate the ratio of the high to low value of each security for the current year. If values of this ratio for several years are available, then these ratios should be averaged out over, say, four or five years. The securities can then be listed in decreasing magnitude of this ratio, i.e. the most volatile at the top of the list. Frequently situations can be found in which the premium is an incorrect reflection of the volatility of the share, and such situations can usually be turned to advantage.

Intrinsic Value of Put Options

The above discussions of intrinsic values and time values apply only to call options. The relationship between share prices, strike prices, premiums, intrinsic values and time values is different for put options. A put option becomes more valuable as the share price falls.

The intrinsic value of an equity put option is therefore given by the relationship:

Intrinsic value = strike price – share price

For FTSE100 Index put options, the relationship is:

Intrinsic value = strike price – FTSE100 Index

The intrinsic value is zero for the situation where the strike price is equal to the share price (at-the-money) or where the share price is higher than the strike price (out-of-the-money). It is only where the share price has fallen below the strike price that the option has an intrinsic value.

Thus, taking as an example the three British Aerospace February puts of 750, 800 and 850, we find on 3rd January 1996 that the share price was 787p. By the above definition, we see that the 750 put has an intrinsic value of zero, while the 800 put has an intrinsic value of 13p and the 850 puts an intrinsic value of 63p. Thus on 3rd January we could exercise the February

Table 5.4 Intrinsic values for some put options on 3rd January 1996

Share	Share price	Strike price	Intrinsic value
Allied Domecq	549	500	0
		550	1
		600	51
British Aerospace	787	750	0
		800	13
		850	63
Barclays	778	700	0
		750	0
		800	22
FTSE100 Index	3715.6	3550	0
		3600	0
		3650	0
		3700	0
		3750	34.4
		3800	84.4
		3850	134.4

850 option so that a writer of these puts is forced to buy British Aerospace shares at 850p at a time when they can be bought in the market at 787p.

In order to help in understanding intrinsic values as applied to put options, in Table 5.4 are shown the intrinsic values of Allied Domecq, British Aerospace, Barclays and FTSE100 puts.

The concept of intrinsic value for put options can be depicted graphically as shown in Figure 5.3. Here we have taken a put option with a strike price of 300p and show the effect of an increase in the share price on the intrinsic value. The intrinsic value stays at zero for the situation where the share price is equal to the strike price (at-the-money) or where the

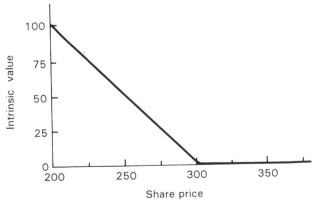

Figure 5.3 Intrinsic value of a 300-put option with increasing share price

share price is higher than the strike price (out-of-the-money). The line then rises at a slope of 45°, as the share price falls, since every 1p fall of share price below 300p gives an equal increase in intrinsic value of 1p.

Time Value of Put Options

As with call options, we can use the same argument to explain why there should still be a premium payable for a put option even though it has no intrinsic value. Once again, it is the expectation for the price that generates a premium value. Some investors feel that the price will fall some time before the expiry of the option, and they are willing to pay money in the form of the premium for the option to back their view of the course of events. Again, as with call options, this remaining time until expiry has a value, which differs from one option to another; this is called the time value.

The time value of a put option can be defined as:

Time value = option premium – intrinsic value

For at-the-money options and out-of-the-money options, where the intrinsic value is zero, the relationship becomes:

Time value = option premium

Just as was the case with call options, it can be seen that a higher intrinsic value (more in-the-money) will lead to a higher premium. Also the higher the time value, the higher the premium. Thus the most expensive options are the deepest in-the-money with the longest time to expiry, while the cheapest are the furthest out-of-the-money which are just about to expire. In Table 5.5 are shown the premiums, intrinsic values and calculated time values for the Allied Domecq, British Aerospace and Barclays put options. As was the case with call options, a specific relationship between time values and share price cannot be deduced. In the case of British Aerospace, the extra six months given by the August over the February option is worth an increase in time value of 22p, 25p and 20p for the 750, 800 and 850 puts respectively relative to a share price of 787p. In the case of Barclays, the extra six months given by the September over the March option is worth an increase in time value of 14p, 22p and 25p for the 700, 750 and 800 puts respectively relative to a share price of 778p. In the case of Allied Domecq options, the extra six months given by the July option over the January option is worth an increase in time value of 9p, 21p and 10p for the 500, 550 and 600 puts respectively relative to a share price of 549p.

To complete the comparison with call options (Table 5.3), in Table 5.6 are shown similar data for various FTSE100 put options.

The time values of put options can be shown graphically as in Figure 5.4, where we have assumed a constant share price. The decay of time value is

Table 5.5 Intrinsic values and time values for some equity put options on 3rd January 1996

Share (price)	Strike price	Expiry date	Premium	Intrinsic value	Time value
Allied Domecq (549)	500	January	1	0	1
		April	5	0	5
		July	10	0	10
	550	January	8	1	7
		April	20	1	19
		July	29	1	28
	600	January	51	51	0
		April	53	51	2
		July	61	51	10
British Aerospace (787)	750	February	10	0	10
		May	23	0	23
		August	32	0	32
	800	February	30	13	17
		May	45	13	32
		August	55	13	42
	850	February	66	63	3
		May	78	63	15
		August	86	63	23
Barclays (778)	700	March	6	0	6
		June	12	0	12
		September	20	0	20
	750	March	20	0	20
		June	29	0	32
		September	38	0	42
	800	March	30	22	8
		June	45	22	23
		September	55	22	33

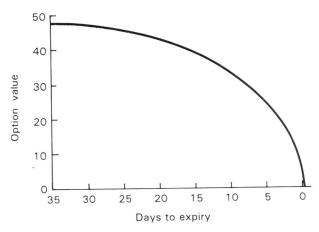

Figure 5.4 The decay of time value of put options as expiry day approaches. The share price is assumed to remain constant

Table 5.6 Intrinsic values and time values for FTSE100 put options on 3rd January
1996

FTSE100 Index	Strike price	Expiry date	Premium	Intrinsic value	Time value
3715.6	3550	January	2	0	2
		February	8	0	8
		March	20	0	20
		April	38	0	38
3715.6	3600	January	4	0	4
		February	14	0	14
		March	29	0	29
		April	50	0	50
		September	75	0	75
3715.6	3650	January	9	0	9
		February	24	0	24
		March	42	0	42
		April	67	0	67
3715.6	3700	January	20	0	20
		February	39	0	39
		March	60	0	60
		April	85	0	85
		September	107	0	107
3715.6	3750	January	44	34.4	9.6
		February	63	34.4	28.6
		March	82	34.4	47.6
		April	108	34.4	73.6
3715.6	3800	January	85	84.4	0.6
		February	95	84.4	10.6
		March	111	84.4	26.6
		April	134	84.4	125.6
		September	156	84.4	148
3715.6	3850	January	135	134.4	0.6
		February	135	134.4	0.6
		March	146	134.4	11.6
		April	167	134.4	32.6

similar to that shown earlier for call options. As expiry date approaches, the
value, which consists of time value plus intrinsic value, falls due to the dimin-
ishing time value, until on expiry day its value is just the intrinsic value.

The same relationship for the nine-month, six-month and three-month
option premiums holds as for call options, i.e. they fall in the approximate
relationship of 3 to 2 to 1 for out-of-the-money and 2 to 1.5 to 1 for at-the-
money options. As was the case with call options, there is a further aspect
that we have yet to consider in this discussion of premiums, and that is the
nature of the underlying share. If we take two shares which are standing at
the same price and have similar put option series, then we would be
unlikely to find that each series has the same premium. In general, just as
for call options, the more volatile the share, the higher will be the premium

for a particular option series. However, since the intrinsic values for the option series of the respective shares are calculated only from the share price and the strike price, which are identical, then the intrinsic values will be the same. Because of this fact, the effect of the differing volatility of the shares is to be found incorporated into the time values:

Premium 1 = intrinsic value 1 + time value 1

Premium 2 = intrinsic value 2 + time value 2

If premium 1 is not equal to premium 2, then time value 1 is not equal to time value 2.

Since the timescales are identical, then time value 1 includes some value for the volatility of share 1 and time value 2 includes some value for the volatility of share 2.

As was stressed for call options, the measure of volatility for each share based upon the ratio of the high to low value of each security for the current year is very useful. Frequently, situations can be found in which the premium is an incorrect reflection of the volatility of the share, and such situations can usually be turned to advantage.

CORRELATION BETWEEN OPTION AND SHARE PRICES

It would be perfectly logical to assume that there is a simple direct relationship between share prices and call option prices and a simple inverse relationship between share prices and put option prices. We would therefore expect that if the share price rises by a small amount, then so should the price of a call option, while the price of a put option should fall. Conversely, if the share price falls, then the price of a call option should fall and the price of a put option should rise. Naturally, the effect of gearing should magnify the responses of the options if these responses are expressed as percentage changes, but we would still, on a simple view, expect that a penny change in share price should cause a penny change in the option price, either upwards or downwards. Some further thought on this subject should lead us to a further conclusion that, of course, the options themselves are subject to their own individual supply and demand, which might from time to time, depending upon the circumstances, be independent of the supply and demand position of the underlying shares. In such a situation, the option price might move independently of the share price to a limited extent. Certain investors have a knack of spotting when an option price is out of line with the price or direction of movement of the underlying shares. Working on the assumption that all things eventually find their own level, and that the anomaly will disappear, they can fairly consistently make a profitable investment in such options.

As is apparent from the preceding chapters of this book, our approach is quite different. We have illustrated methods of determining when share price movements will change direction, and the approximate length of time for which the new direction will continue, as well as the new target area for the share price. Quite clearly, therefore, we are concerned with options which behave themselves, moving consistently in the same direction (for call options) or the opposite direction (for put options) as the share price. We therefore have to find some method of deciding which options will behave logically. The answer lies in the statistical technique of correlation. There are quite complex statistical methods which can be employed which are tedious unless carried out on a computer, but for our purposes a simple, graphical approach which does not require "A" level mathematics is perfectly adequate. The Greek letter delta is widely used in science and mathematics to mean the amount of change in a quantity. As far as options are concerned, delta means the change that will occur in the option price for a small change in the share price, assuming other factors to be constant. Theoretical deltas for call options range from 0 to 1, while for put options values range from 0 to –1. The negative value of the latter reflects the fact that the put options lose value as the share price increases, while of course call options gain value with rising share price, and therefore have positive deltas. A delta value of 1 means that a call option gains 1p in value for every 1p rise in the share price, while a delta value of 0 means that the call option price remains unchanged for a 1p rise in the share price.

Note here the reason why we use a small change in the share price in order to determine delta values—a large change, say 50p for example, will have an effect on all options, however far out-of-the-money they may be, and so would render meaningless a delta calculated on such a basis. A deep in-the-money call option, with high intrinsic value, should have a delta value of 1, since every 1p rise in share price will give a 1p rise in the option price. There is obviously a strong relationship between option price and share price in such a case. On the other hand, a far out-of-the-money option with no intrinsic value will show a zero rise for a 1p rise in share price, i.e. a delta of 0. There is then a very weak relationship between option and share prices. Obviously, options between these two extremes will have delta values other than 0 or 1. For example, at-the-money options should have a delta of 0.5. These delta values can be computed approximately from perusal of daily option prices in the quality newspapers by looking for small changes (1p to 3p) in the share prices and relating all changes to a notional change of 1p in the share price (i.e. for a 3p share price change, divide the option price change by 3). For put options, the delta values are based on the rise in option price for a fall in share price, and have negative values. Thus a heavily in-the-money put option with a high intrinsic value will have a delta of –1, while a heavily out-of-the-money option has a delta of 0. At-the-money options have deltas of –0.5.

The above theoretical discussion is useful for giving an insight into the relationship between option prices and share prices, but cannot be carried too far in practical application. As we discussed in the opening section of this chapter, many anomalous situations exist, and it is easy to find in the option price tables in your newspaper call options which rise more than 1p for a 1p rise in the underlying share price, and put options which rise more than 1p for a 1p fall in share price. There are some periods when most options seem to misbehave rather than follow the theoretical relationship discussed above. As we mentioned earlier, this must be due to the unquantifiable effect of supply and demand, a larger than normal demand for an option causing a larger than normal increase in the option price.

A more practical method of showing how strong a relationship exists between the option price and the share price is to plot the option price change from one day to the next against the share price change over the corresponding period for both call and put options. Strong and weak correlations can then be easily determined. As stated above, it is essential to stay with those options that exhibit strong correlation, and avoid those where the correlation is weak. This has the useful effect of reducing the vast array of options available to a much more manageable level, simplifying the task of selecting the correct option for the particular circumstances. Note, though, that shares which have shown weak correlation in the immediate past can gradually change to a stronger correlation. This means that your current list of "good" shares should be checked at frequent intervals to weed out any that are changing their behaviour. Such shares can then be replaced with some from the "bad" list that are changing for the better.

Two diagrams can be drawn, one for call options and one for put options (Figure 5.5(a) and (b)). The values which are plotted can fall into each of the quadrants shown in the diagrams. The shaded areas represent values which have a positive correlation, while the unshaded areas represent values where there is a negative correlation, for both call and put options. The dashed line at an angle of 45° in each diagram is the line where a change in share price gives exactly the same change in the option price, i.e. delta values of 1 or −1 in terms of the theoretical correlations discussed earlier. When we carry out our plotting of real-life share and option prices, we are looking for shares where the majority of the points fall into the shaded areas, since we are looking for positive correlation. If we really wish to fine-tune our selections, we can divide the graph into octants, rather than quadrants. This will highlight shares which show stronger than theoretical correlation (areas marked + +), less than theoretical correlation (areas marked +), weak correlation (areas marked −) and very weak correlation (areas marked − −). In fact, it might be better to describe shares which fall into the − and − − areas as truly perverse, showing an inverse correlation between option and share prices. For those investors interested in options which are way out of line with expectation, shares which fall into these − and − − sectors offer a fruitful area of investigation.

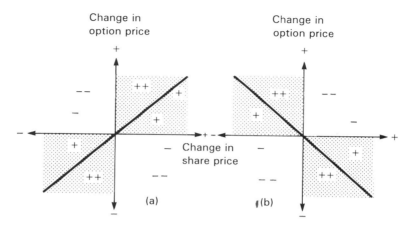

Figure 5.5 Theoretical correlation plots for (a) call options and (b) put options. Shaded quadrants have a positive correlation and points falling on the heavy 45° lines would have perfect correlation. Points falling in unshaded quadrants have a negative correlation

Real data are plotted for several shares during a period in December 1995 in the next four figures. Figure 5.6 shows the behaviour of the Allied Domecq January 550 calls over about 35 business days up to early January 1996. Correlation is not very good since it can be seen that there are a few points in the top left and bottom right quadrants. In addition there are some 13 points where there was a change in share price, but no corresponding change in option price.

On the other hand the Grand Metropolitan February 460 calls shown in Figure 5.7 are about as good a correlation between share price changes

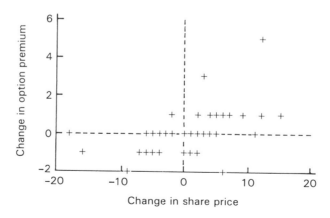

Figure 5.6 Correlation plot for Allied Domecq January 550 calls up to early January 1996

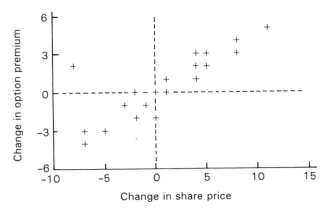

Figure 5.7   Correlation plot for Grand Metropolitan February 460 calls

and option premium changes that you will find. Only one rogue point mars the display of points lying along the 45° line.

A perfect example of a correlation plot for put options is shown in Figure 5.8. The BP July 550 puts have no points in the negative correlation quadrants, and the points lie very close to the theoretical 45° line.

In the case of British Steel October 180 calls, as shown in Figure 5.9, most points are in the correct quadrants for good correlation. However, the correlation is not particularly good because the points are widely scattered within these quadrants, i.e. they do not fall very close to the 45° line.

These few examples should serve to show the power and simplicity of this method of determining the degree of correlation between the share price and the option price, and the reader is urged to adopt it in order to

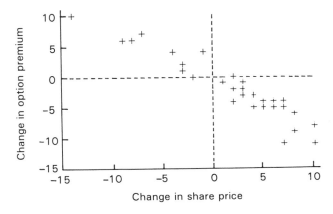

Figure 5.8   Correlation plot for BP July 550 puts

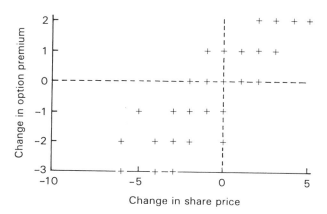

Figure 5.9   Correlation plot for British Steel October 180 calls

avoid the disappointment of failing to capitalise to the maximum when the future movement of a share price has been correctly forecast.

COST PER PERCENTAGE POINT—THE SENSIBLE WAY OF EVALUATING PREMIUMS

As was shown in *Stocks and Shares Simplified*, it is extremely important to devise methods to reduce, rapidly and virtually automatically, the vast range of investment possibilities down to a much more manageable handful. As far as traded options are concerned, we have already shown that the list can be reduced considerably by means of the concept of correlation, so that we focus on options which will behave as we expect them to behave if we have made the correct decision about the progress of the share price itself. Another consideration of vital importance is the premium associated with the particular option. The purchaser of call options (see Chapter 7) or put options (see Chapter 9) is interested in options which are cheap in terms of the premium that must be paid for a certain profit expectation. It is important that we do not confuse the actual option premium itself with what we pay for this expectation. Many beginners to traded options go for those options with the lowest premiums, in the belief that they are getting much better value for money, but have not given much consideration to the amount of risk involved with the various options. As in many other things in life, what appears cheap may well be expensive. For writers of call options (see Chapter 8) and put options (see Chapter 10), the opposite arguments will apply. The writers wish to write options as expensively (to the buyer) as possible. Thus we need a much better method than the mere value of the premium itself to determine if we are paying over the odds for call or put options, or receiving less than we should for writing call and put options for the realistic return that we may expect.

A powerful way of deciding on the cost of an option is to focus on the movement of the share price required before we start to generate a profit from the premium. In order to be able to compare one share with another, we should express this movement as a percentage of the original share price. We can develop the method by referring to call options, but the ideas that we put forward here are equally applicable to put options. Having calculated the movement in share price required, we can then quite easily compare the various premiums we have to pay if purchasing, or the premium we would receive if writing options, on this logical basis. Thus an option with a high premium may only require a relatively small share price movement for profitability, whereas an option with a low premium may require a large movement. In such circumstances, the lowest premium turns out to be the most expensive of the two, since we have to take a much greater risk with our money. Conversely, the writer of the same option with a high premium may see the option exercised and the profit thereby limited. Thus quite obviously, the purchaser and the writer should be looking for opposite properties associated with the premium.

CPPs of Call Options

The very simple way of calculating the cost per percentage point (CPP) of a call option is best illustrated by reference to an example such as Bass. Thus, the necessary data for Bass call options on 21st December 1995 were:

Share price 685p
January 650s, 40p; January 700s, 9p; January 750s, 1p

Taking the January 650s first, we can see that the share price of 685p is already above the striking price. The price has to move to 690p (strike price + premium) before the purchase moves into profit. For January 700s, the price has to move to 709p before the purchase starts to move into profit. For the January 750s, the share price has to move to 751p for the purchase to move into profit. Expressed as a percentage gain:

January 600s require a 5p share price rise, i.e. 0.73%
January 650s require a 24p share price rise, i.e. 3.5%
January 700s require a 66p share price rise, i.e. 9.6%

By dividing the premium by this required percentage share price rise, we get the cost per percentage point, CPP:

January 600s = 40/0.73 = 54.8
January 650s = 9/3.5 = 2.57
January 700s = 1/9.6 = 0.1

For those who prefer a mathematical equation:

$$\text{CPP (call)} = \frac{(0.01 \times \text{premium} \times \text{share price})}{(\text{striking price} + \text{premium} - \text{share price})}$$

Using this formula, we can now proceed to calculate the CPPs of the call options listed on 21st December 1995. To conserve space, only the CPPs of the out-of-the-money options are given in Table 5.7.

Table 5.7 Cost per percentage point (CPP) values for call options on 21st December 1995

Share	Strike price	Jan prem.	Apr prem.	Jul prem.	Jan CPP	Apr CPP	Jul CPP
Allied Domecq	550	1	12	19	0.13	1.20	1.67
Argyll	330	8	20	24	2.38	2.84	2.91
Asda	120	5	9	13	0.11	0.40	0.56
BAA	500	4	17	23	0.8	2.21	2.57
British Airways	500	2	13	20	0.28	1.39	1.84
Boots	600	6	22	30	1.45	3.2	3.64
British Steel	160	4	8	11	0.62	0.88	1.00
British Petroleum	550	4	16	24	1.02	2.58	3.12
Bass	700	9	28	38	2.57	4.46	4.91
	750	1	11	19	0.10	0.99	1.55
Commercial Union	650	7	21	31	1.41	2.92	3.53
Cable & Wireless	460	29	26	36	0.25	3.35	3.61
	500	3	13	21	0.26	0.95	1.35
Courtaulds	420	4	16	22	0.73	1.89	2.21
Glaxo	900	16	36	52	5.07	6.66	7.21
	950	4	18	32	0.54	2.00	3.02
HSBC	1000	26	55	70	9.27	9.63	9.70
	1050	9	33	50	1.47	3.87	4.89
ICI	800	5	16	28	0.77	2.02	2.94
Kingfisher	550	11	29	35	3.52	4.51	4.64
	600	1	11	17	0.10	0.89	1.27
NatWest Bank	650	17	30	43	6.50	6.50	6.50
	700	3	14	24	0.37	1.42	2.11
PowerGen	550	4	20	27	0.70	2.28	2.67
Reuters	600	10	27	39	2.55	3.96	4.40
Sainsbury	390	4	13	18	0.79	1.74	2.05
Shell Transport	900	1	11	20	0.17	1.59	2.51
Standard Chartered	550	20	44	60	4.36	4.89	5.03
	600	7	25	41	0.62	1.70	2.33
Storehouse	360	2	9	15	0.23	0.83	1.19
Thames Water	600	3	16	23	0.35	1.48	1.91
Unilever	1350	6	27	41	1.60	5.04	6.38
Zeneca	1250	22	55	78	6.44	9.02	9.79

Share	Strike price	Feb prem.	May prem.	Aug prem.	Feb CPP	May CPP	Aug CPP
British Aerospace	800	25	42	59	4.23	5.19	5.75

Share	Strike price	Feb prem.	May prem.	Aug prem.	Feb CPP	May CPP	Aug CPP
BAT Industries	600	11	18	27	1.38	1.96	2.51
BTR	330	7	10	16	1.17	1.45	1.82
British Telecom	360	6	15	21	1.51	2.30	2.55
	390	2	6	11	0.18	0.48	0.79
Cadbury Schweppes	550	16	21	32	2.0	2.34	2.89
Eastern Electricity	1000	1	1	–	0.35	0.35	
GEC	360	4	11	16	0.54	1.17	1.47
Grand Metropolitan	460	12	21	31	2.58	3.16	3.50
Guinness	460	15	24	29	4.04	4.23	4.28
	500	4	9	15	0.40	0.81	1.21
Hanson	200	–	6	8	–	0.71	0.84
Ladbroke	160	7	11	16	0.55	0.71	0.85
LASMO	180	8	12	17	1.29	1.42	1.50
	200	2	5	10	0.14	0.32	0.54
Lucas Industries	180	7	11	15	1.12	1.29	1.39
	200	2	5	8	0.14	0.30	0.44
P&O	500	7	14	20	0.84	1.42	1.80
Prudential	420	16	22	30	3.16	3.38	3.56
	460	5	9	16	0.41	0.69	1.09
RTZ	950	25	38	54	6.34	7.13	7.67
	1000	9	20	34	1.19	2.29	0.32
Redland	390	14	23	28	0.84	3.16	3.27
	420	6	12	16	0.56	0.98	1.21
Rolls-Royce	200	3	7	12	0.31	0.59	0.82
Royal Insurance	390	9	21	28	1.80	2.57	2.80
	420	2	11	18	0.18	0.82	1.18
Tesco	300	8	12	17	1.37	1.66	1.90
United Biscuits	260	11	16	20	1.88	2.05	2.13
Vodaphone	240	5	12	17	0.51	0.92	1.12
Williams	330	8	13	16	1.61	1.99	2.15
	360	1	4	7	0.08	0.31	0.50

Share	Strike price	Mar prem.	Jun prem.	Sep prem.	Mar CPP	Jun CPP	Sep CPP
Abbey National	650	21	31	41	2.92	3.53	3.95
Amstrad	220	14	19	25	1.79	1.87	1.94
	240	7	12	17	0.51	0.74	0.92
Barclays	750	28	39	48	5.45	5.89	6.12
	800	10	21	30	1.06	1.92	2.47
Blue Circle	330	18	22	28	2.95	3.01	3.06
	360	7	11	17	0.59	0.84	1.14
British Gas	260	14	19	22	2.12	2.22	2.26
	280	7	11	14	0.60	0.83	0.97
Dixons	460	11	19	26	0.95	1.41	1.71
Fisons	280	1	1	–	0.16	0.16	–
Forte	330	15	17	25	2.57	2.64	2.81
	360	5	6	13	0.42	0.49	0.90
Hillsdown	160	9	10	12	1.60	1.60	1.60
	180	3	4	5	0.21	0.27	0.32

Share	Strike price	Mar prem.	Jun prem.	Sep prem.	Mar CPP	Jun CPP	Sep CPP
Lonrho	180	8	13	15	1.59	1.66	1.68
	200	3	6	8	0.22	0.40	0.49
Marks and Spencer	460	2	10	15	0.29	1.14	1.51
National Power	460	16	28	34	2.47	3.05	3.23
	500	7	15	19	0.52	0.99	1.18
Scottish Power	390	5	11	15	0.57	1.05	1.30
Sears	110	2	4	6	0.20	0.34	0.44
SmithKlineBeecham	700	8	24	38	1.75	3.46	4.22
Tarmac	110	5	8	11	0.52	0.65	0.72
TSB	420	3	6	–	0.39	0.71	–
Tomkins	280	10	17	21	1.61	1.93	2.05
	300	4	9	13	0.35	0.68	0.89

What we are interested in, of course, is any correlation between CPP value and the future gain that may be made from the particular option. Taking the period between 21st December 1995, when the CPP values were calculated, and a point a few weeks further on in time, i.e. 8th January 1996, the CPP values from Table 5.7 are shown with the gains (or losses) made in the option premiums over the period in Table 5.8.

Table 5.8 Cost per percentage point (CPP) values for call options on 21st December 1995 and gain in option prices by 8th January 1996

Share	Strike price	Jan CPP	Apr CPP	Jul CPP	Jan % gain	Apr % gain	Jul % gain
Allied Domecq	550	0.13	1.20	1.67	1000.0	150.0	50.8
Argyll	330	2.38	2.84	2.91	62.5	30.0	33.3
Asda	120	0.11	0.40	0.56	−80.0	−55.6	−85.7
BAA	500	0.8	2.21	2.57	50.0	47.0	56.5
British Airways	500	0.28	1.39	1.84	200.0	92.3	80.0
Boots	600	1.45	3.2	3.64	33.3	27.3	23.3
British Petroleum	550	1.02	2.58	3.12	50.0	23.8	33.3
Bass	700	2.57	4.46	4.91	300.0	107.4	100.0
	750	0.10	0.99	1.55	300.0	154.5	152.6
Commercial Union	650	1.41	2.92	3.53	−71.4	−23.8	−16.1
Cable & Wireless	500	0.26	0.95	1.35	−66.7	−7.7	−4.8
Courtaulds	420	0.73	1.89	2.21	350.0	118.8	90.9
HSBC	1000	9.27	9.63	9.70	23.1	20.0	17.1
	1050	1.47	3.87	4.89	42.1	24.2	16.0
ICI	800	0.77	2.02	2.94	500.0	187.5	114.3
Kingfisher	550	3.52	4.51	4.64	0.0	10.3	11.4
	600	0.10	0.89	1.27	0.0	0.0	11.8
NatWest Bank	650	6.50	6.50	6.50	−29.4	−6.7	0.0
	700	0.37	1.42	2.11	−66.7	−21.4	−4.2
PowerGen	550	0.70	2.28	2.67	−75.0	−35.0	−25.9
Reuters	600	2.55	3.96	4.40	20.0	33.3	28.2
Sainsbury	390	0.79	1.74	2.05	0.0	30.7	27.8

Share	Strike price	Jan CPP	Apr CPP	Jul CPP	Jan %gain	Apr %gain	Jul %gain
Shell Transport	900	0.17	1.59	2.51	0.01	54.5	35.0
Standard Chartered	550	4.36	4.89	5.03	95.0	43.2	36.7
	600	0.62	1.70	2.33	28.6	48.0	39.0
Storehouse	360	0.23	0.83	1.19	−50.0	−22.2	−6.7
Thames Water	600	0.35	1.48	1.91	−66.7	−31.3	−21.7
Unilever	1350	1.60	5.04	6.38	183.3	77.8	46.3
Zeneca	1250	6.44	9.02	9.79	−9.1	0.0	5.1

Share	Strike price	Feb CPP	May CPP	Aug CPP	Feb %gain	May %gain	Aug %gain
British Aerospace	800	4.23	5.19	5.75	24.0	21.4	18.6
BAT Industries	600	1.38	1.96	2.51	−54.5	−33.3	−18.5
BTR	330	1.17	1.45	1.82	71.4	70.0	43.8
British Telecom	360	1.51	2.30	2.55	−16.7	−6.7	−4.8
Cadbury Schweppes	550	2.0	2.34	2.89	43.8	57.1	40.6
GEC	360	0.54	1.17	1.47	250.0	109.1	87.5
Grand Metropolitan	460	2.58	3.16	3.50	0.0	23.8	16.1
Guinness	460	4.04	4.23	4.28	153.3	87.5	75.9
	500	0.40	0.81	1.21	200.0	122.2	93.3
Hanson	200	–	0.71	0.84	–	66.7	62.5
Ladbroke	160	0.55	0.71	0.85	14.2	18.2	12.5
LASMO	180	1.29	1.42	1.50	12.5	16.7	11.8
	200	0.14	0.32	0.54	0.0	20.0	10.0
Lucas Industries	180	1.12	1.29	1.39	−28.6	−9.1	−6.7
	200	0.14	0.30	0.44	−50.0	−20.0	−12.5
P&O	500	0.84	1.42	1.80	42.9	21.4	25.0
Prudential	420	3.16	3.38	3.56	56.3	40.9	50.0
	460	0.41	0.69	1.09	40.0	55.6	56.3
RTZ	950	6.34	7.13	7.67	−68.0	−50.0	−33.3
Redland	390	0.84	3.16	3.27	−40	−17.4	−10.7
	420	0.56	0.98	1.21	−50.0	−25.0	−12.5
Rolls-Royce	200	0.31	0.59	0.82	66.7	42.9	25.0
Royal Insurance	390	1.80	2.57	2.80	−33.3	0.0	3.5
	420	0.18	0.82	1.18	−50.0	0.0	5.2
Tesco	300	1.37	1.66	1.90	42.9	66.7	52.9
United Biscuits	260	1.88	2.05	2.13	45.5	31.2	30.0
Vodaphone	240	0.51	0.92	1.12	−40.0	−33.3	−23.5
Williams	330	1.61	1.99	2.15	75.0	46.1	50.0
	360	0.08	0.31	0.50	100.0	100.0	57.1

Share	Strike price	Mar CPP	Jun CPP	Sep CPP	Mar %gain	Jun %gain	Sep %gain
Abbey National	650	2.92	3.53	3.95	38.0	32.2	24.4
Barclays	750	5.45	5.89	6.12	35.7	30.8	27.1
	800	1.06	1.92	2.47	50.0	38.1	26.7
Blue Circle	330	2.95	3.01	3.06	22.2	18.2	14.3
	360	0.59	0.84	1.14	28.6	36.4	11.8
British Gas	260	21.2	2.22	2.26	−14.3	−10.5	−9.1

Share	Strike price	Mar CPP	Jun CPP	Sep CPP	Mar %gain	Jun %gain	Sep %gain
	280	0.60	0.83	0.97	−28.6	−18.2	−14.3
Dixons	460	0.95	1.41	1.71	0.0	5.3	7.7
Hillsdown	160	1.60	1.60	1.60	66.7	70.0	58.3
	180	0.21	0.27	0.32	66.7	75.0	80.0
Lonrho	180	1.59	1.66	1.68	100.0	61.5	60.0
	200	0.22	0.40	0.49	100.0	83.3	75.0
Marks and Spencer	460	0.29	1.14	1.51	−50.0	−10.0	0.0
National Power	460	2.47	3.05	3.23	−25.0	−10.7	−14.7
Scottish Power	390	0.57	1.05	1.30	100.0	72.7	66.7
Sears	110	0.20	0.34	0.44	0.0	−25.0	−16.7
Forte	330	2.57	2.64	2.81	53.3	52.9	20.0
	360	0.42	0.49	0.90	40.0	66.7	0.0
SmithKlineBeecham	700	1.75	3.46	4.22	125.0	66.7	47.4
Tarmac	110	0.52	0.65	0.72	20.0	25.0	9.1
Tomkins	280	1.61	1.93	2.05	80.0	52.9	47.6
	300	0.35	0.68	0.89	100.0	77.8	53.8

Out of all the options in Table 5.8, the 10 with the highest CPPs (averaging 7.22) gave an average loss of 14.5% over the period, while those 10 with the lowest CPPs (averaging 0.15) gave an average gain of 122.0%. Looked at another way, the purchaser of the top 10 CPP call options would have put at risk four to eight times as much money (as a cost per percentage gain) and achieved a loss of 14.5%, while the investor in the bottom 10 CPP call options made a gain of 122%. This is not just an aberration during the period from February to March 1988. The same general type of result is obtained from any period of time since the beginning of the traded options market in London and is applicable to out-of-the-money options as well as in-the-money options.

The message is quite clear: purchasers should avoid those options which fall in the top half of the league table of CPP values and concentrate on those in the bottom half. The writers of call options, as we shall see in Chapter 8, take a completely opposite view of premiums. While the purchaser is wishing to keep the premium, expressed as a CPP, as low as possible, the writer wishes to receive as high a premium as possible against the risk that the share price will rise. The purchaser is interested in the gain in the premium itself, but the writer is interested in the premium falling to zero by the time the option expires, so that it is not exercised against him. Because of this fact, the writer should be looking closely at the relationship between CPP values and the ensuing change in the share price. Since we drew the conclusion earlier that there was no advantage for a purchaser in buying call options with high CPPs, then high CPP call options must give an advantage to the writer. The advantage is that these options provide a return, in terms of the premium received, which is as high as possible for the degree of risk which is being accepted by the writer. This aspect is covered more fully in Chapter 8.

CPPs of Put Options

The points which have been made about call options and CPP values apply in exactly the same way to put options. Taking British Airways as an example, the data for put options on 21st December 1995 were:

Share price 469p
January 420s, 1p; January 460s, 7p; January 500s, 32p

Taking the January 420s first, we can see that the share price has to fall to 419p (striking price – premium) before the purchaser starts to move into profit. For the January 460s, the price has to fall to 453p and for the January 500s to 468p before the purchaser starts to move into profit. Expressed as percentage fall:

January 420s require a 50p (469p – 419p) price fall, i.e. 10.7%
January 460s require a 16p (469p – 453p) price fall, i.e. 3.4%
January 500s require a 1p (469p – 468p) price fall, i.e. 0.2%

By dividing the premium by this required percentage share price fall, we get the cost per percentage point, CPP, for the put option:

January 420s = 1/10.7 = 0.09
January 460s = 7/3.4 = 2.05
January 500s = 32/0.2 = 160.0

Note the inverse relationship between the CPPs for call options and the CPPs for put options. With put options the CPP values increase as the strike price increases, whereas with call options the CPP values decrease as the strike price increases. CPP values are high for in-the-money call and put options, and low for out-of-the-money call and put options.

The equation for a put option (compare this with that for call options given earlier) is:

$$\text{CPP (put)} = \frac{(0.01 \times \text{premium} \times \text{share price})}{(\text{share price} + \text{premium} - \text{strike price})}$$

The CPP values of out-of-the-money put options are shown in Table 5.9. The gains and losses calculated for those options in Table 5.9 for which data were available are shown in Table 5.10. The vast majority showed a loss for a very simple reason—the FTSE100 Index rose over the period 21st December to 8th January, and so most of the shares did as well. Hence the climate for the purchasers of put options was adverse. The 10 options with the highest CPPs gave an average loss of 63.3%, while the 10 with the lowest CPPs gave a loss of only 15.0%. Thus, as was the case with call options, it makes sense to stick with put options of small CPP values.

Table 5.9 Cost per percentage point (CPP) values for put options on 21st December 1995

Share	Strike price	Jan prem.	Apr prem.	Jul prem.	Jan CPP	Apr CPP	Jul CPP
Alled Domecq	460	1	4	8	0.10	0.37	0.69
	500	6	14	22	1.80	2.86	3.41
Argyll	300	1	5	10	0.12	0.51	0.88
Asda	100	1	4	5	0.09	0.30	0.35
	110	4	8	10	0.89	0.99	1.01
British Airways	420	1	3	8	0.09	0.27	0.66
	460	7	13	22	2.05	2.77	3.33
Boots	550	2	9	17	0.34	1.28	2.20
British Steel	140				0.10	0.27	0.51
British Petroleum	500	2	7	12	0.30	0.93	1.42
Bass	650	3	11	18	0.54	1.64	2.33
Commercial Union	600	6	22	27	1.17	2.87	3.19
Cable & Wireless	420	3	10	17	0.40	1.10	1.60
Courtaulds	360	1	4	8	0.09	0.35	0.64
	390	4	11	19	1.00	1.92	2.46
ICI	700	1	13	18	0.13	1.42	1.84
	750	11	32	39	4.89	6.37	6.55
Kingfisher	500	1	10	17	0.12	1.01	1.52
NatWest Bank	600	2	15	22	0.25	1.50	1.99
	650	14	38	44	6.50	6.50	6.50
PowerGen	460	1	3	7	0.08	0.16	0.38
	500	3	11	18	0.58	1.65	2.25
Sainsbury	330	1	2	5	0.08	0.16	0.38
	360	3	8	14	0.63	1.30	1.81
Shell Transport	800	1	10	14	0.16	1.37	1.81
	850	11	28	33	7.21	7.95	8.03
Standard Chartered	500	2	21	31	0.23	1.73	2.22
Thames Water	550	1	5	14	0.10	0.46	1.11
Unilever	1250	3	18	26	0.65	3.14	4.09
	1300	23	50	65	8.91	10.99	11.34
Zeneca	1200	15	47	59	4.10	7.51	8.15

Share	Strike price	Feb prem.	May prem.	Aug prem.	Feb CPP	May CPP	Aug CPP
British Aerospace	750	15	27	37	2.66	3.76	4.37
BAT Industries	500	2	8	15	0.17	0.61	1.05
	550	11	25	33	2.31	3.45	3.81
BTR	300	2	8	10	0.32	0.98	1.14
British Telecom	330	6	8	15	0.75	0.94	1.43
Cadbury Schweppes	460	2	9	13	0.16	0.65	0.88
	500	9	22	27	1.43	2.51	2.77
GEC	300	1	2	5	0.08	0.17	0.39
	330	6	9	15	1.36	1.69	2.12
Guinness	420	3	9	12	0.34	0.88	1.10
Hanson	180	3	5	7	0.44	0.63	0.78
LASMO	160	2	5	7	0.19	0.40	0.52
Lucas Industries	160	2	4	6	0.2	0.35	0.48

Share	Strike price	Feb prem.	May prem.	Aug prem.	Feb CPP	May CPP	Aug CPP
P&O	420	3	9	13	0.28	0.74	1.00
	460	12	25	30	2.81	3.55	3.69
Prudential	390	6	14	19	0.80	1.49	1.79
RTZ	900	10	24	31	1.95	3.63	4.21
Redland	360	4	13	16	0.53	1.32	1.50
Royal Insurance	360	4	17	22	0.63	1.75	1.99
Tesco	280	6	11	14	1.03	1.45	1.63
United Biscuits	240	5	10	13	0.61	0.98	1.15
Vodaphone	200	3	5	7	0.26	0.40	0.52
	220	9	12	15	1.67	1.78	1.86
Williams	300	2	7	9	0.27	0.78	0.93

Share	Strike price	Mar prem.	Jun prem.	Sep prem.	Mar CPP	Jun CPP	Sep CPP
Abbey National	600	20	29	39	2.72	3.30	3.76
Amstrad	200	6	8	10	0.57	0.69	0.80
Barclays	700	16	25	32	2.11	2.85	3.29
Blue Circle	300	4	11	14	0.41	0.93	1.09
British Gas	240	6	11	12	0.67	1.01	1.06
Dixons	390	8	13	17	0.84	1.22	1.46
	420	18	25	30	3.80	3.91	3.96
Hillsdown	140	1	4	6	0.08	0.27	0.37
	160	8	13	15	1.60	1.60	1.60
Lonrho	160	2	4	7	0.17	0.31	0.48
National Power	420	5	14	17	0.70	1.53	1.73
Scottish Power	330	4	6	10	0.39	0.56	0.84
	360	14	17	23	2.99	3.09	3.21
Sears	90	1	2	3	0.08	0.15	0.20
	100	4	6	7	0.68	0.76	0.79
Forte	300	4	7	8	0.43	0.69	0.77
SmithKlineBeecham	650	4	15	22	0.87	2.42	3.04
Tarmac	100	5	7	10	0.52	0.61	0.70
Tomkins	260	7	10	14	0.96	1.19	1.42

Table 5.10 Cost per percentage point (CPP) values for put options on 21st December 1995 and gain in option prices by 8th January 1996

Share	Strike price	Jan CPP	Apr CPP	Jul CPP	Jan %gain	Apr %gain	Jul %gain
Allied Domecq	500	1.80	2.86	3.41	−83.3	−72.6	63.6
Argyll	300	0.12	0.51	0.88	0.0	−60.0	−30
Asda	100	0.09	0.30	0.35	0.0	−50.0	−20.0
British Airways	460	2.05	2.77	3.33	−85.7	−61.5	45.5
Boots	550	0.34	1.28	2.20	−50.0	−44.4	−23.5
British Petroleum	500	0.30	0.93	1.42	−50.0	−42.9	33.3
Commercial Union	600	1.17	2.87	3.19	−66.7	0.0	3.7
Cable & Wireless	420	0.40	1.10	1.60	−66.7	−40.0	23.5

Share	Strike price	Jan CPP	Apr CPP	Jul CPP	Jan % gain	Apr % gain	Jul % gain
Courtaulds	390	1.00	1.92	2.46	−75.0	72.7	−57.9
ICI	750	4.89	6.37	6.55	−90.1	−71.9	−61.5
Kingfisher	500	0.12	1.01	1.52	0.0	−40.0	−17.6
NatWest Bank	600	0.25	1.50	1.99	−50.0	−26.7	−9.1
	750	6.50	6.50	6.50	−50.0	−15.8	−6.8
PowerGen	460	0.08	0.16	0.38	0.0	0.0	14.2
Sainsbury	360	0.63	1.30	1.81	−66.7	−37.5	−28.6
Shell Transport	800	0.16	1.37	1.81	0.0	−50.0	−42.9
	850	7.21	7.95	8.03	−90.1	−42.9	−30.3
Thames Water	550	0.35	1.48	1.91	900.0	340.00	171.00
Unilever	1300	8.91	10.99	11.34	−93.3	−54.0	−43.5
Zeneca	1250	6.44	9.02	9.79	−27.3	−9.1	−17.9

Share	Strike price	Feb CPP	May CPP	Aug CPP	Feb % gain	May % gain	Aug % gain
British Aerospace	750	2.66	3.76	4.37	−60.0	−29.6	−24.3
BAT Industries	500	0.17	0.61	1.05	−50.0	0.0	6.7
	550	2.31	3.45	3.81	18.2	12.0	12.1
BTR	300	0.32	0.98	1.14	−50.0	−50.0	−40.0
British Telecom	330	0.75	0.94	1.43	−66.7	−25.0	−25.0
Cadbury Schweppes	500	1.43	2.51	2.77	−66.7	−50.0	−37.0
GEC	330	1.36	1.69	2.12	−83.3	−55.6	−40.0
Guinness	420	0.34	0.88	1.10	−66.7	−77.8	−58.3
LASMO	160	0.19	0.40	0.52	−50.0	−40.0	−28.6
Lucas Industries	160	0.2	0.35	0.48	−50.0	0.0	0.0
P&O	420	0.28	0.74	1.00	−66.7	−44.4	−30.8
Prudential	390	0.80	1.49	1.79	−50.0	−35.7	−26.3
RTZ	900	1.95	3.63	4.21	50.0	50.0	41.9
Redland	360	0.53	1.32	1.50	0.0	0.0	5.9
Royal Insurance	360	0.63	1.75	1.99	−75.0	−23.5	13.6
Tesco	280	1.03	1.45	1.63	−83.3	−54.5	−42.8
United Biscuits	240	0.61	0.98	1.15	−60.0	−40.0	−30.8
Vodaphone	200	0.26	0.40	0.52	−33.3	20.0	28.6
	220	1.67	1.78	1.86	11.1	16.7	20.0
Williams	300	0.27	0.78	0.93	−50.0	−57.1	−44.4

Share	Strike price	Mar prem.	Jun prem.	Sep prem.	Mar CPP	Jun CPP	Sep CPP
Abbey National	600	2.72	3.30	3.76	−50.0	−34.5	−33.3
Amstrad	200	0.57	0.69	0.80	233.3	187.5	130.0
Barclays	700	2.11	2.85	3.29	−50.0	−40.0	−31.5
British Gas	240	0.67	1.01	1.06	−33.3	0.0	0.0
Dixons	390	0.84	1.22	1.46	−12.5	−23.1	−11.8
	420	3.80	3.91	3.96	−16.7	−16.0	−10.0
Hillsdown	140	0.08	0.27	0.37	0.0	−75.0	−50.0
	160	1.6	1.6	1.6	−62.5	−46.2	−50.0
Lonrho	160	1.60	1.60	1.60	−50.0	−50.0	−42.9
National Power	420	0.70	1.53	1.73	0.0	7.1	11.8

Share	Strike price	Mar prem.	Jun prem.	Sep prem.	Mar CPP	Jun CPP	Sep CPP
Scottish Power	360	2.99	3.09	3.21	−64.3	−47.0	−39.1
Sears	90	0.08	0.15	0.20	0.0	0.0	0.0
	100	0.68	0.76	0.79	0.0	0.0	0.0
Forte	300	0.43	0.69	0.77	−50.0	−57.1	−50.0
SmithKlineBeecham	650	0.87	2.42	3.04	−75.0	−60.0	−45.5
Tarmac	100	0.52	0.61	0.70	−40.0	−14.3	−30.0
Tomkins	260	0.96	1.19	1.42	−57.1	−40.0	−35.7

While the purchaser of put options should obviously be seeking those options where the CPPs are lowest, the writer of puts has the opposite view, and should therefore be writing those options where the CPPs are highest.

Although CPPs can be calculated for call and put options in the FTSE100 Index in exactly the same way as we have done for equity options, there is no point in doing so, since the main value of CPPs is that they allow you to compare options in different underlying securities. Since the Index options are unique, their CPPs are not readily compared with the CPPs of equity options.

Finally, the discussion in this chapter shows that by taking note of the concept of correlation, both between share price and option premiums and between cost per percentage point and option premiums, the very large number of available options can be reduced to a mere handful, say about six classes. This considerably simplifies the task of selecting which option will be the vehicle for investment, where the other consideration, addressed in the remaining chapters, will revolve around the degree of risk which the investor is prepared to accept.

6

Option Strategies

There are two main categories of investor active in the traded options market. There are those who wish to make a profit out of an anticipated movement in the price of the underlying security, and there are those who wish to insure an existing portfolio against an adverse market move by taking out an option position to cover this eventuality. If there is any difference between these two categories of investor, it is probably that the first category has a more positive feeling about the direction of the market. The second category, like a person taking out house insurance, hopes that the worst will not happen, but knows that at least he will be compensated if it does. He is therefore less positive that the market will move against him because of course if he were surer about the future course of events he could adjust the portfolio by selling or buying as appropriate.

Whichever category of investor we consider, their reason for involvement in the traded options market at a particular time is that they have come to some conclusion about the probable behaviour of the market in general or a share in particular in the near future. They may have used techniques such as those discussed in Chapters 3 and 4; they may have some information whose significance the general public has not yet come to appreciate; or they may just have a hunch about the likely course of events.

These future events can follow only three paths:

1. The share price/market will rise.
2. The share price/market will fall.
3. The share price/market will stay more or less constant.

Investors will naturally hold one of the above views of the direction of a share price or the market in the immediate future. These investors can obviously be described as bulls, bears or neutrals respectively. If they restrict their activities to the normal share market, then only the bulls can make a good profit. Because of the limited opportunity for short selling (i.e. selling a share before you have bought it) in the UK market, bears would have to rely on a drastic fall in price within the account period or over two account periods in order to make a profit after covering the costs of the transaction. The neutral investor would make no profit at all. By turning to the traded options market, each of these types of investor can make a profit, provided he has taken the correct view of the future movement of the underlying share price.

Within each of these categories of investor, there will be different shades of opinions as to the certainty that events will unfold as predicted. There will be different shades of opinion as to the extent of any rises or falls, and in the case of neutrals, the upper and lower limits within which the price will move in the future. As will be shown in this chapter, there will be an optimum strategy for each of these various shades of opinion.

CATERING FOR SHADES OF OPINION

Investors in traded options have four simple routes open to them, and may combine several of these simple routes into increasingly complex strategies, some of the latter being so complex that a great deal of mathematics has to be applied.

These simple routes involve the buying or selling of simple call options and the buying or selling of simple put options:

- **Call options:** buyers expect a rise in share price; sellers ("writers") do not expect the share price to rise significantly.
- **Put options:** buyers expect a share price fall; writers do not expect the share price to fall significantly.

Even neglecting complex mixed strategies the above four routes can cause confusion. The reader may come to the conclusion that the buyer of a call option and the writer of a put option are expecting the same outcome, i.e. a rise in the share price. Conversely it might appear that the buyer of a put option and the writer of a call option expect a fall in the share price. While it is true that a call option buyer and a put option writer will both profit from a share price rise, and a put option buyer and a call option writer will both profit from a share price fall, the put option and call option writers can profit from a share price standstill while the others cannot. Therefore, quite obviously, there are subtle and not-so-subtle differences in their expectations, and these differences will become more apparent when we discuss the question of risk. The whole thrust of investing in traded options is that the degree of risk taken on board can be tailored, using either simple or complex strategies, to the degree of certainty in the mind of the investor as to the future movement in the price of the underlying security.

DEGREES OF RISK

Taking a very simplified view, the various strategies discussed in the remainder of this book can be listed in order of decreasing risk as follows:

- **High risk:**   writing uncovered call options
                    writing covered calls
                    writing puts
                    writing straddles
- **Medium risk:** buying call options
                    buying put options
- **Low risk:**   bull spreads
                    bear spreads
                    calendar spreads
                    buying straddles

A more exact analysis of the risk/reward position for each strategy will be undertaken in the appropriate chapter, but Table 6.1 shows in simple terms the risk and reward associated with each strategy.

Covered options are those where the underlying shares are also held, hence the writer of a covered call option can supply the shares if the option is called (exercised) by the buyer. The writer of an uncovered option does not hold the shares and therefore if called will have to buy them in the market to supply the caller.

The above view of the various possibilities is simplified, since the amount of risk implicit in any of the strategies will depend upon the expiry dates and striking prices of the options involved. As will be seen later, the amount of risk within one of the above strategies can be adjusted as required by the circumstances. Therefore it is, as an example, possible to open a spread position where the risk is high and not low as listed above.

What might appear paradoxical is the fact that the simplest option strategies to understand, i.e. the buying of a call or a put option, are not

Table 6.1 Reward and risk for various option strategies

Strategy	Reward	Risk	Chapter
Buy calls	unlimited	limited	7
Write covered calls	limited	unlimited	8
Write uncovered calls	limited	unlimited	8
Buy puts	unlimited	limited	9
Write puts	limited	unlimited	10
Bull spread	limited	limited	11
Bear spread	limited	limited	11
Calendar spread	limited	limited	11
Buy straddle	unlimited	limited	12
Write straddle	limited	unlimited	12

those with the lowest risk, but this becomes apparent as we discuss the risk associated with each strategy more fully.

OPTION STRATEGIES

Writing Uncovered Call Options

These are profitable if the share price falls, remains static, or shows only a very small rise. The degree of tolerance to a small rise depends upon the extent to which the option is out-of-the-money. The investor has almost unlimited exposure in the event of a sharp upward price movement due, for instance, to a takeover bid. He will have to buy a similar option to offset the one he has written, and may well have to pay a large multiple of the original cost in order to do this. Alternatively the call may be exercised against him and he will have to buy the shares in the market at a price well above the strike price in order to supply the buyer of the option. Note that the call can be exercised at any time, and therefore the writer is in a situation over which he has no control.

Writing Put Options

These are profitable only if the share price rises, remains static, or shows a very small fall. In the latter case, the extent of the fall which can be tolerated depends upon the degree to which the option is out-of-the-money. The investor has a high exposure in the event of a sharp fall. Although this is limited to the difference between the striking price and the share price, the potential loss is very high since (in theory, anyway) the share price can fall all the way to zero. Again, as with call options, the option can be exercised agianst the writer at any time, the writer having no control over this.

Buying Call and Put Options

Here there is a profit only if the share price rises (call options) or falls (put options). The loss is limited to the amount of premium that has been paid, although this can vary from a small amount, say £20 per contract, up to a much larger amount, say £1000 per contract.

Writing Covered Calls

These are profitable if the share price falls, remains static or shows a very small rise. The degree of tolerance to a small rise depends upon the extent to which the option is out-of-the-money. In the event of a price rise the buyer may exercise the option. The real loss then will be the difference between the share price and the strike price, less any premiums received. The loss may turn out to be relatively small.

Complex Strategies

These strategies involve the buying or writing of at least two different options, and therefore the loss usually involves the difference between two premiums, which is usually comparatively small. However, some strategies could lead to the loss of two premiums and hence involve higher risk than the buying of simple call and put options.

It is helpful at this stage to subdivide further the bull, bear and neutral categories. This can be done either from the degree of certainty they feel about their view of the future security price, or from whether they think a price rise, price fall or the price band within which prices will move will be small, medium or large.

CATEGORIES OF INVESTOR

The degree of risk which an investor is prepared to carry should be in direct proportion to the certainty he or she has about the future course of the particular share price of interest. Since the above strategies were collated with their associated risk, it is therefore possible to correlate the strategy the investor should employ with his or her view about the share price. This is done in Table 6.2.

Within these strategies there are of course varying degrees of risk, so that bullish investors can select the appropriate strategy for their own circumstances. Within each strategy there are once again varying degrees of risk, so that the investor can really fine-tune his or her selection.

The non-neutral category is the one that covers the situation where the investor does not expect the price to remain stable, but has no idea

Table 6.2 Option strategies for various views of share price movement

Bullish	Buy call
	Bull spread
	Calendar spread
	Write put
	Write covered call
Bearish	Buy put
	Bear spread
	Calendar spread
	Write uncovered call
Neutral	Write straddle
	Calendar spread
Non-neutral	Buy straddle

whether the price will rise or fall. Although rarely employed, it can be used to cover the case where a share with a volatile history has traded within a narrow range for some time. Chartists would expect a break-out from this range within a certain time, and therefore can cover themselves with this strategy. The author's view is that since there are such a large number of shares for which traded options are available, then by using the techniques discussed in Chapters 3 and 4 it is always possible to find a share about which you can be much more positive about the direction and extent of its price movement.

7

Buying Call Options

An equity call option gives the buyer of the option the right to buy a number, usually 1000, shares of the underlying security at a fixed price— the striking price—at any time up to the expiry date of the option. Since the FTSE100 Index is an abstract entity, the buyer has no right to buy it, but will make a profit or loss from movement in the Index and hence the premiums over the course of time. The premiums given for equity options, being in pence, have to be multiplied by 1000 in order to determine the consideration for one contract before dealing costs are taken into consideration. The premiums for FTSE100 Index options, being in points, have to be multiplied by £10.

The purchase of call options is the strategy for investors with bullish expectations for the particular share price or the FTSE100 Index, and this strategy is attended by a moderate amount of risk. The purchaser expects the value of the option to rise as the share price (or the FTSE100 Index) rises, but also expects a high degree of gearing, i.e. the increase in the value of the option, expressed as a percentage, is very much greater than the increase in the value of the underlying shares over the same period of time. Within the bounds of normal behaviour of share prices and option prices, the holder of a call option has an almost unlimited potential for gain, while his potential for loss is limited solely to the premium he has paid for the option, plus the expenses involved in the deal. The potential for gain with FTSE100 options, while still very high, is not quite as unlimited, since the FTSE100 Index is not as volatile, and does not rise by a factor of five or ten in the space of less than a year as is the case with some shares.

A major attraction of call options is that the buyer can select from a variety of options, thereby tailoring the amount of risk he is prepared to accept to his own particular psychological and financial circumstances. By and large the profit potential will be proportional to the amount of risk which is accepted, although, as is shown in the chapter, it is possible to find options which have lower premiums than expected. These will provide a lower-risk vehicle for the more astute investor.

LIMITED LOSS, UNLIMITED GAIN

The profit or loss potential of a call option at the expiry date can be plotted as a function of the share price or Index value at expiry to give a graph of characteristic shape as shown in Figure 7.1. The point A shown on the share price axis represents the striking price. Obviously at any value below this there is a total loss of the premium, hence the horizontal line. This is of course the maximum loss that can be sustained. As the share price or Index value rises, the loss gets less until at point B the option value is the same as the original premium paid, and the loss then becomes zero. It is only above this point B that the position moves into profit. Note, however, that the profit continues upwards as a sloping line, i.e. there is essentially no upper limit. In practice, of course, there is some limit since share prices and Index values do not rise to an infinite level, but there are many instances, e.g. due to takeover bids, of share prices rising to very high levels extremely rapidly.

The graph illustrates the major attribute of the purchase of call options in that the loss is limited while the gain is unlimited. Actual values have been left off the axes in Figure 7.1, because the purpose is to convey the shape of the graph and the concept of limited loss, unlimited gain. Values can be put on the axes depending upon the premium paid and the extent to which the options are in-the-money or out-of-the-money.

OPTION PREMIUMS

Table 7.1 shows the premiums for various call options on 31st January 1996, one class being taken from each of the three available time cycles. Two points which are of general application, irrespective of which companies' shares are being considered, can be illustrated by the data in Table 7.1:

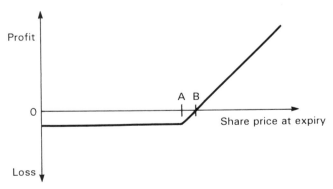

Figure 7.1 Profit/loss potential of a call option for different share prices at expiry time

Table 7.1 Premiums for various call options on 31st January 1996

Share	Share price	Exercise price	Expiry date and premium		
			Feb	**May**	**Aug**
Guinness	457	420	38	43	48
		460	7	18	25
		500	1	5	11
			Mar	**Jun**	**Sep**
Dixons	416	390	34	46	52
		420	16	29	36
		460	4	13	20
			Apr	**Jul**	**Oct**
Boots	623	550	79	86	90
		600	37	48	55
		650	12	22	31
			Feb	**Mar**	**May**
FTSE100	3759.3	3600	161	174	198
		3650	113	134	162
		3700	72	97	131
		3750	36	66	102
		3800	15	41	78
		3850	4	24	58
		3900	1	13	43

1. The least expensive option is always the nearest expiry, furthest out-of-the-money, e.g. Guinness February 500s, Dixons March 460s, Boots April 650s, and FTSE100 February 3900s.
2. The most expensive option is always the furthest expiry, deepest in-the-money, e.g. Guinness August 420s, Dixons September 390s, Boots October 550s, FTSE100 May 3600s.

A perusal of any table of option premiums in the quality newspapers will establish that these two observations are always true. The reason that the nearest expiry, furthest out-of-the-money options are cheapest is because they have no intrinsic value, and there is very little time left for an upward share price movement to put them in-the-money at expiry day. The opposite is true for the most expensive option. These have the highest intrinsic values, since they are furthest in-the-money, and in addition they have plenty of time left for the share price to make an upward move to add to their value.

This is about as far as we can go in generalising from one class of options to another. The April 300 option premium for one share, for example, is unlikely to be the same as the April 300 premium for another share. Even if by chance they were the same, you would find a difference in say the July 300s. This is because investors will have different perceptions of the volatility of the particular share price and the direction of the trend. What we can do, however, is generalise about the behaviour of option prices within an option class, based upon logical analysis of premiums in terms of their intrinsic values and time values. Such an analysis will guide us in the choice of the best option for the particular circumstances, since we can achieve a firmer grasp of the risk and reward associated with the various option series.

RELATIONSHIP BETWEEN PREMIUMS AND SHARE PRICE

In deciding to buy any type of call option, the investor will have made reasoned decisions as to the extent to which the share price will rise, and also the timescale over which this will happen. This will have been done by using the principles discussed in Chapters 3 and 4. The best insight into the relationship between the option prices and the share price is to consider the case where the price movement upwards is expected to occur over the short time between the purchase of the option and the nearest expiry date. Three scenarios can be envisaged:

1. The share price remains static—the *risk*.
2. An upward share price movement occurs—the *reward*.
3. The share price falls—the *risk*.

Since all premiums are composed of an intrinsic value (which might be zero) and a time value, the effect on these of each of the above three outcomes can be discussed, thus giving a picture of the overall effect on the option premium.

Intrinsic Values

Because of the mathematical fact that intrinsic values are the difference between the share price and the striking price, if positive, then the following will be true:

1. Static share price movement will leave intrinsic values unchanged.
2. Upward share price movement will increase intrinsic values on a penny for penny basis, and some options with zero intrinsic value will move into a state of positive intrinsic value as the movement continues.
3. Downward share price movement will decrease intrinsic values on a penny for penny basis, and some options will move to zero intrinsic value as the movement continues.

The theoretical effect of an upward share price movement on call options which initially have no intrinsic value (because the share price is below the striking price) is shown in Figure 7.2(a). At some point the upward price movement takes the share price past the striking price, at

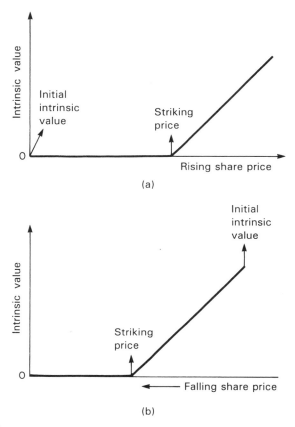

Figure 7.2 (a) Effect of upward share price movement on options with no initial intrinsic value; (b) effect of downward price movement on shares which have initial intrinsic value

which point the graph takes on a slope of 45°, i.e. the increase is on a penny for penny basis.

The effect of a downward movement on call options which initially do have an intrinsic value is shown in Figure 7.2(b). Here the graph falls at a slope of 45° due to the penny for penny fall in the intrinsic value with share price. Once the share price becomes equal to the striking price, the intrinsic value becomes zero and remains so with further fall in share price.

Time Values

The situation with intrinsic value is of course perfectly straightforward, because intrinsic values are simply the difference between the share price and the striking price, if this difference is positive. Time values are not based upon such a mathematical relationship, but on what investors think will happen to the share price over the period of time remaining to expiry. Depending upon the date at which a snapshot view is taken, this time can vary from a day to nine months. As a rough guide, the following reactions might be expected:

1. A static share price should not have a positive effect on time values, and as stated above, normal behaviour under such circumstances is for the time value to fall rapidly during the last six weeks or so of the life of the option, becoming zero at expiry.
2. An upward price movement should have a positive effect on time values, with the greatest effect being on the more distant expiry dates. Since time values where the share price remains constant tend to decrease during the last month or two of the life of an option, becoming zero at expiry, the positive effect of the upward share price movement should cancel this normal decrease, leaving options with say two to eight weeks lifetime virtually unchanged. Options with very little time left to expiry should still exhibit the normal decrease unless a very substantial share price rise occurs to cancel out the disappearing time value.
3. A downward price movement should have most effect on the time values of those options of nearest expiry, causing these to fall even more rapidly than in the static share price case. This is because investors should see that there is very little time left for the adverse trend to reverse itself. Options with more distant expiry dates should see their time values remain more or less constant unless the share price fall becomes substantial, in which case time values will be eroded.

These various cases are best illustrated by means of examples, and these examples will also serve to underline the very approximate nature of the above comments, since they must not be taken as rigid rules which will apply in every situation. There will always be many anomalies. Very often these anomalies can provide situations which can be exploited for improved profit, provided that the investor is correct about his fundamental view of the future share price movement.

The least approximate case, and therefore the one case which can be represented graphically, is where the share price remains more or less constant over the last weeks before expiry of the option. This is shown in Figure 7.3.

EXAMPLES

Static Share Prices—LASMO and British Aerospace Call Options

The most useful example to analyse in order to understand more clearly the relationship between share prices and options prices is the case where

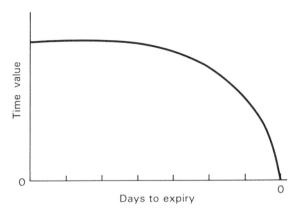

Figure 7.3 Loss of time value of an option up to expiry time, assuming the share price remains constant

the share price remains more or less static. Two such examples will serve for this purpose. February 1996 options expired on 21st February, and to reduce the amount of data, Friday values up to the Friday before expiry are used in these two examples.

Between 12th January and 16th February 1996 the LASMO share price moved in narrow limits of 166p to 179p, ending at 179p. Table 7.2 shows the movement of the various option premiums over the same time period.

The prediction above was that a static share price would lead to static option premiums, except for those near to expiry, which would show a rapid erosion of time values. Table 7.2 shows this prediction to be fairly close to reality, with the near-term February 160 and 180 call premiums falling rapidly as time values diminished up to 9th February. Longer-term options such as the May 160s and August 160s showed virtually no change in time values over the period, while some others, e.g. the May and August 180s, showed modest declines in premiums and time values compared with the February equivalents.

The data do highlight an interesting change in outlook for holders of the February 180s, as well as illustrating how enormous profits can be made by taking more risk, since with the share price at 166p on 9th February, the time value was simply 1p. Thus investors held the view that the price was unlikely to pick up in the remaining eight business days to expiry on 21st February, making the options virtually valueless. An investor with a contrary view would have made a 400% profit, since the price moved up by 13p over the following week, bringing the options to a point only 1p out-of-the-money. The changed hopes for the share were reflected in a premium and hence time value which jumped to 4p, even though only three more days were left to expiry. That there was any time value still left at this point showed that the expectation was for a continued rise in the LASMO share price (the price reached 184p on 21st February).

Table 7.2 Movement of LASMO share prices, call option premiums and time values from 12th January 1996 to 16th February 1996

Date Share price		12 Jan 176	19 Jan 171	26 Jan 174	2 Feb 169	9 Feb 166	16 Feb 179
Feb	140s premiums				30	27	
	time values				1	1	
Feb	160s premiums	18	13	16	11	8	19
	time values	2	2	2	2	2	0
Feb	180s premiums	6	3	4	2	1	4
	time values	6	3	4	2	1	4
Feb	200s premiums	1	1	1	1	1	1
	time values	1	1	1	1	1	1
May	140s premiums				31	28	
	time values				2	2	
May	160s premiums	22	18	20	16	13	23
	time values	6	7	6	7	7	4
May	180s premiums	10	8	10	7	5	13
	time values	10	8	10	7	5	13
May	200s premiums	4	3	4			7
	time values	4	3	4			7
Aug	140s premiums				34	32	
	time values						
Aug	160s premiums	27	22	25	21	18	28
	time values	11	11	11	12	12	9
Aug	180s premiums	16	12	15	12	10	18
	time values	16	12	15	12	10	18
Aug	200s premiums	9	6	8			11
	time values	9	6	8		11	

The data for British Aerospace in Table 7.3 are quite close to expectation as far as changes in time values are concerned. Thus the February 800s showed a steady fall in time value from 25p to 1p over the course of the five weeks. The fall in share price to 844p on 9th February produced a rise in the time values for all of the 850s, irrespective of expiry date. This is an effect which is seen quite often, i.e. a substantial share price movement which takes the price closer to a strike price will increase the time value just that once. For some reason investors expect a positive reaction in the share price from such levels, making such occasions attractive ones for the purchase of the option. The same effect was noticed in the last example caused by the rise in LASMO to 179p on 16th February. The time values for all 180 options rose significantly over the time values for the previous week.

Modest Rising Share Price—Lucas and Rolls-Royce

As buyers of call options, expecting the share price to rise, then naturally we are much more interested in what happens when the price rises than

Table 7.3 Movement of British Aerospace share prices, call option premiums and time values from 12th January 1996 to 16th February 1996

Date			12 Jan	19 Jan	26 Jan	2 Feb	9 Feb	16 Feb
Share price			835	876	878	878	844	836
Feb	800s	premiums	51	81	82	81	50	37
		time values	25	5	4	3	6	1
Feb	850s	premiums	22	43	40	36	14	5
		time values	22	16	12	8	14	5
Feb	900s	premiums	8	15	14	9	2	1
		time values	8	15	14	9	2	1
May	800s	premiums	70	99	97	95	73	60
		time values	35	23	19	17	29	24
May	850s	premiums	43	65	63	62	44	33
		time values	43	39	35	34	44	33
May	900s	premiums	25	61	39	35	24	17
		time values	25	61	39	35	24	17
Aug	800s	premiums	91	118	100	93	83	
		time values	56	42	22	16	39	
Aug	850s	premiums	65	87	86	84	65	57
		time values	65	61	58	56	65	57
Aug	900s	premiums	45	67	60	58	44	
		time values	45	67	60	58	44	

when it falls or remains the same. In order to gain as much information as possible about the effect on option premiums of a rising share price, it is useful to compare two shares which made similar gains over a short period of time. Such a pair is Lucas Industries and Rolls-Royce, which both made gains of just under 10% between 12th January and 16th February 1996. The data for these are given in Tables 7.4 and 7.5.

Our earlier general prediction from first principles was that an upward share price movement may have the effect of turning a zero intrinsic value into a positive one, and also have a positive effect on time values, being greatest on the more distant expiry dates, and probably causing the nearest ones to remain steady rather than experience their normal fall. While the predictions were naturally correct for intrinsic value, since that is simply a mathematical relationship, they were totally incorrect as far as time values are concerned. What becomes immediately obvious from Tables 7.4 and 7.5 is that there is an interaction between intrinsic value and time value. During the period of the rise in share prices (12/1/96 to 16/2/96) only options which stayed out-of-the-money, i.e. had zero intrinsic values, showed a rise in time values. Examples are the Rolls-Royce 220s and Lucas 200s (in the latter case this applied during the rise to 2nd February). In-the-money options with intrinsic values exhibit a fall in time values. Examples are the Rolls-Royce 180s and 200s and the Lucas 180s. Where there are rises in time values, the more distant expiry dates seem to enjoy

Table 7.4 Movement of Lucas share prices, call option premiums and time values from 12th January 1996 to 16th February 1996

Date			12 Jan	19 Jan	26 Jan	2 Feb	9 Feb	16 Feb
Share price			176	188	196	202	194	193
Feb	160s	premiums	19	29				
		time values	3	1				
Feb	180s	premiums	6	11	18	23	15	13
		time values	6	3	2	1	1	0
Feb	200s	premiums	1	2	5	7	2	1
		time values	1	2	5	5	2	1
Feb	220s	premiums			1	1	1	1
		time values			1	1	1	1
May	160s	premiums	22	31				
		time values	6	3				
May	180s	premiums	10	16	23	27	19	18
		time values	10	8	7	5	5	5
May	200s	premiums	4	7	11	13	8	7
		time values	4	7	11	11	8	7
May	220s	premiums			5	6	3	2
		time values			5	6	3	2
Aug	160s	premiums	26	34				
		time values	10	6				
Aug	180s	premiums	15	21	27	31	24	23
		time values	15	13	11	9	10	10
Aug	200s	premiums	8	12	16	19	14	13
		time values	8	12	16	17	14	13
Aug	220s	premiums			9	11	7	7
		time values			9	11	7	

less of a rise than nearer expiry dates. Note again the observation made in the previous examples that when the price rises sharply to a value around a strike price, the time value increases markedly. This happens for Lucas with the rise from 188p to 196p between 19th and 26th January. The time values for the 200s shoot up considerably, as do those for the Rolls-Royce 220s on 2nd February.

Strongly Rising Share Price—P&O

It is of interest to compare the changes in time values for the call options in a share which has risen strongly over a short period of time. Such an example is P&O, where the share price rose from 474p to 545p between 12th January and 16th February 1996, i.e. a gain of just under 15%. Broadly similar conclusions can be drawn as for the moderately rising share price examples. The data for P&O are given in Table 7.6. There was a large jump in price from 489p to 542p between 19th and 26th January. As with Lucas and Rolls-Royce, the time values for the in-the-money options

Table 7.5 Movement of Rolls-Royce share prices, call option premiums and time values from 12th January 1996 to 16th February 1996

Date Share price			12 Jan 196	19 Jan 201	26 Jan 200	2 Feb 214	9 Feb 206	16 Feb 215
Feb	180s	premiums	19	23	20	36	27	
		time values	3	2	0	2	1	
Feb	200s	premiums	6	8	6	14	8	15
		time values	6	7	6	0	2	0
Feb	220s	premiums	1	1	1	3	1	1
		time values	1	1	1	3	1	1
Feb	240s	premiums				1		1
		time values						
May	180s	premiums	23	25	23		28	
		time values	7	4	3		2	
May	200s	premiums	11	13	11	19	14	19
		time values	11	12	11	5	8	4
May	220s	premiums	5	5	5	9	6	9
		time values	5	5	5	9	6	9
May	240s	premiums				4		4
		time values				4		4
Aug	180s	premiums	27	30	28		32	
		time values	11	9	8		6	
Aug	200s	premiums	16	18	16	24	20	26
		time values	16	17	16	10	14	11
Aug	220s	premiums	9	10	9	14	11	15
		time values	9	10	9	14	11	15
Aug	240s	premiums				8		9
		time values				8		9

actually fell for all three expiry dates. On the other hand, the time values for the out-of-the-money options rose strongly.

From these examples, we can draw some general conclusions about the interaction between rising share prices and intrinsic and time values.

Our earlier prediction from first principles was that an upwards share price movement may have the effect of turning a zero intrinsic value into a positive one, and also have a positive effect on time values, being greatest on the more distant expiry dates, and probably cause the nearest ones to remain steady rather than experience their normal fall. While the predictions were naturally correct for intrinsic value, since that is simply a mathematical relationship, they were totally incorrect as far as time values are concerned. What becomes immediately obvious from Tables 7.4 to 7.6 is that there is an interaction between intrinsic values and time values. During the period of the rise in share prices (12th January to 16th February 1996) only those options which stayed out-of-the-money, i.e. had zero intrinsic values, showed a rise in time values. In-the-money options with

Table 7.6 Movement of P&O share prices, call option premiums and time values from 12th January 1996 to 16th February 1996

Date Share price			12 Jan 474	19 Jan 489	26 Jan 542	2 Feb 538	9 Feb 524	16 Feb 545
Feb	460s	premiums	24	34	84			
		time values	10	5	2			
Feb	500s	premiums	5	9	46	40	25	45
		time values	5	9	4	2	1	0
Feb	550s	premiums	1	3	12	7	2	5
		time values	1	3	12	7	2	5
Feb	600s	premiums				1	1	1
		time values				1	1	1
May	460s	premiums	31	40	88			
		time values	17	11	6			
May	500s	premiums	12	17	53	48	35	52
		time values	12	17	11	10	11	7
May	550s	premiums	3	6	22	18	11	19
		time values	3	6	22	18	11	19
May	600s	premiums				6	3	
		time values				6	3	
Aug	460s	premiums	38	46	89			
		time values	24	17	7			
Aug	500s	premiums	20	26	58	55	44	59
		time values	20	26	16	17	20	14
Aug	550s	premiums	9	13	31	28	20	30
		time values	9	13	31	28	20	30
Aug	600s	premiums				13	9	14
		time values				13	9	14

intrinsic values showed a fall in time values. Where there are rises in time values, the more distant expiry dates seem to enjoy less of a rise than sometimes the middle-term and sometimes the near-term expiring options.

The effect of share price rises on both intrinsic values and time values as an average for the three shares (Lucas, Rolls-Royce and P&O) is shown in Table 7.7. As far as in-the-money options are concerned, all show a rise in their intrinsic values, simply because they move to a more in-the-money position. On the other hand, the near-expiry options lose all of their time values, the medium-term expiry options lose 62% of their time value, and the distant expiry options lose 31%. The relative changes between these three expiries are what one would expect.

In the case of the out-of-the-money options, there is, of course, no intrinsic value. The time values all show good rises of well over 100%, with those for the medium-term options rising by 229%. The average of these rises is enhanced by the very large rise in the P&O time values, which is caused by the large rise in the P&O share price over the short time covered by the data. The medium-term P&O time values rose by over 500%.

Table 7.7 General conclusions on the effect of share price rise on time values and intrinsic values of call options. Percentages are average values from Lucas, Rolls-Royce and P&O, 12th January and 16th February 1996

Type of option	Effect on intrinsic value	Effect on time value
Short term in-the-money	rise	large fall (−100%)
Short term out-of-the-money	stays zero	large rise (+133%)
Medium term in-the-money	rise	large fall (−62%)
Medium term out-of-the-money	stays zero	modest rise (+229%)
Long term in-the-money	rise	modest fall (−31%)

Falling Share Price—Guinness

We can now attempt to draw some general conclusions about the behaviour of intrinsic values and time values of options where the underlying share price has fallen.

Earlier it was pointed out that the most marked effect on premiums where the share price falls over a month or so should be on the time values of the nearest expiry option. In addition, those options which are in-the-money could become out-of-the-money, and hence lose all their intrinsic value. The net result should be a rapid erosion of the short-term premiums and a rather less rapid erosion of the longer expiry options.

The data for Guinness shown in Table 7.8 support the expected reaction perfectly. The time values of most of the options fell away regularly over the period of time. Taking the furthest expiry first, the out-of-the-money 500s lost 58% of their value, the middle expiry saw a loss of 68% and the nearest a loss of 86% of their value over the period of six weeks.

The main exception to the erosion of time values is in the 460s, i.e. those that are nearest to the share price. These either maintained their time values, or in the case of the furthest expiry saw a modest rise in time values as the share price fell away. The furthest expiry 420s also showed a gain. These gains were established when the share price fell between the 12th and 19th January.

Behaviour of the FTSE100 Index Call Options

In Table 7.9 are shown the various premiums for a range of strike prices from 3650 to 3800 for February, March and April expiries of the FTSE100 Index options. Exactly the same behaviour is shown by these options as by the equity options just discussed. Thus the in-the-money 3650s and 3700s showed a fall in time value during the rise in the FTSE100 Index from 12th January to 19th January, and another fall in time value during the rise in the Index from 9th February to 16th February. Conversely, the well out-

Table 7.8 Movement of Guinness share prices, call option premiums and time values from 12th January 1996 to 16th February 1996

Date			12 Jan	19 Jan	26 Jan	2 Feb	9 Feb	16 Feb
Share price			484	471	467	459	458	456
Feb	420s	premiums	67	53	49	40	39	37
		time values	3	2	2	1	1	1
Feb	460s	premiums	30	18	15	7	6	3
		time values	6	7	8	7	6	3
Feb	500s	premium	7	3	2	1	1	1
		time values	7	3	2	1	1	1
May	420s	premiums	70	57	54	46	44	41
		time values	6	6	7	7	6	5
May	460s	premiums	37	27	25	19	17	15
		time values	13	16	18	19	17	15
May	500s	premiums	16	10	9	6	6	5
		time values	16	10	9	6	6	5
Aug	420s	premiums	73	61	58	50	49	47
		time values	7	10	11	11	11	11
Aug	460s	premiums	44	35	32	26	25	24
		time values	20	24	25	26	25	24
Aug	500s	premiums	24	17	15	12	11	10
		time values	24	17	15	12	11	10

of-the-money 3750s and 3800s showed a substantial rise in time values during these two one-week rises.

The loss in time values over the whole period for the in-the-money options was less for the further expiry April and March than for the near expiry February, as expected. On the other hand the gain in time values for the out-of-the-money options was greater for the near expiry options than for the further expiry March and April options.

In general therefore, the Index options behave in a similar way to equity options.

POTENTIAL FOR PROFIT AND LOSS

The foregoing discussion of intrinsic values and time values for falling, rising and static share prices and FTSE100 Index options is intended to give a background against which investors can select the correct option for the degree of risk and the potential reward that they require. As a result of the correlation approach discussed in Chapter 5, we are now of course faced with a greatly reduced number of options from which to choose. This reduced list of options has to be considered in the light of the two important dimensions—the gap between the actual share price and the striking price (i.e. the extent to which the option is in- or out-of-the-money), and the length of time to expiry (i.e. short, medium or long).

Table 7.9 Movement of the FTSE100 Index, call option premiums and time values from 12th January 1996 to 16th February 1996

Date		12 Jan	19 Jan	26 Jan	2 Feb	9 Feb	16 Feb
FTSE100 Index		3657.3	3748.4	3734.7	3761.5	3716.3	3770.9
Feb	3650s premiums	62	129		144	101	134
	time values	55	31		33	35	14
Feb	3700s premiums	37	84	87	105	68	94
	time values	37	36	53	44	52	24
Feb	3750s premiums	18	53	56	72	42	59
	time values	18	53	56	72	42	39
Feb	3800s premiums	8	27	33	44	22	31
	time values	8	27	73	44	22	31
Mar	3650s premiums	87	150	130	154	114	143
	time values	80	52	46	43	48	23
Mar	3700s premiums	62	111	99	120	84	109
	time values	62	63	65	59	68	39
Mar	3750s premiums	40	79	74	89	60	79
	time values	40	79	74	78	60	59
Mar	3800s premiums	25	53	51	65	40	55
	time values	25	53	51	65	40	55
Apr	3650s premiums	101	160	146	170	138	165
	time values	94	62	62	59	72	45
Apr	3700s premiums	78	129	115	138	107	133
	time values	78	81	81	77	91	63
Apr	3750s premiums	56	97	91	107	83	102
	time values	56	97	91	96	83	82
Apr	3800s premiums	40	74	63	83	58	77
	time values	40	74	63	83	58	77

Just to give an approximate idea of the potential gains, we can consider a matrix containing nine boxes, with one pair of opposite sides representing the gap between striking price and share price and the other pair of sides the length of time to expiry. The gains made from a rise in share price or Index value are shown on a scale of 1 to 5. It must be stressed that this is approximate, and there will often be exceptions, but the diagram (Table 7.10) will be helpful to the discussion.

Table 7.10 Expected gains, on a scale of 1 to 5, for various categories of call options

	Short expiry	Medium expiry	Long expiry
In-the-money	+ + +	+ +	+
At-the-money	+ + + +	+ + +	+ +
Out-of-the-money	+ + + + +	+ + + +	+ + +

Quite clearly, therefore, the potential for the largest gain lies in the short-term, out-of-the-money options, while the long-term, in-the-money options offer the lowest potential for gain.

As far as the degree of risk is concerned, we might be tempted to say that we could use the same pluses to represent the risk for each option, i.e. long-term, in-the-money options being the safest, and short-term, out-of-the-money being the riskiest. This is much too simple a view. It is sensible to look at risk in terms of being completely wrong about the direction of the share price. If the share price falls drastically, then much more capital will be lost with short-term, in-the-money options than any of the others. In these terms, therefore, it is these that are the riskiest, not their out-of-the-money counterparts. A slightly rosier view of risk may be taken if we look at the position where we are only half right about the movement of the share price, i.e. it neither rises nor falls. In such a case the risk is approximately proportional to the potential gains shown in Table 7.10.

The expected gains shown in Table 7.10 are intended to give an approximate idea of the relative potential for gain in the various types of option available to the investor. Naturally, most investors are attracted to options because of their gearing effect, i.e. they multiply the gains that would have been made simply by investing in the underlying share, provided of course that the investor has correctly forecast the future direction of the share price. We now move to a more detailed consideration of the level of gearing obtained from in-the-money and out-of-the-money options.

When to Buy In-the-Money Call Options

Since Table 7.10 shows that the potential for profit with in-the-money options is always less than with their out-of-the-money equivalents, it is not surprising that most of the action in traded options takes place in the latter. Although the profit potential of in-the-money option is less, never forget that this potential is very much greater than the potential for profit in the underlying shares themselves. Thus there are attractions in these options for the investor who may be considering buying the shares. The key here is to find options which have been so ignored by other investors that their time values have become too low, offering an extremely good buy. A good example which has already appeared in this chapter is Rolls-Royce (Table 7.5). Here the time value for the February 180s on 26th January was down to zero when the share price was 200. Such options— short expiry, reasonably heavily in-the-money—approach a delta value of 1 (Chapter 5), i.e. will rise penny for penny with the share price. Thus in the Rolls-Royce case, over the following week the share price rose by 14p to 214p (7%), while the option premium rose from 20 to 36p, i.e. 80%. It is usually possible to find one such example every few weeks. The investor employing such a successful strategy now has two courses open to him: he can take his profit in the options, or, if he still requires the shares, he can exercise into them. Do not forget also the other source of income during this exercise: he could have invested the balance of the sum he had intended to invest in the shares in the money market, partly offsetting the 20p premium he has had to pay.

Note that it is in the short-term expiry options that opportunities such as that with Rolls-Royce exist. The longer expiry options are unlikely to throw up many situations where the time values are absurdly low.

The level of gains to be made from the in-the-money options are shown for the period 12th to 19th January 1996 in Table 7.11. Most shares made fairly modest gains over these two weeks, the average gain for all of the shares being 2.1%.

Table 7.11 Gains in share prices and in-the-money call option premiums between 12th and 19th January 1996

Share	Strike price	Share price	12th January Jan pre	Apr pre	Jul pre	19th January Jan pre	Apr pre	Jul pre	Share price	Jan gain	Apr gain	Jul gain	Share gain
Allied Dom.	500	534	35	48	55	43	50	56	550	22.9	4.2	1.8	3.0
Argyll	300	342	43	49	53	60	65	69	351	39.5	32.7	30.2	2.6
Asda	100	114	15	17	20	14	17	18	111	−6.7	0	−10.0	−2.6
BAA	460	491	21	36	42	39	47	53	486	85.7	30.6	26.2	1.0
British Airws.	460	491	31	44	51	67	74	78	519	109.7	68.2	52.9	5.7
Boots	550	593	43	57	65	60	68	73	597	39.5	19.3	12.1	0.7
British Steel	140	165	25	28	30	29	31	32	166	16.0	10.7	6.7	0.6
British Petrol.	460	526	66	70	75	68	73	77	526	3.0	4.3	2.7	0
	500	526	26	36	46	35	45	49	526	160.0	23.1	12.5	
Bass	700	703	8	35	55	54	71	82	734	575.0	102.9	49.1	4.4
Comm. U.	550	624	73	81	84	73	77	81	619	0	−4.9	−3.6	−0.8
	600	624	24	42	50	35	44	50	619	45.8	4.6	0	
Cable & W.	420	460	41	54	61	52	59	66	462	26.8	9.3	8.2	0.4
	460	460	6	28	37	26	35	43	462	333.3	25.0	16.2	
Courtaulds	390	429	39	49	56	56	62	66	438	43.6	26.5	17.8	2.1
	420	429	10	28	36	33	41	47	438	230.0	46.4	30.6	
Glaxo	850	873	26	49	64	75	81	99	912	188.5	65.3	54.7	4.5
HSBC	1000	1001	12	49	60	98	115	130	1076	733.3	134.7	97.0	7.5
ICI	750	802	54	64	75	82	89	96	825	51.9	39.0	28.0	2.9
Kingfisher	500	531	35	49	56	49	55	62	536	40.0	12.2	10.5	0.9
Land Secs	600	627	28	42	50	42	48	52	625	50.0	14.3	4.0	4.5
M & S	420	431	12	26	32	35	42	46	445	191.7	34.7	43.8	3.2
NatWest	600	635	35	46	57	70	78	84	665	100.0	69.6	47.4	4
PowerGen	460	504	45	57	64	69	74	79	519	53.3	29.8	23.4	2.9
	500	504	9	30	38	38	46	53	519	322.2	53.3	39.4	
Reuters	550	599	50	62	75	68	79	90	609	36.0	27.4	20.0	1.7
Sainsbury	390	404	14	28	34	37	42	47	416	164.3	50.0	38.2	2.9
Shell Transpt	800	840	40	54	60	58	63	72	847	45.0	16.7	20.0	0.8
SmithKline	650	690	41	56	70	67	78	89	707	63.4	39.3	27.0	2.4
Standard Ch.	550	564	19	50	68	84	103	115	618	342.1	106.0	69.1	9.6
Storehouse	280	297	17	26	32	23	30	34	296	35.2	15.4	6.3	−0.3
Thames Wat.	500	533	33	48	55	54	81	64	542	63.6	27.1	16.7	1.7
Unilever	1300	1317	20	50	65	74	85	106	1347	270.0	70.0	63.1	2.3
Zeneca	1200	1230	34	70	95	114	138	155	1275	235.3	97.1	63.2	3.6
Average gain										**138.5%**	**38.4%**	**27.2%**	**2.5%**
Gearing										55	15	10	

Share	Strike price	Share price	12th January			19th January			Share price	Feb gain	May gain	Aug gain	Share gain
			Feb pre	May pre	Aug pre	Feb pre	May pre	Aug pre					
British Aero.	800	835	51	70	91	81	99	118	876	58.9	41.4	29.7	4.9
BAT Inds	550	551	19	28	37	35	43	51	577	84.2	53.6	37.8	4.7
BTR	300	333	35	37	39	36	38	39	334	2.9	2.7	0	0.3
British Tele.	360	361	11	20	28	18	28	35	375	63.6	40.0	25.0	3.9
Cadbury-Sch.	500	534	41	49	59	46	54	63	541	12.1	10.2	6.8	1.3
GEC	330	365	39	46	51	38	45	49	366	−2.6	−2.1	−3.9	0.3
	360	365	15	24	31	13	23	29	366	−13.3	−4.2	−6.5	
Grand Met.	420	444	31	43	51	36	47	56	451	16.1	9.3	9.8	1.6
Guinness	420	484	67	70	73	53	57	61	471	−20.9	−18.6	−16.4	−2.7
	460	484	30	37	44	18	27	35	471	−4.0	−27.0	−20.5	
Ladbroke	140	154	18	21	25	26	30	33	164	44.4	42.9	32.0	6.5
LASMO	160	176	18	22	27	13	18	22	171	−27.8	−18.2	−18.5	−2.8
Lucas	160	176	19	22	26	29	31	34	188	52.6	40.9	30.8	6.8
P&O	460	474	24	31	38	34	40	46	489	41.7	29.0	21.1	3.2
Prudential	390	429	44	48	56	47	51	59	434	6.8	6.3	5.3	1.2
	420	429	22	28	41	22	29	42	434	0	3.6	0	
RTZ	850	885	47	59	73	47	57	73	889	0	−3.4	0	0.5
Redland	330	364	38	45	48	28	36	39	354	−26.3	−20.0	−18.8	−0.3
	360	364	15	25	29	9	18	23	354	−40.0	−28.0	−20.7	
Rolls-Royce	180	196	19	23	27	23	25	30	201	21.0	8.7	11.1	2.6
Royal Ins.	360	386	27	36	44	42	50	56	396	55.6	38.9	27.3	2.6
Tesco	280	300	24	29	34	30	34	38	307	25.0	17.2	11.8	2.3
	300	300	10	16	22	13	20	25	307	30.0	25.0	13.6	
Utd Biscuits	240	254	19	24	30	20	25	31	256	5.3	4.2	3.3	0.8
Vodaphone	200	214	18	25	29	27	33	37	227	50.0	32.0	27.6	6.1
Williams	300	330	33	38	39	42	46	47	339	27.3	21.1	20.5	2.7
Average gain										**17.8%**	**10.4%**	**5.4%**	**2.2%**
Gearing										**8**	**4**	**2**	

Share	Strike price	Share price	12th January			19th January			Share price	Mar gain	Jun gain	Sep gain	Share gain
			Mar pre	Jun pre	Sep pre	Mar pre	Jun pre	Sep pre					
Abbey Nat.	600	639	52	61	69	67	75	82	660	28.8	23.0	18.1	3.3
Amstrad	160	183	27	33	38	29	35	38	184	7.4	6.1	0	0.5
Barclays	700	750	62	71	79	79	84	93	772	27.4	18.3	17.7	2.9
	750	750	29	41	51	39	50	62	772	34.4	22.0	21.6	
Blue Circle	300	325	31	36	41	45	48	52	339	45.2	33.3	26.8	4.3
British Gas	240	265	29	32	36	19	23	28	252	−34.5	−28.1	−22.2	−4.9
	260	265	15	19	23	9	14	18	252	−4.0	−26.3	−27.8	
Dixons	390	409	31	42	49	36	47	53	417	16.1	11.9	8.2	2.0
Forte	360	369	17	19	20	20	24	26	375	17.6	26.3	30.0	1.6
Hillsdown	160	174	18	19	21	20	22	23	178	11.1	15.5	9.5	2.3
Lonrho	180	196	17	24	27	23	28	32	203	35.3	16.7	18.5	3.6
Nat. Power	390	435	52	60	63	55	64	66	441	5.8	6.7	4.8	1.4
	420	435	28	38	44	30	42	46	441	7.1	10.5	9.6	
Scot. Power	360	376	20	29	35	26	34	40	383	30.0	17.2	14.3	1.9
Sears	90	97	9	11	12	9	11	12	98	0	0	0	1.0
Tarmac	100	104	9	13	15	12	15	17	108	33.3	15.4	13.3	3.8
Tomkins	260	279	23	30	34	21	29	32	276	−8.7	−3.3	−5.9	−1.1
Average gain										**14.8%**	**9.7%**	**8.0%**	**1.6%**
Gearing										**9**	**6**	**5**	

In order to gain more of an insight into the relationship between the gain in share prices and the gain in option premiums, it is best to split the options into the January, February and March expiry cycles. Taking the nearest expiries from these three cycles, the average gain in the January options was 138.5%, in the February options 17.8% and in the March options 14.8%. The gains in the three groups of shares were 2.5%, 2.2% and 1.6%. Because of these slightly different gains in the three groups of shares, it is best to compare the three gearings, i.e. the ratio of the gain made in the options compared with the gain made in the shares. In round numbers the gearings were 55, 8 and 9.

Taking the middle expiry options, i.e. the April, May and June expiries, the gains in the options were 38.4%, 10.4% and 9.7% respectively, with gearings of 15, 4 and 6.

Finally, the furthest expiry options made average gains of 27.2%, 5.4% and 8.0% respectively, with gearings of 10, 2 and 5.

The case for investing in the nearest expiry, in-the-money options at a time when modest gains are expected in the share price is fully vindicated, with an enormous gearing of 55 for the options which had only a couple of weeks to run. Even choosing from the next cycles with about six weeks and ten weeks to run gave excellent gearings of 15 and 10.

Out-of-the-Money Options

As was stated earlier, most of the action in the traded options market occurs in the out-of-the-money options. In these options the length of time to expiry becomes of paramount importance. Before looking in more detail at these options, some general observations are in order.

1. Volatility is of prime importance. A share of low volatility will rise so slowly that short-expiry options may see little movement in the time remaining to expiry. Do not consider far out-of-the-money options unless the share is in the top half of the volatility league table.
2. Base your decision as to whether to invest in short, medium or long expiry times on the result of channel analysis on the underlying share. This should give you a firm idea of the length of time for which the coming share price rise will endure. Expiry dates should be chosen so as to coincide as near as possible to this period of rise in order to maximise the gearing obtained.

It is interesting to compare the gains made in the out-of-the-money versions of the options which were shown in Table 7.11. These values are given in Table 7.12. Taken as an average, the gains made are approximately ten times as much for the January expiry options, four times as much for the February options and three times as much for the March expiries. Other expiries give gains of about double their in-the-money counterparts.

Table 7.12 Gains in share prices and out-of-the-money call option premiums between 12th and 19th January 1996

Share	Strike price	Share price	12th January			19th January			Share price	Jan gain	Apr gain	Jul gain	Share gain
			Jan pre	Apr pre	Jul pre	Jan pre	Apr pre	Jul pre					
Allied Dom.	550	534	1	18	26	15	23	31	550	1400.0	27.8	19.2	3.0
	600		1	6	11	4	9	15		300.0	50.0	36.4	
Argyll	360	342	1	12	17	15	21	26	351	1400.0	75.0	52.9	2.6
Asda	120	114	1	5	8	3	6	8	111	200.0	20.0	0	
BAA	500	491	1	14	21	14	23	31	486	1300.0	64.3	47.6	1.0
British Airws	500	491	2	20	30	35	44	51	519	1650.0	120.0	70.0	5.7
			1	5	13	1	20	27		0	300.0	107.7	
Boots	600	593	3	23	33	25	35	42	597	733.0	52.2	27.3	0.7
	650		1	7	14	7	15	22		600.0	114.3	57.1	
British Steel	180	165	1	5	7	5	7	9	166	400.0	40.0	28.6	0.6
British Petrol.	550	526	1	10	20	9	19	24	526	800.0	90.0	20.0	0
Bass	750	703	1	14	33	25	45	55	734	2400.0	221.4	66.7	4.4
Comm. U.	650	624	1	16	26	12	22	29	619	1100.0	37.5	11.5	−0.8
Cable & W.	500	460	1	12	20	1	18	27	462	0	50.0	35.0	0.4
Courtaulds	460	429	1	10	17	12	21	27	438	1100.0	110.0	58.8	2.1
Glaxo	900	873	2	24	41	40	57	69	912	1900.0	137.5	68.3	4.5
	950		1	10	24	18	34	46		1700.0	240.0	91.7	
HSBC	1050	1001	1	28	46	63	85	103	1076	6200.0	203.6	123.9	7.5
ICI	850	802	1	12	25	18	32	41	825	1700.0	166.7	64.0	2.9
Kingfisher	550	531	1	20	29	19	28	37	536	1800.0	40.0	27.6	0.9
Land Secs	650	627	1	14	21	13	19	24	625	1200.0	35.7	14.3	4.5
M & S	460	431	1	8	13	13	19	25	445	1200.0	137.5	92.3	3.2
NatWest	650	635	3	18	33	32	47	55	665	966.7	161.1	66.7	4.0
	700		1	8	17	14	26	34		1300.0	225.0	100.0	
PowerGen	550	504	1	10	17	14	21	30	519	1300.0	110.0	76.5	2.9
Reuters	600	599	7	30	45	33	48	60	609	371.4	60.0	33.3	1.7
	650		1	11	24	13	26	38		1200.0	136.4	58.3	
Sainsbury	420	404	1	13	19	18	24	30	416	1700.0	84.6	57.9	2.9
Shell Transpt.	850	840	2	21	31	24	32	42	847	1100.0	52.4	35.5	0.8
	900		1	6	13	6	14	22		500.0	133.3	69.2	
SmithKline	700	690	3	25	41	33	46	58	707	1000.0	84.0	41.5	2.4
	750		1	9	22	12	23	35		1100.0	155.6	59.1	
Standard Chr.	600	564	1	28	46	51	73	88	618	5000.0	160.7	91.3	9.6
Storehouse	300	297	3	13	21	13	18	23	296	333.3	38.5	9.5	−0.3
Thames Water	550	533	1	19	27	23	31	35	542	2200.0	63.2	29.6	1.7
	600		1	6	12	6	12	17		500.0	100.0	41.7	
Unilever	1350	1317	1	25	38	40	53	74	1347	3900.0	112.0	94.7	2.3
Zeneca	1250	1230	5	44	69	64	88	105		1180.0	100.0	56.3	6.3
	1300		1	26	49	39	62	80		3800.0	138.5	63.3	
Average gain										1449.6%	108.9%	54.0%	2.5%
Gearing										579	43	21	

Share	Strike price	Share price	12th January			19th January			Share price	Feb gain	May gain	Aug gain	Share gain
			Feb pre	May pre	Aug pre	Feb pre	May pre	Aug pre					
British Aero.	850	835	22	43	65	43	65	87	876	95.5	51.2	33.8	4.9
	900		8	25	45	15	40	61		87.5	60.0	35.6	4.9
BAT Inds	600	551	4	12	20	8	18	28	577	100.0	50.0	40.0	4.7
BTR	360	333	1	4	9	1	5	9	334	0	25.0	0	0.3
British Tele.	390	361	1	8	14	3	12	22	375	200.0	50.0	57.1	3.9

Share	Strike price	Share price	12th January Feb pre	May pre	Aug pre	19th January Feb pre	May pre	Aug pre	Share price	Feb gain	May gain	Aug gain	Share gain
Cadbury-Sch.	550	534	11	23	34	12	25	36	541	0.1	8.7	5.9	1.3
	600		2	9	19	2	11	21		0	18.2	10.5	
GEC	390	365	4	11	16	2	10	15	366	−50.0	−9.1	−6.3	0.3
Grand Met.	460	444	8	20	30	9	23	33	451	12.5	15.0	10.0	1.6
	500		1	8	16	1	9	18		0	12.5	12.5	
Guinness	500	484	7	16	24	3	10	17	471	−57.1	−37.5	−29.2	−2.7
Ladbroke	160	154	7	12	16	12	19	22	164	71.4	58.3	27.3	6.5
LASMO	180	176	6	10	16	3	8	12	171	−50.0	−20.0	−25.0	−2.8
	200		1	4	9	1	3	6		0	−25.0	−33.3	
Lucas	180	176	6	10	15	11	16	21	188	83.3	60.0	40.0	6.8
	200		1	4	8	2	7	12		100.0	75.0	50.0	
P&O	500	474	5	12	20	9	17	26	489	80.0	41.7	30.0	3.2
Prudential	460	429	6	12	22	4	13	23	434	−33.3	8.3	4.5	1.2
RTZ	900	885	16	31	46	15	28	46	889	−6.3	−9.7	0	0.5
	950		4	15	27	3	11	27		−25.0	−26.7	0	
Redland	390	364	4	12	17	3	8	12	354	−25.0	−33.3	−29.4	−0.3
Rolls-Royce	200	196	6	11	16	8	13	18	201	33.3	18.2	12.5	2.6
	220		1	5	9	1	5	10		0	0	11.1	
Royal Ins.	390	386	4	18	29	21	33	40	396	425.0	83.3	37.9	2.6
	420		1	9	18	10	21	28		900.0	133.3	55.6	
Tesco	330	300	2	5	10	2	7	12	307	0	40.0	20.0	2.3
Utd Biscuits	260	254	8	14	20	8	14	21	256	0	0	5.0	0.8
	280		2	8	13	3	8	13		50.0	0	0	
Vodaphone	220	214	7	14	19	12	20	26	227	71.4	42.9	36.8	6.1
	240		2	7	12	3	11	17		50.0	57.1	41.7	
Williams	330	330	9	17	20	15	22	26	339	66.7	29.4	30.0	2.7
	360		1	6	9	2	8	12		100.0	33.3	33.3	
Average gain										**71.3%**	**25.3%**	**16.2%**	**2.2%**
Gearing										**32**	**11**	**7**	

Share	Strike price	Share price	12th January Mar pre	Jun pre	Sep pre	19th January Mar pre	Jun pre	Sep pre	Share price	Mar gain	Jun gain	Sep gain	Share gain
Abbey Nat.	650	639	22	34	44	31	43	53	660	40.9	26.5	20.5	3.3
	700		7	17	26	11	23	33		57.1	35.3	26.9	
Amstrad	200	183	6	13	18	8	15	18	184	33.3	15.4	0	0.5
Barclays	750	750	29	41	51	39	50	62	772	34.5	30.0	21.6	2.9
	800	750	9	22	31	13	27	39	772	44.4	22.7	25.8	2.9
Blue Circle	330	325	12	19	21	20	27	33	339	66.7	31.6	52.4	4.3
	360		4	10	14	7	15	20		75.0	50.0	42.9	
British Gas	280	265	7	10	15	3	7	12	252	−57.1	−30.0	−20.0	−4.9
Dixons	420	409	15	26	33	18	30	37	417	20.0	15.4	12.1	2.0
	460		5	13	19	6	14	21		20.0	7.7	10.5	
Forte	390	369	2	8	6	4	7	8	375	100.0	−12.5	33.3	1.6
Hillsdown	180	174	6	8	10	7	10	12	178	16.7	25.0	20.0	2.3
	200		2	3	4	2	4	5		0	33.3	25.0	
Lonrho	200	196	7	12	16	10	16	20	203	42.9	33.3	25.0	3.6
	220		2	6	9	3	8	12		50.0	33.3	33.3	3.3
Nat. Power	460	435	8	17	25	9	20	26	441	12.5	17.6	4.0	1.4
Scot. Power	390	376	2	14	20	9	17	23	383	350.0	21.4	25.0	1.9
Sears	100	97	3	5	7	4	5	7	98	33.3	0	0	1.0
	110		1	2	4	1	2	4		0	0	0	
Tarmac	110	104	5	8	10	6	9	12	108	20.0	12.5	20.0	3.8
Tomkins	280	279	10	19	23	9	17	21	276	−10.0	−10.5	−8.7	−1.1
Average gain										**50.0%**	**18.8%**	**19.5%**	**1.6%**
Gearing										**31**	**11**	**12**	

Thus, quite obviously, the out-of-the-money options are attractive in terms of their potential for gain compared with the in-the-money options. This potential is, of course, obtained at the expense of increased risk. The risk is highest particularly with the short expiry options, since time values are falling off rapidly.

Tired Options

Note that as the share price continues to rise, the gains being made on a week-by-week basis in a particular option, especially one with the nearest expiry, will start to fall off. This is shown in Figure 7.4 for the theoretical case where the share price continues upwards at a constant rate. It can be seen that the gain in the option starts to flatten out as time goes on. There are several reasons for this. As discussed earlier, the time values of the options start to erode over the last six weeks or so of the life of the option, putting the brake on the upward movement in the premium. A further factor is that the longer the upward movement in the share price continues, the more does the traded options market consider that it is coming to an end, so that the demand for that particular option declines. This naturally has an adverse effect on the option premium. The logic of this situation is that, if we neglect the impact of the buying and selling costs, there comes a point at which we should close the position and open a different one, even though the share price is still rising. As shown in the next section, if we feel that the share price rise still has some steam left in it, it is sensible to close the current position and open another one in a different option of that share.

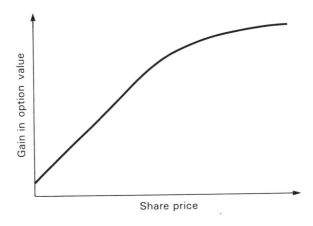

Figure 7.4 Fall-off in the gain of an option with time even though the share price continues upwards at a constant rate

SUBSEQUENT ACTION

Once an option has been bought, then the position must be constantly monitored to see that the expected upward share price trend is maintained within the timescale of the option expiry date. Two outcomes require that action is taken other than that intended when the option was purchased. The first is a fall in the share price, and the second is when the upward trend in the share price appears to be exceeding the original expectation and you wish to profit further from the extended movement.

Falling Share Price

Action here depends upon whether you feel the price will continue to fall or whether it will rally from what you consider is a temporary situation. In the former case the best thing is to close the position. In the latter case you could sweat it out by doing nothing and waiting for the share price recovery to improve the value of your option. A much better strategy which will reduce the risk in your position is to roll down.

Rolling Down

This strategy will reduce the risk in your position at the cost of reducing the potential profit. There are two legs to this strategy, which will end up with you holding a bull spread (see Chapter 11). A bull spread is one where you write a call with one striking price and buy a call with a lower striking price, and since the share price is falling, obviously we will have to buy another call with a lower striking price than the present one. In order to convert our holding of the higher strike price call into a written position on that option, we will have to write two contracts on the option series that we originally held. Thus:

1. Write two contracts for the same option that we held originally.
2. Buy one contract in an option with a lower striking price.

All of these transactions should be carried out on options of the same expiry date as the original, provided of course that there is sufficient time left to expiry. If the latter is the case, then move out into further expiring options if you are convinced that the amended timescale you see for the upward turn to the current downward trend is appropriate.

Rising Share Price

If the upward trend is as you expected, then maintain the present position in the option or close if you have achieved your objective. If you are convinced that the price rise will be prolonged, then the appropriate strategy is to roll up. *Note that you should only undertake this action if you are convinced that the opportunity for profit by staying with this share is greater or more imminent than opportunities with other shares which may just be entering a new upward phase.*

Rolling Up

This is the strategy to employ where you feel that a share price movement, which has given you a useful profit in your selected call option, may continue for some considerable time, possibly past the expiry date of your option. In such a case therefore you need to continue your involvement with options in that share. However, you will be putting at risk profits that you have already made from the current option that you hold, and therefore you must be convinced that the upward price trend will continue for some time.

The strategy involves the following actions:

1. Closing your current position in the option.
2. Buying an option with a higher striking price.

The strategy takes into account the comments made in the last section about tired options. Since the most gearing will be obtained with the shorter expiry options, the investor should stick with these, with the proviso that they should only be bought if they have more than about six weeks left to expiry. This is because, as we have stated previously, time values start to decay rapidly over this final period. Because of this, the amount of gearing available from the option starts to fall off compared with that from options with a further out expiry date. We also pointed out (Table 7.8) that as the option moves into the at-the-money or in-the-money position due to the share price rise, the fall off in time values becomes more marked. Thus, as a general rule, we can say that it is time to move out of the option once the share price has more or less reached the striking price. This gives us an automatic selling signal for the option. The new option should be the most out-of-the-money option, which will of course have been newly introduced as a result of the share price rise (see Chapter 2).

Thus our strategy becomes:

1. Sell once the share price reaches the striking price, or if the option was initially in-the-money, sell when there are only a few weeks left to expiry.
2. Buy the most out-of-the-money option with the nearest expiry date that has at least six weeks to run.

This policy will bring to bear the maximum gearing, and hence the maximum profit during the course of the share price rise. The number of contracts being bought will escalate dramatically. A close watch has to be kept on the share price using all available techniques, especially channel analysis, in order to determine the point at which the strategy should be terminated.

This is essential, since at the end of a successful series of these transactions, an enormous sum of money will be at risk relative to the initial starting sum. This is well illustrated by an example based on a prediction of the future course of the Dixons share price made on 17th March 1995, using the Sigma-p probability program (Figure 7.5). The prediction was that a rising trend had already started, and would probably end towards the end of July, giving at least four months of a rising price. Table 7.13 shows the rolling-up strategy adopted in this example.

The gain of 34.6% in the share price was transformed by the gearing of options into a gain of 2413% by using this strategy over just three complete buying and selling operations (Table 7.13). This resulted in just £900 being converted into over £22 000! Note also that the £22 000, riding on the last buying transaction, could have been lost quite quickly with an adverse price move in Dixons, emphasising the necessity for the utmost vigilance during this last phase of the share price rise.

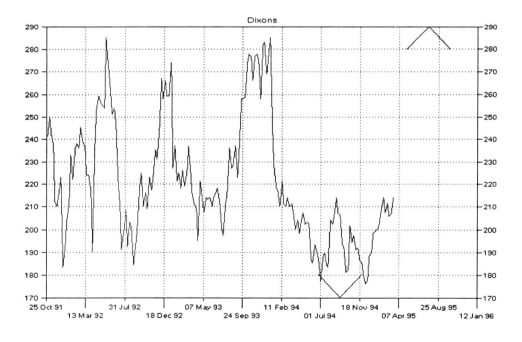

Figure 7.5 The Sigma-p probability program applied to the Dixons share price on 17th March 1995. This shows that an upward trend in the Dixons share price had already started, and predicted the trend to end about late July 1995

Table 7.13   The mechanics of a rolling-up strategy in Dixons

Date	Share price	Transaction			£
17/03/95	214	Buy 10 contracts	Jun 220s	@ 9p	900
20/03/95	222	Sell 10 contracts	Jun 220s	@ 15p	1500
		Buy 18 contracts	Jun 240s	@ 8p	1440
25/05/95	246	Sell 18 contracts	Jun 240s	@ 13p	2340
		Buy 78 contracts	Sep 260s	@ 3p	2340
07/07/95	288	Sell 78 contracts	Sep 260s	@ 29p	22 620

Percentage gain = 2413%   Annualised % gain = 2413 × 52/17 = 7380%

8

Writing Call Options

The writer of a call option receives a premium from a buyer of the option and in return undertakes to sell the shares at the striking price if a buyer exercises the option.

Much time was spent in the last chapter on a discussion of the relationship between share prices and option premiums, including a careful consideration of time values. These relationships are also, of course, of paramount importance to the seller, i.e. the writer of a call option, but since the topic has been covered in detail, it will not be repeated here. The writer of a call option is naturally at the opposite side of the transaction to the purchaser, and therefore on a simple view he takes a diametrically opposed position about the future movement of the share price.

While the purchaser expects a rise in the share price during the lifetime of the option, and can buy an option which will reflect his view of the extent of the rise and the timescale over which it will occur, the writer expects either a fall in the share price, a static share price, or a rise so limited that it would not be profitable for the buyer to exercise the option. This reference to exercising the option draws attention to a major important difference which a newcomer to the purchase of call options can overlook: the buyer of the option has control of the situation while the writer does not. The buyer can exercise the option at any time during its lifetime, in which case the writer has to provide the requisite number of shares in the underlying security, usually 1000 shares per option contract (see Chapter 2).

There are then two positions in which the writer can find himself—he already owns the shares and can deliver, or he will have to buy the shares in the market in order to deliver. The first type of investor is called a "covered" writer, and the second category an "uncovered" or "naked" writer.

As the discussion proceeds, it will become apparent that the naked writer is exposed to a very high level of risk, while the covered writer can be considered to be quite a conservative investor.

NAKED OPTION WRITING

The opposed positions of a purchaser of a call option and the writer of the call option are most obviously illustrated by the naked option writer. In the last chapter we defined the option purchaser's position as being one of limited loss and unlimited gain. The naked writer is in the unfortunate position of having a position of unlimited loss and limited gain. The gain is limited because it is simply the premium, less expenses, obtained by selling the option. The loss is unlimited because the writer has to buy the shares in the market if the option is exercised. In theory he may have to pay an infinitely high price for them.

Loss/gain Potential—Unlimited Loss, Limited Gain

Just as in the last chapter, we can draw a diagram to illustrate this concept of limited gain and unlimited loss for the naked option writer by plotting the profit or loss potential against the share price. This is shown in Figure 8.1.

At point A, the share price is equal to the striking price and the purchaser would be considering exercising the option. The profit, i.e. the original premium, has remained constant up to this point, but as the share price moves above the striking price, the writer has to pay an increasing amount to buy the shares in order to deliver them when the option is exercised. At point B, the original premium received has been wiped out. Since the share price has in theory no upper limit, then the loss incurred will also have no limit.

Because of this relationship between profit and loss for naked option writing, it is not to be recommended to the novice in the traded options market. Financial disaster can be the outcome of an incorrect decision

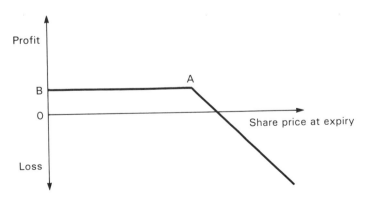

Figure 8.1 Profit/loss situation for a naked call option writer with changing share price. Point A is the striking price and point B is the premium received

about the future share price movement. The writer must be extremely confident of a fall in the price of the underlying security. Although, of course, the written position can be cancelled simply by the purchase of an identical number of contracts in the same option, this cannot be done, under the rules of the traded options market, once the writer has received an exercise notice. The writer is therefore vulnerable to the sort of sharp upward price movements that occur upon the news of a takeover bid. In such situations the writer may simply not have the time to take corrective action by closing the position. The naked option writer should always adopt the policy of closing his position at the first hint that matters are going against him, rather than wait in the hope that the situation will change.

Margin Requirements for Writing Call Options

An option writer must deposit cover with the London Clearing House by 10 a.m. the business day following the day of the bargain. This can be arranged via the broker. The cover can be in several forms, such as a bank confirmation that it holds the share certificates, or convertible issues, bearer bonds, etc., of the company in whose shares the option is being written, to the order of the London Option Clearing House. In the case of a naked writer, he must deposit a margin of 25% of the value of the underlying security, adjusted by the extent to which the option series stands in- or out-of-the-money. The sum deposited by the naked option writer has to be adjusted on a daily basis as the share price moves. As the share price moves upwards, the required margin increases, and it decreases as the share price falls.

Exercise of Call Options

The discussion so far has had to consider the position when the option is exercised against the writer. Since the writer does not wish the option to be exercised, then from the writer's point of view such exercise of the option is not a good outcome of the investment position. Simplistically, it might be thought that an option would be exercised once it moves sufficiently in-the-money to more than cover the premium paid and any expenses involved in the purchase of the option and the purchase of the shares. That this does not happen is due to the fact that, early in the life of an option, the purchaser is generally not looking towards the purchase of the shares as the means to generating a profit, but to the selling of the option at a much higher value than he has paid for it. Thus, early in the life of options, only a very small proportion are exercised, while the majority, if they do not expire worthless, are exercised in the last few weeks prior to expiry.

   As we have pointed out, however, the writer is completely at the mercy of the purchaser, and should not take for granted that the option will not be exercised against him, however much time is left until expiry. Note that the purchaser and writer of the corresponding option are matched against each other in a random selection by computer as being the fairest way to do this.

COVERED OPTION WRITING

While the writing of uncovered options is an extremely aggressive investment stance, the writing of covered options is extremely conservative, and is frequently less risky than simply buying shares themselves. The writing of a covered option can be used in the sense of an insurance against a fall in share price, thereby reducing the downside exposure. It can be used also as a means of improving the overall return on an investment. The improvements in the potential for loss obviously have to be paid for, and this payment is the loss of the potential for gain beyond a certain point (the striking price), since a rise in the share price can result in the option being exercised and the consequent loss of the shareholding.

Compared with simply holding the shares, covered option writing is superior when:

1. The share price falls.
2. The share price remains static.
3. The share price enjoys a small rise.

In the latter case, the extent to which the written option is in-the-money or out-of-the-money is of vital importance. The further the option is out-of-the-money, the greater is the tolerance to small share price rises.

Loss/gain Potential—Limited Loss, Limited Gain

This fundamental property of covered option writing can be illustrated by a diagram (Figure 8.2) similar to that used for naked options, by plotting the potential profit or loss against the share price.

Ignoring dealing costs, the maximum loss which can be incurred is the cost of the shares less the premium received for writing the options, and of course this loss will only occur if the value of the shares falls to zero. Point A, where the share price is above the sum of the striking price plus the premium which the purchaser has paid for the option, we can assume is the lowest share price at which the option will be exercised. The maximum profit is therefore obtainable at point A, and will not change as the share price rises further above this point. The profit is equal to the premium obtained plus the difference between the striking price (the price at which the writer has to deliver the shares to the purchaser) and the share price which was paid when the shares were bought. Quite clearly, this difference may be positive or negative, depending upon whether the option is out-, at-, or in-the-money. Since the profit can be described by the relationship

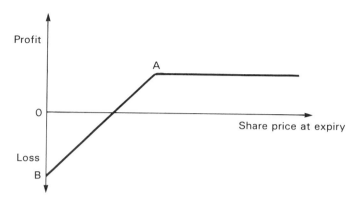

Figure 8.2   Profit/loss situation for a covered call option writer with changing share price. Point A is the striking price and point B is equal to the striking price – share price + premium received

$$\text{Profit} = \text{premium (A)} + \text{striking price (B)}$$
$$- \text{price originally paid for shares (C)}$$

and bearing in mind that option premiums get lower as we proceed from in-the-money to out-of-the-money, we can make the following generalisations:

Type of option	A	B – C
In-the-money	* * *	negative
At-the-money	* *	zero
Out-of-the-money	*	positive

Thus the higher premium for the in-the-money option is offset by the fact that when the shares are called, the investor receives less than he has paid for them. At the other extreme, the lower premium for out-of-the-money options will have an additional amount added, thereby improving the profit. Since the pricing of options is not an exact science, we would not expect the net result of adding A to (B – C) to be the same for all types of options. This fact is best illustrated by an actual example based on the data presented for Rolls-Royce in Table 7.5 in the last chapter. On 19th January 1996, the data for Rolls-Royce were as follows:

Share price 201p;   February 180s, 23p; 200s, 8p; 220s, 1p
May 180s, 25p; 200s, 13p; 220s, 5p
August 180s, 30p; 200s, 18p; 220s, 10p

We will assume that the investor buys the shares at this price of 201p. For our purpose, the 200 options can be considered to be at-the-money, since

Table 8.1 Potential profit to be made from Rolls-Royce February options, share price 201p

Type of option		If exercised	If not exercised
In-the-money	180s	23 + 180 − 201 = 2	23
At-the-money	200s	8 + 200 − 201 = 7	8
Out-of-the-money	220s	1 + 220 − 201 = 20	1

the share price was 201p. Taking just the February options, the potential profit to be made from the options is shown in Table 8.1.

The outcome that the writer of call options does not wish to happen is to have the option exercised, since he will then be in the position of losing the additional profit which would be obtained from the shares themselves if the rising market which has triggered the exercise continues to rise. The outcome he does want is for the options to expire without being exercised. We can take the exercise of the options as being the bad outcome, and the expiration without exercise as being the good outcome. Thus, the "if exercised" column represents the bad outcome and the "If not exercised" column the good outcome. Note that the values in the "If exercised" column represent maximum values, since as already pointed out, additional profit would have been lost if the share price continued to rise after exercise. Accepting this proviso, then on this basis therefore we can see that the following is true:

- In-the-money call options writing: high gain for good outcome, low protection for bad outcome.
- At-the-money call options writing: moderate gain for good outcome, moderate protection for bad outcome.
- Out-of-the-money call options writing: low gain for good outcome, high protection for bad outcome.

Protection in this sense is relative, simply meaning that the investor pockets slightly more in one "bad" situation than another, but has foregone the profit which his shares would have made subsequently in the rising market. We will see shortly that this concept of "good" and "bad" outcomes can be quantified numerically in order to help the decision making process.

Thus, before considering in more detail which particular option should be written, it is important for the option writer to define his objectives in terms of profit potential and protection against incorrect forecasts.

TIMESCALE

As was the case with the purchase of call options, the prime consideration with option writing is to obtain a view of the timescale of the trend that you are taking advantage of, preferably by means of channel analysis. Since a prime consideration is to avoid having your shares called away, the expiry date of the option being written should be nearer than the antici- pated length of time for which the trend will continue. It is best to take an opposite view of time from that taken by the purchaser of the option. Purchasers will tend to take the view that it might be worth paying the higher premiums for longer expiry options because there is more time for an adverse trend to reverse direction and put the option into profit. As far as the writer of a call option is concerned, he has already pocketed the premium, and therefore the sooner the option expires the better, since there is less chance of the option being exercised. Of course, this comes down to a straight trade-off between extra premium that can be obtained for writing longer expiry options and the additional risk that the option will be exercised.

A further point here is to consider the return from the investment as a weekly return (WR). If the premiums for the nine-month, six-month and three-month options were in the ratio of 3 to 2 to 1 in cost, then of course the WRs would be the same. The relationship between short-, medium- and long-term expiry premiums can be examined by extracting some data from Table 7.1 from the last chapter. The data are shown in Table 8.2, where the premiums have been divided by the number of months to expiry, thus giving a value for the premium to be paid or received per month to expiry.

Quite obviously with a particular option class, the further out the expiry date, the less is the premium per month remaining. This is fine for the purchasers of the option, since they are reducing their costs per month by

Table 8.2 Premiums per month (p.m.) remaining to expiry for the options listed in Table 7.1. The data are for 31st January 1996 and share prices are given in parentheses

Option		Expiry month	Prem. p.m.	Expiry month	Prem. p.m.	Expiry month	Prem. p.m.
Guinness	420	February	38	May	10.8	August	6.8
(457)	460		7		4.5		3.6
	500		1		1.3		1.6
Dixons	390	March	17	June	9.2	September	6.5
(416)	420		8		5.8		4.5
	460		2		2.6		2.5
Boots	550	April	26.3	July	14.3	October	9.0
(623)	600		12.3		8		5.5
	650		4		3.7		3.1
FTSE100	3600	February	161	March	87	May	49.5
(3759.3)	3650		113		67		32.4
	3700		72		48.5		26.2
	3750		36		33		20.4
	3800		15		33		15.6
	3850		4		12		11.6
	3900		1		6.5		8.6

going for the longer term. As far as the writer of an option is concerned, he is receiving less premium per month for the longer expiry options, i.e. his WR is less.

With these constraints, more attention can be given to option premiums and time values with a view to moving the odds in the favourable direction for the option writer. Two major areas for consideration here will be those options with anomalous time values, and options with high CPPs.

Anomalous Time Values

The purchaser of a call option can frequently spot an anomalous situation where the time value is ludicrously small for the amount of time remaining to expiry. Thus, in the last chapter in Table 7.5, the time value for the Rolls-Royce February 180s was zero on 26th January, with one month still to run to expiry. Exactly the opposite view has to be taken by the writer of the option—he is looking for situations where the time value appears too high for the circumstances, i.e. for the amount of time remaining to expiry. This means he will receive a higher premium than normal for a certain risk. It should be borne in mind that time values are at their highest for options which are at-the-money, or at least very close to that position.

Probably the most fruitful area, since it will be more easily spotted and understood, will be the short expiry options, which of course we have already indicated are the most sensible for the option writer in any case. Options where the time values are high for the amount of time remaining to expiry should stand out from the rest. Of course the main reason for high time values is an upward surge in the share price, so we have to ignore those options where the underlying share price has been particularly buoyant. We have to look for options where the share price has remained static or has fallen, but where the time values are too optimistic for the situation.

There are sometimes situations where, although the share price has risen over a few weeks and looks as though it has topped out for the time being, channel analysis or moving average analysis shows that the price peak is still a few weeks away, after which the price will then start to move downwards. To rush in and write such an option under such circumstances is to take an unnecessary risk. It is vital, if channel analysis shows that a peak or trough is about to be reached in the near future, that the investor waits until this peak or trough has just been passed, i.e. that the prediction has been confirmed. If the investor tries instead to anticipate peaks and troughs, this will inevitably lead to failure, since there are many occasions where a channel will develop an adverse hook to its previous direction. Besides the reduction in risk that will accompany this way of approaching the investment, there is a more direct value to the option writer—the rise in share price to its peak value will carry the option premium with it, and therefore the profit potential in writing that particular option will have increased.

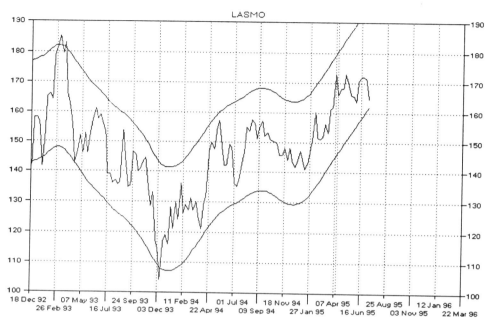

Figure 8.3 The LASMO share price up to 7th July 1995, with 25-week channel superimposed

This point can be well illustrated by taking LASMO as an example. In Figure 8.3 is shown the share price chart up to 7th July 1995, along with the channel produced from the 25-week weighted average. In the absence of the channel, the investor would come to the conclusion that the price has now passed its peak, and is on the way down. Thus the investor would feel relatively comfortable in writing a call option at this point.

On this date, the share price and options premiums were as follows:

Share price 164.5p; August 140s, 26p; August 160s, 9p; August 180s, 2p

An analysis of the good/bad relationship is as follows:

Option	If exercised ("bad")	If not exercised ("good")	Good/bad ratio
August 140s	26 + 140 − 164.5 = 1.5	26	17.3
160s	9 + 160 − 164.5 = 4.5	9	2.0
180s	2 + 180 − 164.5 = 17.5	2	0.1

Note as before that the "If exercised" column represents maximum values since the investor would lose additional profit if the share price continued to rise after exercise. The investor using channel analysis would not be writing options at this time, but would wait for the subsequent peak to be passed. This position was reached a few weeks later on 26th July. The relevant prices then were:

Share price 178p; August 160s, 18p; August 180s, 5p; August 200s, 1p

These options give the following figures for upside potential and downside protection:

Option	If exercised ("bad")	If not exercised ("good")	Good/bad ratio
August 160s	$18 + 160 - 176 = 2$	18	9.0
180s	$5 + 180 - 176 = 9$	5	0.6
200s	$2 + 200 - 176 = 25$	1	0.04

Not only are the premiums which can be obtained far superior to those of a month earlier, but the good/bad ratios are much better, for example a ratio of 9 compared with 2 for the August 160s, and the investor would have the added advantage that only a few weeks were left to expiry. It turned out that the share price was little changed at expiry of the August options and therefore the August 180s and 200s would not have been exercised.

The above example illustrates quite clearly the improvement that is obtained when timing of the investment is improved by means of channel analysis.

The above strategy was one of waiting for the correct opportunity to write an option in a particular share. Naturally, some investors are impatient, and do not relish having to wait before they can take action. If you happen to be the impatient type of investor who has to get involved immediately then the simplest answer is to look for another option which is not giving conflicting signals. After all, there are plenty to choose from.

Returning to the simple approach of anomalous time values, we can take, as an example, the premiums of the out-of-the-money options (and therefore the premiums will equal the time value) on 25th August 1995 and 8th September 1995. For the short expiry November options, these are shown in Table 8.3.

Of the 22 shares in Table 8.3, nine fell in price over the period. These were BTR, Cadbury, Lucas, P&O, Prudential, Rolls-Royce, Royal Insurance, United Biscuits and Williams. The premiums/time values for these on 25th August were 4, 16, 4, 8, 6, 5, 7, 8 and 8. For our purposes, not only are we looking at the size of the premium, but also at the degree to which the option is standing out-of-the-money, since as we have seen earlier, we have a greater upside potential the further out-of-the-money the option is. Ignoring those where the premiums were less than 8p, we have to look more closely at Cadbury-Schweppes, P&O, United Biscuits and Williams.

Table 8.3 Premiums and share prices for November call options on 25th August and 8th September 1995

Share	Series	25th August 1995 Premium	Share price	8th September 1995 Premium	Share price
British Aerospace	Nov 650s	32	650	31	655
BAT Industries	Nov 550s	11	517	10	519
BTR	Nov 360s	4	340	3	336
British Telecom	Nov 420s	10	408	8	409
Cadbury-Sch.	Nov 500s	16	498	13	494
GEC	Nov 330s	5	311	7	321
Grand Met.	Nov 460s	3	413	6	429
Guinness	Nov 550s	4	501	7	523
Ladbroke	Nov 180s	3	167	3	168
LASMO	Nov 200s	3	179	3	181
Lucas Industries	Nov 200s	4	187	3	186
P&O	Nov 600s	8	564	4	552
Pilkington	Nov 220s	6	206	6	210
Prudential	Nov 360s	6	339	5	338
RTZ	Nov 950s	8	891	17	927
Redland	Nov 420s	8	395	6	395
Rolls-Royce	Nov 200s	5	188	1	177
Royal Insurance	Nov 360s	7	346	7	344
Tesco	Nov 360s	5	337	5	338
United Biscuits	Nov 300s	8	286	6	282
Vodaphone	Nov 280s	9	269	11	272
Williams	Nov 330s	8	324	5	321

The Cadbury-Schweppes November 500s were about 0.4% out-of-the-money, the P&O November 600s about 6% out-of-the-money, the United Biscuits November 300s about 4.7% out-of-the-money, and the Williams November 330s about 1.8% out-of-the-money. On this basis the P&O and United Biscuits call options offer by far the best writing opportunity. Neither of these shares moved into an in-the-money position up to expiry time and so resulted in useful profits. It must be reiterated that the investor should not write options simply on the basis of two weeks' data such as those given above, but should have come to a view about the near-term direction of the share price. Table 8.3 has to be used in the sense of confirming the direction of the price movement as being downwards over a short period such as two weeks, and then making the best selection of the option to be written.

At the time of writing of these options on 25th August 1995, the "good" and "bad" situations for P&O and United Biscuits were:

- *P&O:*
  Bad outcome = 8 + 600 − 564 = 44p
  Good outcome = 8p
  Good/bad ratio = 0.18

- *United Biscuits:*
  Bad outcome = 8 + 300 − 286 = 22p
  Good outcome = 80p
  Good/bad ratio = 0.36

On these figures P&O offer an advantage in giving a better return for the bad outcome where the option is exercised, since the investor would receive 44p as against 22p.

Cost per Percentage Point (CPP)

The method of calculating CPPs was discussed in Chapter 5. It was shown that options with low CPPs were advantageous for the buyer. Conversely, therefore, options with high CPPs are going to be advantageous to the writer of options. The CPPs for the same options as were listed in Table 8.3 are given in Table 8.4. Since there are 22 options entered in the table, we can select the top 10, and these are RTZ, Cadbury-Schweppes, British Telecom, Vodaphone, GEC, British Aerospace, BAT, Williams, Guinness, and Royal Insurance.

Of these top 10, all were on a rising trend on 8th September (judged by the change in price from 25th August) except for Cadbury-Schweppes,

Table 8.4 Cost per percentage point (CPP) values for various call options on 8th September 1995

Share	Series	Premium	Share price	CPP	Share price at expiry
British Aerospace	Nov 700s	0	655	1.38	733
BAT Industries	Nov 550s	10	519	1.27	554
BTR	Nov 360s	3	336	0.37	333
British Telecom	Nov 420s	8	336	1.72	361
Cadbury-Sch.	Nov 500s	13	494	3.38	545
GEC	Nov 330s	7	321	1.40	324
Grand Met.	Nov 460s	6	429	0.7	440
Guinness	Nov 550s	7	523	1.08	470
Ladbroke	Nov 180s	3	168	0.34	127
LASMO	Nov 200s	3	181	0.25	157
Lucas Industries	Nov 200s	3	186	0.33	196
P&O	Nov 600s	4	552	0.42	496
Pilkington	Nov 220s	6	210	0.79	200
Prudential	Nov 360s	5	338	0.63	423
RTZ	Nov 950s	17	927	3.94	909
Redland	Nov 420s	6	395	0.76	370
Rolls-Royce	Nov 200s	1	177	0.07	171
Royal Insurance	Nov 360s	7	344	1.05	382
Tesco	Nov 360s	5	338	0.63	284
United Biscuits	Nov 300s	6	382	0.7	261
Vodaphone	Nov 280s	11	272	1.57	251
Williams	Nov 330s	5	321	1.15	334

Williams and Royal Insurance. If channel analysis is not applied, then logic would dictate that one of these three should be the selected vehicle for writing. The "good" and "bad" situations for each of these are:

- *Cadbury-Schweppes:*
  Bad outcome = 13 + 500 – 494 = 19p
  Good outcome = 13p
  Good/bad ratio = 0.68

- *Williams:*
  Bad outcome = 5 + 330 – 321 = 14p
  Good outcome = 5p
  Good/bad ratio = 0.36

- *Royal Insurance:*
  Bad outcome = 7 + 360 – 344 = 23p
  Good outcome = 7p
  Good/bad ratio = 0.3

Cadbury-Schweppes would be the choice here, since it has the highest good/bad ratio and the highest profit potential, the investor pocketing the largest premium, 13p.

The last column in the table shows the share prices at expiry of the November options. Most showed a rise in share price between 8th September and the November expiry, including Cadbury-Schweppes which had been on a falling trend up to 8th September. The rise to 545p at expiry means that the November 500s would have been exercised by the purchaser, an outcome which the writer does not want.

It is interesting to look at channel analysis on Cadbury-Schweppes, in order to see whether the investor would take a different view of the future price movement.

The Sigma-p chart of the Cadbury-Schweppes share price to the relevant date, 8th September 1995, is shown in Figure 8.4. We can see clearly that the channel is still rising, and that there are still many weeks to go before the anticipated downturn. This would cause the investor to have second thoughts about writing call options in this share in spite of the favourable good/bad ratio.

SUBSEQUENT ACTION

We have already stated that the covered call outperforms a straightforward purchase of the shares if the share price subsequently falls, stays static or rises slightly. Our constant theme as traded options investors must be to monitor the position constantly and react rapidly if the share price starts to behave differently from our initial projection. The two extreme trends which will require a reaction other than to do nothing are, firstly, a

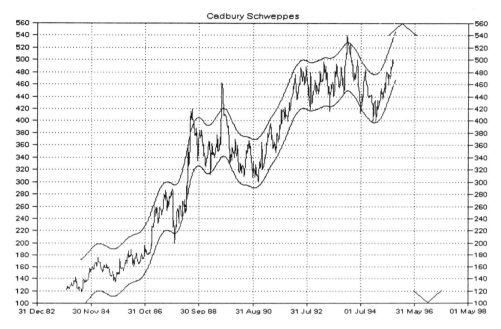

Figure 8.4   The plot of Cadbury-Schweppes at 8th September 1995, showing a rising channel and predicted turning point

rapid fall in share price and, secondly, a rise in share price that looks as if it could be the start of a longer upward trend.

Rapid Fall in Share Price

Although a covered call gives you a measure of downside protection in the form of the additional premium that you have received, this is worth most to the investor when the share price fall is modest. Anything more than that will mean a considerable fall in the value of the investment. The best action in this situation is the same as you would take if you simply held the shares themselves: sell when selling signals such as moving averages tell you to (see *Stocks and Shares Simplified*). By virtue of the premium that you have received, you still come out ahead of the investor who did not write options against his shareholding.

Prolonged Rise in Share Price

If the share price rises above the striking price, then you become increasingly at risk to the option being called and thus losing the underlying shares, albeit at a higher price than you paid for them. You will of course receive the return that would have been calculated as the bad outcome when the position was first taken. As an alternative to this, it is possible to carry out a rolling up procedure that can increase the return significantly above that from the initial position.

Rolling up

The procedure and effect on the profit/loss potentials is best illustrated by using an example such as Allied Domecq. On 24th April 1995 the share price was 531p and the out-of-the-money July 550 calls were 9p. An investor buying the shares and selling the call at these prices would have bought the shares at a net cost of 531 − 9 = 522p. By 2nd May the share price had risen to 551p and the July 550s to 16p. The premium for the July 600s was 4p. If the investor was becoming convinced that the share price would continue to rise but decided to take no action, he would eventually see the call exercised against him. In such a situation, his profit would be the exercise price less the net price he paid for the shares, i.e. 550 − 522 = 28p. Thus:

Percentage profit = 28 × 100/522 = 5.4%

Instead of doing nothing, the investor could have rolled up the option. This means closing the July 550 written call by purchasing a July 550 call, now at 16p, and writing a July 600 call, i.e. further out-of-the-money, at 4p. The net cost of the shares is now 531 − 9 + 16 − 4 = 534p. He has now, of course, had to invest 12p more in the position than his original investment. In return, if the share price continues to rise and the option is exercised, he will receive 600p for the shares, giving a profit of 66p. Thus:

Percentage profit = 66 × 100/534 = 12.4%

The net effect of rolling up the position once the investor became convinced that the share price would continue to rise was that the investor was able to participate in this rise to a level of 600p rather than 550p, which was the original striking price. This improved the profit from 5.4% to 12.4%, neglecting dealing costs.

This example serves to illustrate, if such is needed, the flexibility of traded options as an investment vehicle. Even when the original prediction of the investor begins to turn sour, there is still plenty of scope to change the position to take advantage of the changed circumstances.

9

Buying Put Options

A put option gives the purchaser of the option the right to sell a number, usually 1000, shares in the underlying security at a fixed price—the striking price—at any time up to the expiry of the option. As shown in Chapter 6, buying puts is the strategy for those investors who have bearish expectations for the share price. The buyer expects that the value of the option, expressed in terms of its premium, will increase as the share price falls, and just like the buyer of a call option, he expects a high level of gearing (in this case a reverse gearing), i.e. the gain in the value of the option is much greater than the fall in the share price. The strategy is attended by a moderate amount of risk, limited to the amount of the premium that has been paid. The holder of a put option has a large, though limited, potential for gain. The gain is limited by the fact that the share price has an ultimate lower value of just above zero, perhaps 0.5 or 1p. A value of zero would of course imply that the company has ceased trading and the shares therefore have no value. In such a case there would be no dealings, and therefore the right that the option gives to sell the shares at the striking price would no longer apply.

As with call options, a major attraction of put options for the investor with bearish expectations for the share price is that there is a large variety of options available, so that the investor can tailor his investment to the amount of risk he is prepared to accept. As with other options, the potential for profit in a put option is proportional to the amount of risk which is accepted, although there are many instances where options have anomalous premiums which are lower than expected for the particular circumstances. These can provide much lower risk situations for the alert investor.

LIMITED LOSS; LARGE, THOUGH LIMITED, GAIN

The profit or loss potential of a put option can be plotted as a function of the share price at expiry to give a graph of characteristic shape as shown in Figure 9.1. The point A on the horizontal axis represents the striking price.

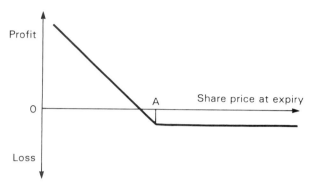

Figure 9.1   Gain or loss for a put option

As the share price at expiry falls below this point, the profit increases as an upward sloping line, being limited only by the lowest possible tradeable share price of just above zero. In the opposite direction, as the share price rises the profit decreases until the value of the option is the same as the original premium paid. A further rise in share price to point A, at which it is equal to the striking price, reduces the value to zero, hence the maximum loss at that point is the original premium paid.

The graph illustrates a major attribute of a put option—the loss is limited while the gain is, although also limited, many times larger.

OPTION PREMIUMS

In order to provide a comparison with call options, we can take the premiums for put options in the same underlying shares, and at the same time, 31st January 1996, as Table 7.1 in Chapter 7.

Bearing in mind the opposite nature of in-the-money, etc., for put options compared with call options, i.e. the higher striking prices are in-the-money for puts whereas the lower striking prices are in-the-money for calls, there are two points which are general in application and which can be seen from Table 9.1:

1. The least expensive option is always the nearest expiry, furthest out-of-the-money option, e.g. Guinness February 420s, Dixons March 390s, Boots April 550s and FTSE February 3600s.
2. The most expensive option is always the furthest expiry, deepest in-the-money options, i.e. Guinness August 500s, Dixons September 460s, Boots October 650s and FTSE May 3900s.

Any table of option prices in a newspaper will confirm these two facts. The nearer expiry, furthest out-of-the-money options are cheaper because

Table 9.1 Premiums for various put options on 31st January 1996

Share	Share price	Exercise price	Expiry date and premium		
			Feb	**May**	**Aug**
Guinness	457	420	1	7	11
		460	10	25	29
		500	45	55	57
			Mar	**Jun**	**Sep**
Dixons	416	390	6	12	17
		420	16	24	31
		460	46	50	51
			Apr	**Jul**	**Oct**
Boots	623	550	1	6	9
		600	10	19	25
		650	36	46	51
			Feb	**Mar**	**May**
FTSE100	3759.3	3600	4	15	45
		3650	6	24	58
		3700	14	37	76
		3750	31	57	97
		3800	60	83	124
		3850	112	118	153
		3900	157	161	188

they have no intrinsic value (being out-of-the-money) and their time values will be lower than the longer expiry options because of the lack of time in which they can move into a profitable position before the expiry date by virtue of a fall in share price. The corollary of this is that the deepest in-the-money options have an intrinsic value and the further expiry options higher time values because there is plenty of time available during which the share price can fall, thereby improving the value of the premium.

As we commented for call options, we can go no further than these two simple statements in trying to generalise from one class of options to another. The premium for the March 200 puts for one share is unlikely to be the same as the premium for the March 200 puts for another share. We can, however, look more closely at the premiums within an option class by looking at their time values and intrinsic values. This sort of analysis will help in selecting the best option for a particular set of investment circumstances.

RELATIONSHIP BETWEEN PREMIUMS AND SHARE PRICE

Before investing in any type of option, the investor will obviously have come to a conclusion about the direction of the share price and the time for which this direction will be maintained. He may have come to the conclusion by using the principles already discussed in this book, or he may have other ways of analysing share prices. Attention will now focus on a correct choice of option, and a knowledge of how put option prices may be expected to move as the underlying share price moves will be of paramount importance. This movement will be magnified in the case of options which are of short expiry date, and therefore these offer the most fruitful area to study. As in the case of call options, there are three scenarios:

1. The share price remains static—the *risk*.
2. A downward share price movement occurs—the *reward*.
3. The share price rises—the *risk*.

Since all premiums are composed of an intrinsic value (which might be zero) and a time value, the effect on intrinsic values and time values for each of the three share price movements listed above can be discussed.

Intrinsic Values

The intrinsic value for a put option is the difference between the striking price and the share price where this difference is positive, i.e. where the share can be put at a higher price than the actual share price. Because of this mathematical fact, the following observations will be true:

1. Static share price movement will leave intrinsic values unchanged.
2. Downward share price movement will increase intrinsic values on a penny for penny basis, and some options with zero intrinsic value will move into a state of positive intrinsic value as the movement continues.
3. Upward share price movement will decrease intrinsic values on a penny for penny basis, and some options will move to zero intrinsic value as the movement continues.

The theoretical effect of a downward share price movement on put options which initially have no intrinsic value (because the share price is above the striking price) is shown in Figure 9.2(a). At some point the downward price movement takes the share price below the striking price, at which point the graph takes on a slope of 45°, i.e. the increase is on a penny for penny basis (in this example) with the price fall.

The effect of an upward share price movement on a put option which initially has an intrinsic value because the share price is below the striking price is shown in Figure 9.2(b). Here the line falls at a slope of 45° due to the penny for penny fall in option value (in this example) with rise in share price. Once the share price and striking price become equal, the intrinsic value becomes zero and stays so with increasing share price.

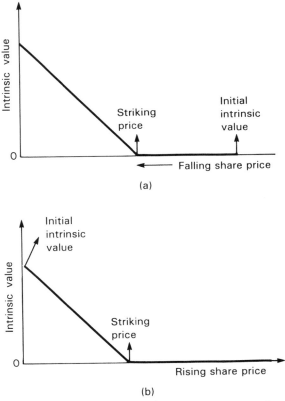

Figure 9.2 (a) Effect of downward share price movement on put options with no intrinsic value; (b) effect of upward share price movement on put options which have an initial intrinsic value

Time Values

Time values are not based on a direct mathematical relationship as is the case with intrinsic values. Time values are simply decided by the balance between purchasers and writers of options, which itself depends upon the view of the future that each of these classes of investor has. We might expect the following reactions in time values for the various share price movements:

1. A static share price should certainly not cause time values to rise. The normal behaviour with no share price movement is for put option premiums to stay more or less constant until about six weeks before the expiry of the option, at which point the time values will fall off rapidly, becoming zero at expiry.
2. A downward share price movement should have a positive effect on time values, with the greatest effect being on the more distant expiry

dates. We have already stated that the normal tendency with a neutral share price is for time values to decrease over the last six weeks of the option's life, and therefore we would expect that the positive effect of the downward share price movement is to cancel this normal decrease, leaving options with say six to eight weeks to expiry having virtually static time values. Options with only one or two weeks to expiry will require a very substantial share price fall to offset the disappearing time value.

3. An upward share price movement should have the most effect on the time value of those options nearest to expiry, making them fall even more rapidly than if the share price is static. This is because there is little time left for the trend to reverse direction. Where options have more distant expiry dates we would expect little effect unless the upward share price move increases in momentum.

As in the case of call options, we have to illustrate these various scenarios by means of concrete examples. It is advantageous to use the same examples as were used for call options, since besides illustrating the trends in put option time values, it gives us the additional chance of comparing the trends in the put options with the trends in the call options.

EXAMPLES

Static Share Prices—LASMO and British Aerospace Put Options

A neutral share price behaviour provides the best circumstances in which to investigate the relationship between share price and the time values of put options, and we can use the same examples as in Chapter 7. Taking LASMO first of all, during the period between 12th January and 16th February 1996 the share price moved only between the limits of 166 and 179p. The behaviour of the time values is shown in Table 9.2.

Our theoretical consideration of the effect of a static share price was that time values would remain more or less constant, but fall off during the last few weeks of the life of the option. This is broadly true for LASMO, except for the last week, which saw a rise from 166 to 179p. This of course has the effect of distorting the time values at that point. In the case of the longer expiry options, such as the August 160s, the time values remained in the band of 6p to 8p over the period.

A better example is British Aerospace from 12th January to 16th February 1996. The data for these put options are given in Table 9.3.

The time values for the February options fall off much more regularly, while as expected, the time values for the longer expiry May and August options stay more or less constant. It can also be clearly seen that, just like the call options, those put options closest to being at-the-money, e.g. the

Table 9.2 Movement of LASMO share prices, put option premiums and time values from 12th January 1996 to 16th February 1996

Date			12 Jan	19 Jan	26 Jan	2 Feb	9 Feb	16 Feb
Share price			176	171	174	169	166	179
Feb	140s	premiums				1	1	
		time values						
Feb	160s	premiums	1	2	1	2	2	1
		time values	1	2	1	2	2	1
Feb	180s	premiums	8	11	9	12	14	4
		time values	4	2	3	1	0	3
Feb	200s	premiums	24	30	26			21
		time values	0	1	0			0
May	140s	premiums				1	1	
		time values				1	1	
May	160s	premiums	4	6	5	6	7	4
		time values	4	6	5	6	7	4
May	180s	premiums	12	15	13	16	18	11
		time values	8	6	7	5	4	10
May	200s	premiums	26	31	28			25
		time values	2	2	2			4
Aug	140s	premiums				2	3	
		time values						
Aug	160s	premiums	7	8	6	7	8	6
		time values	7	8	6	7	8	6
Aug	180s	premiums	15	18	16	18	20	12
		time values	11	9	10	7	6	11
Aug	200s	premiums	28	32	30			25
		time values	4	3	4			

850s on 12th January and 9th and 16th February, have the highest time values, followed by the out-of-the-money options.

Falling Share Price—Guinness Put Options

The buyer of a call option naturally has the view that the share price will fall, and so the behaviour of put options under such circumstances is of prime importance. Since we used Guinness as an example of a falling share price in Chapter 7, we can see the effect of this fall on the Guinness put options between 12th January and 16th February 1996, when the share price fell from 484p to 456p, i.e. a fall of 7.8%. The data are given in Table 9.4.

The time values moved as predicted, showing an initial rise for the first few weeks for the short expiry options before falling again as time runs out. In the case of the longer expiry options, the time values continue to rise as the share price is still falling gently over the last three weeks.

Table 9.3 Movement of British Aerospace share prices, put option premiums and time values from 12th January 1996 to 16th February 1996

Date			12 Jan	19 Jan	26 Jan	2 Feb	9 Feb	16 Feb
Share price			835	876	878	878	844	836
Feb	800s	premiums	10	3	2	2	2	1
		time values	10	3	2	2	2	1
Feb	850s	premiums	31	13	12	7	16	19
		time values	16	13	12	7	10	5
Feb	900s	premiums	68	37	36	31	54	
		time values	3	13	14	9	0	
May	800s	premiums	25	15	14	14	19	22
		time values	25	15	14	14	19	22
May	850s	premiums	49	32	30	29	41	46
		time values	34	32	30	29	35	32
May	900s	premiums	82	57	56	54	72	
		time values	17	33	34	32	16	
Aug	800s	premiums	35	24	23	23	30	32
		time values	35	24	23	23	30	32
Aug	850s	premiums	58	42	41	40	52	56
		time values	43	42	41	41	46	42
Aug	900s	premiums	89	67	66	65	82	
		time values	24	43	44	43	26	

Table 9.4 Movement of Guinness share prices, put option premiums and time values from 12th January 1996 to 16th February 1996

Date			12 Jan	19 Jan	26 Jan	2 Feb	9 Feb	16 Feb
Share price			484	471	467	459	458	456
Feb	420s	premiums	1	1	1	1	1	1
		time values	1	1	1	1	1	1
Feb	460s	premiums	3	6	6	8	7	7
		time values	3	6	6	7	5	3
Feb	500s	premium	20	31	33	42	43	44
		time values	4	2	0	1	1	0
May	420s	premiums	3	5	5	6	6	6
		time values	3	5	5	6	6	6
May	460s	premiums	12	18	18	22	23	24
		time values	12	18	18	21	21	20
May	500s	premiums	33	43	45	52	53	55
		time values	17	14	12	11	11	11
Aug	420s	premiums	6	8	8	10	10	10
		time values	6	8	8	10	10	10
Aug	460s	premiums	17	22	23	27	27	28
		time values	17	22	23	26	25	24
Aug	500s	premiums	38	46	48	54	55	57
		time values	22	17	15	13	13	13

Table 9.5 Movement of British Gas share prices, put option premiums and time values from 12th January 1996 to 16th February 1996

Date			12 Jan	19 Jan	26 Jan	2 Feb	9 Feb	16 Feb
Share price			265	252	240	243	242	241
Mar	220s	premiums			3	2	1	1
		time values			3	2	1	1
Mar	240s	premiums	2	6	9	8	6	6
		time values	2	6	9	8	6	6
Mar	260s	premiums	7	14	22	20	20	20
		time values	7	6	2	3	2	1
Mar	280s	premiums	18	29				
		time values	3	1				
Jun	220s	premiums			8	7	7	7
		time values			8	7	7	7
Jun	240s	premiums	8	13	18	17	16	16
		time values	8	13	18	17	16	16
Jun	260s	premiums	15	24	31	30	30	30
		time values	15	16	11	13	12	11
Jun	280s	premiums	27	37				
		time values	12	9				
Sep	220s	premiums			11	10	10	10
		time values			11	10	10	10
Sep	240s	premiums	9	16	21	20	19	19
		time values	9	16	21	20	19	19
Sep	260s	premiums	18	26	34	32	32	32
		time values	18	18	14	15	14	13
Sep	280s	premiums	30	40				
		time values	15	12				

Strongly Falling Share Price—British Gas Put Options

The data for British Gas over the period from 12th January to 16th February 1996 are shown in Table 9.5. The share price fell from 265p to 240p in two weeks, and then remained more or less stationary for four weeks, ending up the period in question at 241p, for a fall of over 9% during the period.

Naturally, over this initial three-week period, all premiums rose. Interestingly, only those options which were out-of-the-money, i.e. the 240s, showed an increase in time value. The 260s and 280s showed a fall over this period, irrespective of the time left to expiry. The fall-off in time values was particularly marked for the shorter expiry options. Once the steady period from 26th January to 16th February was reached, time values fell off gently as predicted.

This effect of the time values of the slightly in-the-money options falling with a fall in share price is the same effect that we noticed in Chapter 7

Table 9.6 General conclusions on the effect of share price fall on time values and intrinsic values of put options

Type of option	Effect on intrinsic value	Effect on time value
Short term in-the-money	rises	large fall
Short term out-of-the-money	stays zero	uncertain, medium fall or rise
Medium term in-the-money	rises	medium fall
Medium term out-of-the-money	stays zero	uncertain
Long term in-the-money	rises	medium fall
Long term out-of-the-money	stays zero	uncertain

when discussing the behaviour of the time values of call options at a time when the share price was moving favourably. Just as we did for call options, we can make some general conclusions about the effect on time values and intrinsic values of put options when the share price falls. This is shown in Table 9.6.

The only constant effect which can be seen across a wide range of put options is that the short term, in-the-money options show large falls in their time values when the share price falls. One reason for this may be that investors become less certain that a fall occurring over the space of a few weeks will continue, and more certain that it will reverse direction.

Rising Share Price—Rolls-Royce

In our theoretical discussion of time values, we came to the conclusion that a rising share price should cause a rapid erosion of the time values of the options of nearest expiry, because of the lack of time for the adverse trend to reverse itself. Data for Rolls-Royce, where the share price rose from 196p to 215p over the course of five weeks, are shown in Table 9.7.

As we can see, in general the in-the-money options lost time values as the share price rose, with the greatest loss, of course, being in the short expiry February options. Paradoxically, the greatest rise in the share price, between 26th January and 2nd February, saw an increase in time value. Thus a large loss in intrinsic value becomes partially compensated for by an increase in time value. Probably the only obvious correlation is that time values are highest for those options whose striking price is closest to the share price itself, i.e. are close to being at-the-money.

Behaviour of the FTSE100 Index Put Options

Table 9.8 shows the movement of the FTSE100 Index and the premiums for various put options between 9th February and 15th March 1996. During this period the Index rose from 3716.3 to 3770.9 and then fell to 3644.8. Where February options are shown, these of course have no data for March since they expired in February.

Table 9.7 Movement of Rolls-Royce share prices, put option premiums and time values from 12th January 1996 to 16th February 1996

Date			12 Jan	19 Jan	26 Jan	2 Feb	9 Feb	16 Feb
Share price			196	201	200	214	206	215
Feb	180s	premiums	1	1	1		1	
		time values	1	1	1		1	
Feb	200s	premiums	8	6	6	2	3	1
		time values	8	5	6	2	3	2
Feb	220s	premiums	24	21	21	10	15	7
		time values	0	2	0	4	1	2
Feb	240s	premiums				27		26
		time values				1		1
May	180s	premiums	5	4	5		3	
		time values	5	4	5		3	
May	200s	premiums	14	12	13	7	9	6
		time values	10	12	13	7	9	6
May	220s	premiums	28	25	27	17	21	15
		time values	4	6	7	11	7	10
May	240s	premiums				32		30
		time values				6		5
Aug	180s	premiums	7	6	6		5	
		time values	7	6	6		5	
Aug	200s	premiums	16	15	15	9	13	10
		time values	12	15	15	9	13	10
Aug	220s	premiums	30	27	28	19	24	19
		time values	6	8	8	19	10	14
Aug	240s	premiums				33		33
		time values				7		8

Correlation between the movement of the Index and the time values is not good. The rise in the Index from 3716.3 to 3770.9 caused a rapid loss of time value for most of the options except the further expiry in-the-money 3800s. The shorter the time to expiry, the greater this loss in value. Conversely, the fall from 3770.9 to 3740.3 caused a rise in all time values.

Part of the reason for this anomalous behaviour of time values for the Index put options lies in the fact that the fall in value of the FTSE100 Index took place during a period when the long-term trend was upwards. Sentiment was thus swinging between the view that the end of the long upward trend had occurred and the view that the fall was only a blip in the trend, which would become re-established within a few weeks.

POTENTIAL FOR PROFIT AND LOSS

As was the case with call options, the discussion on intrinsic values and time values for shares which are falling, static or rising is intended to

Table 9.8 Movement of the FTSE100 Index, put option premiums and time values from 9th February 1996 to 15th March 1996

Date		9 Feb	16 Feb	23 Feb	1 Mar	8 Mar	15 Mar
FTSE100 Index		3716.3	3770.9	3740.3	3752.7	3710.3	3644.8
Feb	3650s premiums	5	1	16			
	time values	5	1	16			
Feb	3700s premiums	15	1	29			
	time values	15	1	29			
Feb	3750s premiums	42	1	51			
	time values	16					
Feb	3800s premiums	98	34	86			
	time values	14					
Mar	3650s premiums	30	13	40	7	13	1
	time values	30	13	40	7	13	1
Mar	3700s premiums	48	23	60	15	28	38
	time values	48	23	60	15	28	0
Mar	3750s premiums	73	38	84	31	60	87
	time values	49	38	74	31	20	
Mar	3800s premiums	106	62	113	61	109	138
	time values	22	32	53	13	29	0
Apr	3650s premiums	54	34	58	30	44	94
	time values	54	34	58	30	44	94
Apr	3700s premiums	73	49	76	46	65	115
	time values	73	49	76	46	65	59
Apr	3750s premiums	99	68	100	66	93	147
	time values	65	68	90	64	53	41
Apr	3800s premiums	130	94	127	94	128	189
	time values	46	64	67	46	38	33

provide a background to the selection of the correct option. The list of options will of course have been greatly reduced by the use of correlation, as discussed in Chapter 5, so that attention now has to turn to two other aspects. These are the gap between share price and striking price, i.e. the extent to which the option lies in- or out-of-the-money, and the length of time remaining to expiry, i.e. whether the option is short-, medium- or long-term expiry.

Using these three expiry terms and three degrees of gap between share price and striking price, we can arrive at the 3×3 matrix shown in Table 9.9. The gains here are based on the share price moving in the direction anticipated by the buyer of call options, i.e. downwards, and are given on a scale of 1 to 5, and must be considered very approximate. There will be many exceptions, but the overall picture given by Table 9.9 is helpful.

The potential for the largest gain in the option price lies with the out-of-the-money options which are short-term to expiry, while the longer-term expiry, in-the-money options have the least potential for gain.

Losses when the share price rises rather than falls, very approximately, are directly proportional to the gains made when the share price falls, i.e.

Table 9.9 Expected gains, on a scale of 1 to 5, for various put options when the share price falls

	Short	Medium	Long
In-the-money	+ + +	+ +	+
At-the-money	+ + + +	+ + +	+ +
Out-of-the-money	+ + + + +	+ + + +	+ + +

Table 9.10 Approximate level of premiums for various put options

	Short	Medium	Long
In-the-money	+ + +	+ + + +	+ + + + +
At-the-money	+ +	+ + +	+ + + +
Out-of-the-money	+	+ +	+ + +

the higher the potential for profit, the higher is the potential for loss. The obvious deduction from this is that the short-term, out-of-the-money options are the riskiest while the long-term, in-the-money options are the safest. This ignores the actual premiums which are being paid, because the amount of money being risked is also important. The usual levels of premium associated with these various categories of options are shown in Table 9.10.

From this it can be seen that the investor in short-expiry, in-the-money options is risking far more capital than an investor going for out-of-the-money options, so this point should always be borne in mind when considering the risk/reward relationship for a particular option.

When to Buy In-the-Money Put Options

The above discussion shows that the profit potential of in-the-money put options is always less than that of their out-of-the-money counterparts. Thus it is of interest to determine the gearing effect of the options as was done in Chapter 7. Table 9.11 shows the percentage changes in option premiums and share prices over the week from 1st to 8th March 1996. The gearing can be determined from the average change of the list of shares and options, i.e. taking the percentage change irrespective of whether it is a gain or a loss. The options are subdivided into the three different expiry cycles. Thus for the options listed, the share prices averaged changes of 2.5%, 2.7% and 2.8% for the April, May and June expiry cycles, whereas the average gain made in the near-expiry options was 29.5% for the April expiries, 22.3% for the May expiries and 31.5% for the June expiries, with gearings (i.e. change relative to the change in share price) of 11, 8 and 11 respectively. For the medium-term July, August and September expiries the average gains were 18.6%, 18.5% and 19.0%, with gearings of 7, 6 and 6 respectively. For the longer-term October, November and December expiries the average gains were 15.1%, 16.3% and 15.2%, with gearings of 6, 6 and 5 respectively.

Table 9.11 Gains in share prices and in-the-money put option premiums between 1st and 8th March 1996

Share	Strike price	Share price	Apr pre	Jul pre	Oct pre	Apr pre	Jul pre	Oct pre	Share price	Apr gain	Jul gain	Oct gain	Share gain
			1st March			8th March							
Allied Dom.	550	511	41	54	56	47	59	61	503	14.6	9.3	8.9	-1.6
Argyll	300	298	9	20	23	3	13	16	313	-66.7	-35.0	-30.4	5.0
	330		32	41	43	19	31	33		-40.6	-24.4	-23.2	
Asda	110	105	7	9	11	6	8	10	106	-14.2	-11.1	-9.1	1.0
BAA	500	491	16	24	30	8	18	23	504	-50.0	-25.0	-23.3	2.6
	550		60	61	64	47	51	55		-21.6	-16.4	-14.1	
British Airws	550	510	41	50	54	29	40	47	526	-29.3	-20.0	-13.0	3.1
Boots	600	598	15	29	34	10	24	30	605	-33.3	-17.2	-13.3	1.2
	650		54	63	67	45	57	61		-16.6	-9.5	-8.9	
British Steel	200	184	18	25	26	23	30	31	177	27.8	20.0	19.2	-3.8
British Petrol.	550	545	15	22	28	19	28	34	537	26.7	27.3	21.4	-1.5
	600		55	57	61	64	65	68		16.4	14.0	11.5	
Bass	800	763	41	54	60	42	55	61	762	2.4	1.9	1.7	-0.1
Comm. U.	650	614	60	64	71	61	64	72	590	1.7	0	1.4	-3.9
Cable & W.	460	453	19	30	34	21	33	36	447	10.5	10.0	5.9	-1.3
Courtaulds	460	435	29	42	45	39	52	54	424	34.5	23.8	20.0	-7.8
Glaxo	900	899	32	44	58	73	80	89	845	128.1	81.8	53.4	-6.0
HSBC	1100	1084	56	72	88	83	93	107	1047	48.2	29.2	21.6	-3.4
ICI	950	907	67	73	83	67	73	84	909	0	0	1.2	0.2
Kingfisher	550	520	45	50	54	36	43	48	534	-20.0	-14.0	-11.1	2.7
Land Secs	650	613	38	54	56	45	61	63	607	18.4	13.0	12.5	-1.0
M & S	460	429	32	40	42	26	35	38	436	-18.7	-12.5	-9.5	1.6
NatWest	700	693	23	33	43	38	47	58	667	65.2	42.4	34.8	-3.8
PowerGen	550	542	18	33	37	29	43	46	524	61.1	30.3	24.3	-3.3
Reuters	750	706	57	64	73	60	67	74	702	5.3	4.7	1.4	-0.6
Sainsbury	390	376	18	28	31	16	26	29	379	-11.1	-7.1	-6.5	0.8
	420		45	52	53	41	49	50		-8.9	-5.8	-5.7	
Shell Transpt	900	852	70	71	75	77	78	81	847	10.0	9.9	8.0	0.6
SmithKline	700	698	17	29	36	8	19	28	721	-52.9	-34.5	-22.2	3.3
	750		53	60	66	34	45	53		-35.8	-25.0	-19.7	
Standard Chr.	650	640	38	59	68	51	71	80	615	34.2	20.3	17.6	-3.9
Storehouse	330	317	17	23	27	10	18	22	328	-41.1	-21.7	-18.5	3.5
Thames Wat.	550	540	19	36	40	12	30	33	548	-36.8	-16.7	-17.5	1.5
	600		62	75	77	51	67	69		-14.5	-10.7	-10.3	
Unilever	1250	1211	62	70	74	71	76	80	1203	14.5	8.6	8.1	-0.7
Average gain										29.5%	18.6%	15.1%	2.5%
Gearing										11	7	6	

Share	Strike price	Share price	May pre	Aug pre	Nov pre	May pre	Aug pre	Nov pre	Share price	May gain	Aug gain	Nov gain	Share gain
			1st March			8th March							
British Aero.	900	891	43	55	63	59	70	77	864	37.2	27.3	22.2	-3.0
BAT Inds	600	571	49	57	61	63	68	73	557	28.6	19.3	19.7	-2.5
BTR	330	327	17	20	24	19	22	27	324	11.8	10.0	12.5	-0.9
	360		43	43	45	47	47	49		9.3	9.3	8.9	
British Tele.	390	375	21	29	32	29	38	40	364	38.1	31.0	25.0	-2.9
Cadbury-Sch.	600	555	60	63	67	102	105	111	519	70.0	66.7	65.7	-6.5
GEC	390	372	24	33	36	41	48	50	350	70.8	45.5	38.9	-5.9
Grand Met.	460	437	29	38	42	38	44	49	425	31.0	15.8	16.7	-2.7
Guinness	460	459	22	26	31	19	24	28	462	-13.6	-7.7	-9.7	0.7

Share	Strike price	Share price	1st March May pre	1st March Aug pre	1st March Nov pre	8th March May pre	8th March Aug pre	8th March Nov pre	Share price	May gain	Aug gain	Nov gain	Share gain
	500		53	55	58	49	49	52		−7.5	−10.9	−10.3	
Ladbroke	200	186	24	27	30	27	30	32	181	12.5	11.1	6.7	−2.7
LASMO	200	187	18	22	23	23	26	27	181	27.8	18.2	17.4	−3.2
Lucas	200	188	17	20	24	14	17	21	193	−17.6	−15.0	−12.5	2.7
P&O	550	528	47	50	60	49	51	62	526	8.5	2.0	3.3	−0.4
Prudential	460	446	35	40	46	37	43	48	439	5.7	7.5	4.3	−1.6
RTZ	950	913	47	55	59	39	49	55	922	−17.0	−10.9	−6.8	1.0
Redland	460	435	41	46	49	55	59	62	419	34.1	34.8	26.5	−3.7
Rolls-Royce	220	208	19	22	24	18	21	23	210	−5.2	−4.5	−4.1	1.0
Royal Ins.	390	385	25	32	39	28	34	40	365	12.0	15.6	2.6	−5.2
	420		51	54	59	60	68	76		17.6	25.9	28.8	
Tesco	280	271	20	22	26	13	16	22	281	−35.0	−27.3	−15.4	3.7
Utd Biscuits	240	235	18	21	23	20	23	25	232	11.1	9.5	8.7	−1.3
	260		34	36	37	37	38	40		8.8	5.6	8.1	
Vodaphone	240	235	15	20	24	10	17	20	243	−3.3	−15.0	−20.0	3.4
	260		28	33	36	22	28	31		−21.4	−15.2	−13.9	
Williams	360	342	29	30	33	36	36	38	334	24.1	20.0	15.2	−2.3
Average gain										**22.3%**	**18.5%**	**16.3%**	**2.7%**
Gearing										8	6	6	

Share	Strike price	Share price	1st March Jun pre	1st March Sep pre	1st March Dec pre	8th March Jun pre	8th March Sep pre	8th March Dec pre	Share price	Jun gain	Sep gain	Dec gain	Share gain
Abbey Nat.	600	581	38	45	54	35	42	51	565	−7.9	−6.7	−5.6	2.8
Amstrad	220	218	10	18	21	18	25	28	203	80.0	38.9	33.3	−6.9
	240		25	31	34	40	50	53		60.0	61.3	32.5	
Barclays	800	782	40	51	61	67	70	78	733	67.5	37.3	27.9	−6.3
	850		89	90	96	120	122	130		34.8	35.6	35.4	
Blue Circle	360	352	13	28	32	11	26	30	354	−15.4	−7.1	−6.3	0.6
	390		39	50	53	37	48	5		−5.1	−4.0	−3.8	
British Gas	260	241	20	29	31	25	34	35	235	25.0	17.2	12.9	−2.5
Dixons	500	467	35	42	50	34	42	50	467	−2.9	0	0	0
Hillsdown	180	173	9	18	18	2	11	14	183	−77.8	−38.9	−22.2	5.8
	200		28	35	36	18	26	28		−35.7	−25.7	−22.2	
Lonrho	200	196	7	12	14	10	14	17	191	42.9	16.7	21.4	−2.6
	220		25	26	28	29	30	31		16.0	15.4	10.7	
Nat. Power	500	483	19	33	39	25	38	44	475	31.6	15.2	12.8	−1.7
Scot. Power	390	366	24	27	34	35	35	42	356	45.8	29.6	23.5	−2.7
Sears	100	96	5	9	10	5	9	10	95	0	0	0	−1.0
Tarmac	120	120	4	9	12	5	10	13	117	25.0	1.1	8.3	−2.5
	130		11	16	18	13	17	20		18.2	6.3	11.1	
Tomkins	280	267	14	19	25	15	18	25	266	7.1	−5.2	0	−0.4
Average gain										**31.5%**	**19.0%**	**15.2%**	**2.8%**
Gearing										11	6	5	

By any standards, therefore, in-the-money put options can be considered to be an excellent investment vehicle for investors who consider that the share price trend is to show a modest fall over a fairly short time period.

Just as was the case with call options, a key to improving even the large profit potential that exists with put options is to try to find those options which have time values much too low for the circumstances. These anomalous options are most likely to be found in the short-expiry series.

Out-of-the-Money Options

These options offer the investor a higher return than their in-the-money counterparts, but of course at the cost of a higher risk of loss, even though the absolute level of premium at risk is lower. The investor in out-of-the-money options must be as sure as he can be that the trend of the share price is for a considerable fall over the time remaining to expiry of the option. There are two prime considerations:

1. Only buy put options which are substantially out-of-the-money in shares which are at the top of the volatility league. This is because a considerable fall in share price is necessary to put such options into an in-the-money position with intrinsic value. Involatile shares often move so slowly that they have not reached the striking price by expiry time.
2. The question as to which to invest in of the short-, medium-, or long-term expiry options has to depend upon a firm prediction as to the timescale of the anticipated share price fall. This is best carried out by means of channel analysis, so that the expiry date can then be chosen so as to coincide as near as possible with the lowest share price that will be attained.

The gains achieved in the corresponding out-of-the-money options to those given in Table 9.11 are shown in Table 9.12 over the same time period from 1st March to 8th March 1996. The gearings are now 19, 18 and 13 for the near-expiry options, 10, 11 and 9 for the medium expiries and 8, 8 and 7 for the long expiries. When compared with the gearings for the in-the-money options, they can be seen to be approximately double. The investor must remember, of course, that the higher gearing works in both directions, so that while profits will be approximately doubled, losses incurred through an incorrect forecast of the direction of share price movement will also be approximately doubled.

Table 9.12 Gains in share prices and out-of-the-money put option premiums between 1st and 8th March 1996

Share	Strike price	Share price	1st March Apr pre	Jul pre	Oct pre	8th March Apr pre	Jul pre	Oct pre	Share price	Apr gain	Jul gain	Oct gain	Share gain
Allied Dom.	500	511	9	21	24	11	23	27	503	22.2	9.5	12.5	−1.6
	460		2	7	9	2	7	11	5.3	0	0	22.2	
Argyll	280	298	3	10	13	1	6	9	313	−66.7	−40.0	−30.8	5.0
Asda	100	105	2	4	6	1	3	5	106	−50.0	−25.0	−16.7	1.0
BAA	460	491	2	8	12	1	5	9	504	−50.0	−37.5	−25.0	2.6
British Airws	500	510	9	20	24	6	15	21	526	−33.3	−25.0	−12.5	3.1
Boots	550	599	2	9	14	1	7	11	605	−50.0	−22.2	−21.4	1.0

Share	Strike price	Share price	1st March Apr pre	1st March Jul pre	1st March Oct pre	8th March Apr pre	8th March Jul pre	8th March Oct pre	Share price	Apr gain	Jul gain	Oct gain	Share gain
British Steel	160	184	1	4	6	1	5	7	177	0	25.0	16.7	-3.8
	180		5	12	14	7	15	17		40.0	25.0	21.4	
British Petrol.	500	545	1	6	10	2	7	12	537	100.0	16.7	20.0	-1.5
Bass	700	763	2	10	16	1	10	16	762	-50.0	0	0	-0.1
	750		12	27	33	12	27	34		0	0	3.0	
Cable & W.	420	453	5	13	16	5	14	17	447	0	7.7	6.3	-1.3
Courtaulds	390	435	2	8	11	3	11	14	424	50.0	37.5	27.3	-2.5
	420		7	19	22	12	25	28		71.4	31.6	27.3	
Glaxo	850	899	9	21	34	33	45	57	845	266.7	114.3	67.6	-6.0
HSBC	1050	1084	29	47	62	45	62	76	1047	55.2	31.9	22.6	-3.4
Kingfisher	500	520	12	20	26	7	16	22	534	-41.7	-20.0	-15.4	2.7
Land Secs	550	613	1	4	7	1	5	8	607	0	25.0	14.3	-1.0
	600		6	20	23	8	24	28		33.3	20.0	21.7	
M & S	390	429	1	5	8	1	4	6	436	0	-20.0	-25.0	1.6
	420		6	15	18	4	12	16		-33.3	-20.0	-11.1	
NatWest	650	693	5	14	22	10	21	32	667	100.0	50.0	45.5	-3.7
PowerGen	500	542	3	13	15	5	18	20	524	66.7	38.5		
Reuters	650	706	6	14	23	6	16	23	702	0	14.3	0	-0.6
	700		23	34	44	24	36	44		4.3	5.9	0	
Sainsbury	360	376	4	12	14	3	10	13	379	-25.0	-16.7	-7.1	0.8
Shell Transpt	800	852	5	12	19	7	14	22	847	40.0	16.7	15.8	0.6
SmithKline	650	698	2	11	17	1	7	12	721	-50.0	-36.4	-29.4	3.3
Standard Chr.	600	640	15	34	43	23	43	52	615	53.3	26.5	20.9	-3.9
Storehouse	300	317	3	9	12	1	6	9	328	-66.7	-33.3	-25.0	3.5
Thames Water	500	540	2	12	17	1	9	14	548	-50.0	-25.0	-17.6	1.5
Unilever	1150	1211	7	17	23	9	19	25	1203	28.6	11.8	8.7	-0.7
	1200		26	37	44	31	42	47		19.2	13.5	6.8	
Average gain										**44.6%**	**24.8%**	**19.1%**	**2.3%**
Gearing										**19**	**10**	**8**	

Share	Strike price	Share price	1st March May pre	1st March Aug pre	1st March Nov pre	8th March May pre	8th March Aug pre	8th March Nov pre	Share price	May gain	Aug gain	Nov gain	Share gain
British Aero.	850	891	19	32	40	29	42	51	864	52.6	31.3	27.5	-3.3
BAT Inds	500	571	3	10	14	6	13	18	557	100.0	30.0	28.6	2.5
	550		16	28	33	25	35	40		56.2	25.0	21.2	
BTR	300	327	3	6	9	4	7	12	324	33.3	16.7	25.0	-0.9
British Tele.	330	375	1	4	6	2	7	9	364	100.0	75.0	50.0	-2.9
	360		6	13	16	10	18	21		66.7	38.5	31.3	
Cadbury-Sch.	500	555	6	11	16	16	21	28	519	166.7	90.0	75.0	-6.5
	550		23	30	36	48	51	56		108.7	70.0	55.6	
GEC	330	372	2	6	9	4	11	14	350	100.0	83.3	55.6	-5.9
	360		8	16	19	16	26	29		100.0	62.5	52.6	
Grand Met.	390	437	2	8	11	3	9	14	425	50.0	12.5	27.3	-2.7
	420		8	17	21	12	20	26		50.0	17.6	27.3	
Guinness	420	459	5	9	13	4	8	12	462	-20.0	-11.1	-7.7	0.7
Ladbroke	160	186	4	8	10	5	9	10	181	25.0	12.5	0	-2.7
	180		12	16	18	14	17	19		16.7	6.3	5.6	
LASMO	160	187	4	6	6	4	7	7	181	0	16.7	16.7	-3.2
	180		9	11	12	11	14	15		22.2	27.3	25.0	
Lucas	180	188	6	9	13	4	7	11	193	-33.3	-22.2	15.4	2.7
P&O	500	528	15	21	31	16	22	32	526	6.7	4.8	3.2	-0.4
Prudential	420	446	12	19	24	13	20	26	439	8.3	5.3	8.3	-1.6

Share	Strike price	Share price	1st March			8th March			Share price	May gain	Aug gain	Nov gain	Share gain
			May pre	Aug pre	Nov pre	May pre	Aug pre	Nov pre					
RTZ	850	913	6	13	18	4	11	16	922	−33.3	−15.4	−11.1	1.0
	900		19	30	34	15	25	32		−21.0	−16.7	−5.9	
Redland	390	435	6	11	15	10	16	20	419	66.7	45.5	33.3	−3.7
	420		16	22	26	25	31	35		56.3	40.9	34.6	
Rolls-Royce	200	208	7	11	13	6	10	13	210	−14.3	−9.1	0	1.0
Royal Ins.	360	385	8	16	23	9	18	24	365	12.5	12.5	4.3	−5.2
Tesco	260	271	8	11	15	5	7	13	281	−37.5	−36.4	−13.3	3.7
Utd Biscuits	220	235	7	10	13	8	11	14	232	14.2	10.0	7.7	−1.3
Vodaphone	220	235	6	11	14	3	9	11	243	−50.0	−18.2	−21.4	3.4
Williams	300	342	1	3	5	2	4	6	334	100.0	33.3	20.0	−2.3
	330		9	11	15	13	14	18		44.4	27.3	20.0	
Average gain										**50.5%**	**29.8%**	**23.6%**	**2.7%**
Gearing										**18**	**11**	**8**	

Share	Strike price	Share price	1st March			8th March			Share price	Jun gain	Sep gain	Dec gain	Share gain
			Jun pre	Sep pre	Dec pre	Jun pre	Sep pre	Dec pre					
Abbey Nat.	550	581	6	18	27	4	15	24	565	−33.3	−16.7	−11.1	−2.7
Amstrad	200	218	2	9	12	5	14	17	203	150.0	55.6	41.7	−6.9
Barclays	750	782	7	24	34	20	35	46	733	185.7	45.8	35.3	−6.3
Blue Circle	330	352	2	12	16	1	11	15	354	−50.0	−8.3	−6.3	0.6
British Gas	220	241	1	5	8	1	7	10	235	0	40.0	25.0	2.5
	240		5	15	17	7	18	21		40.0	20.0	23.5	
Dixons	420	467	1	7	12	1	6	12	467	0	−14.2	0	0
	460		7	19	27	6	18	27		−14.3	−5.3	0	
Hillsdown	160	173	1	6	8	1	3	5	183	0	−50.0	−37.5	5.8
Lonrho	180	196	1	4	6	1	5	7	191	0	25.0	16.7	−2.6
Nat. Power	460	483	3	12	18	3	15	21	475	0	25.0	16.7	−1.7
Scot. Power	330	366	1	4	6	1	5	9	356	0	25.0	50.0	−2.7
	360		4	10	17	8	14	22	356	100.0	40.0	29.4	
Sears	90	96	1	3	4	1	3	4	95	0	0	0	−1.0
Tarmac	110	120	1	5	7	1	5	8	117	0	0	14.3	−2.6
Tomkins	240	267	1	3	6	1	2	7	266	0	−33.3	16.7	−0.3
Average gain										**35.8%**	**25.3%**	**20.3%**	**2.7%**
Gearing										**13**	**9**	**7**	

Tired Options

As the share price continues to fall, the gains being made on a week by week basis in an option will start to decrease. This is especially noticeable in those options with the nearest expiry dates. One reason for this behaviour is that, as we have discussed previously, the time values of options start to decrease rapidly over the last six weeks or so of the life of the option, so this tends to reduce the gains which are being made. Also, the opinion of investors themselves will be that a downward trend in share prices which has continued for any length of time will certainly come to an end, and therefore demand for put options will start to decrease, thereby having a braking effect on the value of the premium. Just as was the case with call options, the investor who thinks that the share price trend will continue for some time to come should close the present position and open another one in a different put option of the same share by rolling down the options.

SUBSEQUENT ACTION

As with call options, once a put option has been purchased, the position must be monitored constantly to see that the downward trend in share price expected when you bought the option is maintained. Two outcomes require that you take action different from that which you intended when you bought the option. The first is a rise in share price, while the second is when the downward trend in the share price appears to be developing into something much more significant or sustained than was first envisaged. In this case you may wish to benefit even more from this movement than your present position allows.

Rising Share Price

There are basically two actions that you can take if the share price begins to move adversely. If you feel that the downward trend that was the reason for the purchase of the put option has now ended prematurely, then the position should be closed. If, on the other hand, you feel that this new rise in price is just a temporary blip, and you are still of the opinion that the real underlying trend is still downwards, then you could just hold the position, waiting for the original movement to be re-established. There is a less risky alternative to this, and that is the strategy of rolling down.

Rolling Down

This is the strategy to employ if you are quite sure that the downward movement of the share price will continue and wish to continue to increase your profit on its upward trend, but see the current option as becoming tired. You have to be as sure as possible about the share price trend continuing, because you are putting at risk the profit you have already accumulated, and expecting a share price trend which may have continued for some time to continue for a further period. The strategy is called "rolling down" because you sell an option and move to a new option with a lower striking price than previously.

There is one major criterion that can be used to determine when to switch to an option with a lower strike price. This is when the share price has fallen so as to put the current option from an out-of-the-money position with no intrinsic value to a position which is close to being at-the-money. Of course, this only applies if you started with an option which is out-of-the-money. If that is not the case, then stay with your in-the-money option until there are only a few weeks to expiry before moving into a different option.

The new option to move into is the one that is furthest out-of-the-money, which of course will be a new option introduced by the authorities to maintain the balance of striking prices around the share price (see Chapter 2).

Our strategy is therefore:

1. Sell once the share price has reached the striking price or thereabouts; or if the option was initially in-the-money, sell when only a few weeks are left to expiry.
2. Buy the furthest out-of-the-money option with the nearest expiry date that gives you at least a further six weeks to expiry.

This strategy will bring the maximum gearing and therefore the maximum profit during the course of the predicted share price fall. We have already said that once this strategy has been under way for some time, the amount of risk involved is high, and the number of contracts which have been bought will have grown rapidly. It is absolutely essential that all techniques at the disposal of the investor to predict the end of the downward share price trend should be utilised, including of course channel analysis.

10

Writing Put Options

The writer of a put option receives a premium from a buyer of the option and in return has undertaken to buy the shares at the striking price if a buyer exercises the option.

The writer of a put option is of course at the opposite side of the transaction from the purchaser of a put option. The put option buyer is bearish for the future trend of the share price, and can select a put option which reflects the degree of his bearishness and the risk he is prepared to take. The writer, on the other hand, expects primarily a rise in share price, but depending on how far in- or out-of-the-money the particular option is, can also make a profit if the share price remains static or even falls slightly. Just like the writer of call options, the writer of put options has no control over if or when the option might be exercised against him; the decision on exercise rests entirely with the buyer of the option.

The objective of the writer of puts is to receive the premium available by writing, and potentially also to be able to buy the shares at a lower price than the present market price. In the latter case, of course, the writer will acquire the shares at a real cost of the striking price less the premium received plus dealing costs, which usually turns out to be less than the striking price. Both of these objectives imply a bullish nature for the writer. He is prepared to receive the shares because he then expects them to rise to make a profit.

In the case of call option writers, we had two categories: the naked call writer, who did not own the shares corresponding to the option being written, and the covered writer, who did own the shares. In theory it is possible to have two categories of put option writer: the naked put writer, who has no position in the underlying shares themselves, and the covered put writer, who has sold the underlying shares but has yet to deliver them. He would be covered in the sense that if the shares are put to him, he needed them to fulfil his commitment in the shares themselves. Covered put writing is a perfectly viable proposition in United States markets, where it is possible to go short on shares, i.e. sell them without delivering them, for long periods of time provided the seller puts up a sufficient margin. In the UK, however, due to the new rolling five-day settlement, it is not feasible to carry such a short position. In this treatment of put option writing, it is only the naked put writer that will be considered.

The put writer is in the position of having the potential for a limited gain and a large loss. The gain is limited because it is the premium received. The loss is large because, in the worst case, the writer will have to purchase the shares at the strike price at a time when the actual share price may have fallen to just above zero.

MARGIN REQUIREMENTS

The same comments about margin apply as for the writer of call options (see Chapter 8). The required margin is 25% of the prevailing price for the underlying share adjusted by the amount by which the option is in- or out-of-the-money. The margin of course increases as the share price falls, thereby moving against the writer.

EXERCISE OF PUT OPTIONS

In the case of call options, the upside profit potential is limited by exercise of the option, and therefore such exercise is against the interests of the writer. On the other hand, the exercise of a put option may be the very outcome that the writer desires, since it can give him the shares at greatly reduced cost compared with that prevailing at the time he writes the option. It has already been pointed out (Chapter 8) that options are seldom exercised early in their lifetime since the initial objective of the purchaser is to see an increase in the premium value of the options rather than become involved with the shares themselves. The put option writer with the objective of acquiring the shares may thus have to wait until the last few weeks before expiry of the option before seeing its exercise. It goes without saying that the put option writer must see that he has the necessary funds available at all times to cover the cost of the share acquisition, and of course an increasing proportion of these funds will be tied up by the margin requirements of the position.

Loss/gain Potential—Large Loss, Limited Gain

As with the other option positions, we can draw a diagram to illustrate the concept of large loss and limited gain by plotting the profit or loss potential against the share price. This is shown in Figure 10.1.

At point A, the share price is equal to the striking price of the put option, and the purchaser would be considering exercising the option. The profit, i.e. the original premium, has remained constant down to this point,

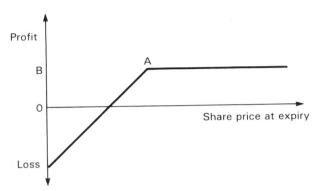

Figure 10.1 Profit/loss situation for a put option writer with changing share price. Point A is the striking price and point B is the premium received

but as the share price falls, the writer, if the put is exercised against him, will have to pay an increasing amount above the share price (the difference between the strike price and the share price) when accepting the shares at the exercise price. Since the share price can go all the way down to a point marginally above zero, the maximum loss that can be sustained is marginally less than the strike price at which the put options were written.

Although the novice put writer may be of the opinion that share price falls may be of limited extent, so that the potential loss is not all that large, it is worth drawing attention to the crash in October 1987 to show what effect share price falls of 20–30% magnitude can have on a put option writer. Data for Dixons, Thorn-EMI, Courtaulds, Trafalgar House, Woolworths and BAA are shown in Table 10.1. The smallest loss is 14p for each BAA share against a premium received of 1p, while the largest loss is 217p for each Thorn-EMI share against a premium received of 50p. Expressed as a ratio, the loss in the case of BAA is 14 times the amount of premium received, while the loss in the case of Thorn-EMI is four times the premium received. Since option writers usually write a sufficient number of contracts to make the premium received a useful sum, it can be seen that the losses, especially in the case of BAA, are horrendous. This is not to suggest that the writing of put options should be avoided, but to emphasise that the writer must be aware at all times of the risk, and stay within sensible limits of exposure. Even share price falls of lesser momentum than those on Black Monday can pose a difficulty, and the writer should always be prepared to close the position at the first sign that things are not going to plan.

The potential for gain for the put option writer is of course simply the value of the premium received, less dealing costs. The potential for loss depends upon three factors: the premium, the striking price and the share price prevailing at the time of exercise. The relationship is

Table 10.1   The October 1987 crash and put option premiums

Share	Exercise price	Share price 10/10/87	Option premiums received (p)			Share price 4/10/87	Loss (p)
			Oct	**Jan**	**Apr**		
Courtaulds	460	513	0.5	7	12	383	77
	500		6	24	28		117
	550		40	52	58		167
Trafalgar House	390	424	2	10	17	319	71
	420		8	22	30		101
	460		37	45	53		141
Woolworth	350	369	3	–	–	314	36
	360		–	–	25		46
	375		17	23	–		61
			Nov	**Feb**	**May**		
BAA	130	150	1	4	7	116	14
	140		3.5	9	11		24
	160		14	19	22		44
			Dec	**Mar**	**Jun**		
Dixons	360	397	7	15	18	271	89
	390		18	24	30		119
	420		34	–	–		149
Thorn-EMI	650	719	7	20	25	533	117
	700		22	32	42		167
	750		50	53	65		217

$$\text{Loss} = \text{premium received (A)} - \text{striking price (B)} + \text{share price (C)}$$

The potential for gain or loss can be summed up in Table 10.2.

Table 10.2   Potential for gain/loss for put options

Type of option	A	– B + C	Result
In-the-money	* * *	negative	loss
At-the-money	* *	zero	gain (= A)
Out-of-the-money	*	positive	gain (= A)

If the at-the-money and out-of-the-money options stay that way until expiry, they will not be exercised and therefore the gain is equal to the premium (A). As we saw previously from Figure 10.1, the loss can increase to a maximum where the share price is just above zero, and this is therefore the potential for loss which the writer has to take into account when deciding on his course of action. These various scenarios are best described by an actual example, Glaxo on 1st March 1996:

Share price 899p; April 850s, 9p; 900s, 32p; 950s, 71p
July 850s, 21p; 900s, 44p; 950s, 78p
October 850s, 34p; 900s, 58p; 950s, 89p

Taking just the April options, the profits from the options (ignoring dealing expenses) at expiry are shown in Table 10.3. By the convention used in Chapter 8, the "good outcome" in the writing of these April put options is the value found in the final column, i.e. 71p, 32p or 9p, while the "bad outcome" is the value found in the "If exercised" column. At the date on which the data were taken, obviously with a share price of 899p the at-the-money and out-of-the-money options would not be exercised. The bad outcome would limit the gain to 20p. However, note that the values in the "If exercised" column are minimum values, applying only if the share price is at the value it was when the option was written. In the worst case, the share price could fall to zero, so that the writer would have to accept shares at the exercise price when they have no value.

Table 10.3 Potential profit from various Glaxo April put options. The share price is 899p

Type of option		If exercised	If not exercised
In-the-money	950s	71 + 899 − 950 = 20	71
At-the-money	900s	would not be exercised	32
Out-of-the-money	950s	would not be exercised	9

The position for the various categories of put option writing can be summarised as follows:

- In-the-money put options writing: good potential with good outcome, very high potential for loss.
- At-the-money put options writing: moderate potential on the upside, high potential for loss.
- Out-of-the-money put options writing: poor potential on the upside, fairly high potential for loss.

As one would expect, therefore, options with the highest potential for gain are also those with the highest potential for loss. The more conservative put option writer would tend to favour the out-of-the-money options, accepting the lower profit potential in return for the lower loss potential.

TIMESCALE

It is as vital for a put option writer as it is with any other option position that he is clear about the timescale of the share price trend he is about to use to make his profit. Although some put option writers might feel re-laxed about the option being exercised so that they have to take delivery of the shares themselves, most would have as their strategy the avoidance of this outcome. In this case the expiry date of the option which is being written should be nearer than the anticipated length of time for which the trend will continue. This will then ensure that the trend does not go into reverse, making exercise of the option become increasingly attractive as the adverse trend continues. Just as with the writer of call options, time is the put option writer's enemy, in the sense that since he has already pocketed the premium, the sooner the option expires worthless the better. On the other hand, the buyer of the put option may consider that it is worth paying extra for time, since even if the share price moves against him initially, this may change in his favour as time goes on. The writer is faced with a simple choice—either to take the higher premium associated with the further expiry dates and also accept a higher risk of events moving against him, or take the lower premium for the shorter expiry options where the risk of adverse movement of the share price is much less.

More light can be thrown on this aspect of put option writing if the premiums are expressed as a weekly return (WR). We can take the data for Guinness, Dixons, Boots and the FTSE100 Index for 31st January 1996 which are given in Table 10.4. Quite obviously, within a particular option class, the further out the expiry date, the less is the premium per month remaining. The buyer of a put option is therefore reducing his costs per month by going for the longer expiry options. On the other hand, the writers of put options will receive less premium per month for these longer expiry options, i.e. his WR is less. Thus, unless there are very valid reasons for the contrary, the writer is better off going for the shorter expiry options.

As with call options, the two major considerations of interest to the option writer will be those situations where there may be anomalous time values, and those where the CPP values are high.

Anomalous Time Values

The purchaser of a put option can frequently spot an anomalous situation where the time value is much too small for the amount of time remaining to the expiry of the option. As far as the put option writer is concerned, this situation has to be avoided, since the premium received will be less than is usual for such an option at that stage of its life. The writer has to take an opposite view, looking for anomalous situations where the time values are too high for the circumstances. In such cases the writer will then receive a higher than usual premium without taking on board any higher risk. Note that time values are highest for those options which are closest to being at-the-money.

Since we have indicated that the short expiry options are the most sensible for the writer, then these are the ones which should be scanned

Table 10.4 Premiums per month remaining to expiry for the options listed in Table 7.1

Share	Share price	Exercise price	Expiry date and premium/month		
			Feb	**May**	**Aug**
Guinness	457	420	38.0	10.75	6.9
		460	7.0	4.5	3.6
		500	1.0	1.25	1.6
			Mar	**Jun**	**Sep**
Dixons	416	390	17.0	9.2	6.5
		420	8.0	5.8	4.5
		460	2.0	2.6	2.5
			Apr	**Jul**	**Oct**
Boots	623	550	26.3	14.3	10.0
		600	12.3	8.0	6.1
		650	4.0	3.7	3.4
			Feb	**Mar**	**May**
FTSE100	3759.3	3600	161.0	87.0	66.0
		3650	113.0	67.0	54.0
		3700	72.0	48.5	43.7
		3750	36.0	33.0	34.0
		3800	15.0	20.5	26.0
		3850	4.0	12.0	19.3
		3900	1.0	6.5	14.3

for anomalies. As an example, we can take the premiums for the out-of-the-money short-expiry February puts (where the premiums will be equal to the time value) on 12th January and 26th January 1996. These are shown in Table 10.5.

Of this list of 19 shares and option premiums, only six shares did not rise in price between the two dates in January. The anomalies we should look for in such a situation are where the time values do not fall substantially in spite of either a rise in share price, or a very modest fall in share price. Three such situations can be seen in Table 10.5. Royal Insurance stood still as far as both share price and premium were concerned, while Cadbury-Schweppes and GEC showed minor falls in share price and minimal change in option premiums. The premiums which Royal and GEC commanded, 11p and 8p respectively, represented very good writing opportunities at a time when, in the absence of any other evidence, the share prices were not showing evidence of any serious fall, i.e. at a time therefore when the risk appeared to favour the writer. At expiry, the share prices were 378p for Royal Insurance and 367p for GEC, so that the options expired worthless from the point of view of the purchaser.

It is worth comparing these two options on the basis of good and bad outcomes:

Table 10.5 Premiums and share prices for February expiry options on 12th and 26th January 1996

Share	Exercise price	Premium	Share price	Premium	Share price
British Aerospace	800	10	835	2	878
British Telecom	360	7	361	9	357
Cadbury-Schweppes	500	5	534	4	534
GEC	360	7	365	8	361
Grand Metropolitan	420	5	444	3	448
Guinness	460	3	484	6	467
Ladbroke	140	3	154	1	169
LASMO	160	1	176	1	174
Lucas	160	1	176	1	196
P&O	460	8	474	1	542
Prudential	420	10	429	10	420
RTZ	850	7	885	2	905
Redland	360	8	364	2	384
Rolls-Royce	180	1	196	1	200
Royal Insurance	360	11	386	11	386
Tesco	380	2	300	2	296
United Biscuits	240	3	254	2	256
Vodaphone	200	2	214	1	231
Williams	300	1	330	1	340

- *Royal Insurance:*
  Good outcome = 15p (the premium)
  Bad outcome = loss of 360p (the striking price you will have to pay if exercised when shares are valueless)
  Good/bad ratio = 0.042

- *GEC:*
  Good outcome = 8p
  Bad outcome = loss of 360p
  Good/bad ratio = 0.022

As far as the good/bad ratio is concerned, the Royal Insurance example is slightly more favourable to the writer.

The above examples, of course, take the very simplistic view that the behaviour in share prices over a two-week period nearly a month before the expiry of the options is a good indicator of their behaviour over the rest of the period to expiry. As we have continued to stress in this book, it is imperative that you hold a clear view of the predicted price movement of the shares in which you are interested before taking any option position. In the case of Royal Insurance, the Sigma-p program predicts that the share is already past its peak price on the date a decision would be taken (Figure 10.2). Thus the risk is high that the price will fall, increasing the chance that the option will be exercised against the writer.

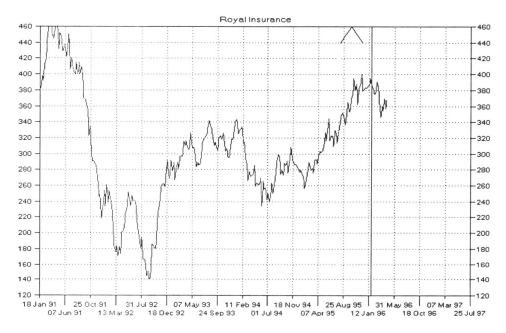

Figure 10.2 The Royal Insurance share price to 25th April 1996. The vertical line corresponds to the date of 26th January 1996. The inverted chevron shows that the Sigma-p program is predicting in January that the peak price has passed

Cost per Percentage Point (CPP)

We have discussed earlier in Chapter 5 the method of calculating CPPs for put options. We saw then that buyers of put options should look for those with low CPPs. Since writers of put options are diametrically opposed, they should avoid those options with low CPPs and look for options with high CPPs. The CPPs are calculated for the same options as are listed in Table 10.5 taking the data for 26th January 1996 and are shown in Table 10.6. Also shown are the share prices at the expiry date of these February options.

Note that the British Telecom option had moved into an in-the-money situation by 26th January, and so the CPP is not relevant amongst the remaining out-of-the-money options. Of the other 18 entries in the table, the top five were Prudential, GEC, Guinness, Royal Insurance and Cadbury-Schweppes. As a reasonable approach, therefore, it would be wise to select the options for writing out of this list, applying in addition any further criteria. It is gratifying that both Royal Insurance and GEC appear in this list. Of these top five, three showed falls and two a standstill in price from the date of the calculation of the CPP to the time of expiry. Thus none of these would have been exercised against the writer, and all five situations would have been profitable.

Table 10.6 CPP values calculated for the options listed in Table 10.5 as at 26th January 1996

Share	Exercise price	Premium	Share price	CPP	Price at expiry
British Aerospace	800	2	878	0.22	837
British Telecom	360	9	357	–	368
Cadbury-Schweppes	500	4	534	0.56	532
GEC	360	8	361	3.21	367
Grand Metropolitan	420	3	448	0.43	440
Guinness	460	6	467	2.16	451
Ladbroke	140	1	169	0.06	186
LASMO	160	1	174	0.12	184
Lucas	160	1	196	–	191
P&O	460	1	542	0.07	533
Prudential	420	10	420	4.20	448
RTZ	850	2	905	0.32	915
Redland	360	2	384	0.30	410
Rolls-Royce	180	1	200	0.10	210
Royal Insurance	360	11	386	1.15	358
Tesco	380	2	296	0.33	282
United Biscuits	240	2	256	0.28	237
Vodaphone	200	1	231	0.07	224
Williams	300	1	340	0.08	334

SUBSEQUENT ACTION

You will have written the put option in the first place because you were bullish of the direction of the share price movement during the time remaining to expiry of the option. The two outcomes where you will have to take a decision other than continue to hold the position is when either the share price falls, or the share price rise turns into something much more significant than you first expected.

Falling Share Price

The sensible course of action here is to close your current position, protecting the profit if you have one, and limiting your loss if you have not made a profit. You should do this unless you are totally convinced that the fall in share price is purely temporary, and that the upward trend will recommence well before the expiry of the option. Two other courses of action are to maintain the current position or roll down the option. Holding the current position is the riskiest tactic with a falling share price, and it goes without saying that you require very good reasons for following this course. Less risky than this is to roll down the option.

Rolling Down

Rolling down for the writer of a put option means closing the current option position and writing an option with a lower strike price. Naturally the risk is thereby reduced because of the lower strike price, but the potential profit is also reduced. To close the current position will of course require a net outlay over the premium you received initially, since the option premium will have risen due to the fall in the share price. This will be offset by writing the option of lower striking price.

As an example, take the Argyll put options between 20th October and 3rd November 1995.

On 20th October, with the share price at 324p, the January 330s were at a premium of 22p and appeared to be an attractive writing opportunity to the investor. By 3rd November the share price had fallen to 299p, but the investor was convinced that this represented the bottom of a short-term trough and that the price would change direction. The January 330s were then at a premium of 35p. The January 300s were at 16p.

Rolling down would give the following position:

- Initial premium received = 22p
- Good outcome is therefore 22p
- Bad outcome is value of striking price, i.e. loss of 330p

The investor closed the initial position by buying back the option at 35p and writing a new option at a lower striking price, the January 300s at 16p. The position is then:

- Initial premium received = 22p
- Less buy-back of option = 35p
- Plus premium from January 300s = 16p
- Premium now in pocket = 22 – 35 + 16 = 3p
- Good outcome is therefore 3p
- Bad outcome is therefore loss of 300p

The investor has therefore reduced his potential for profit from 22p down to 3p, but in doing so has reduced his risk accordingly. The share price is now standing 1p below the striking price, whereas prior to rolling down, the share price was standing 31p below the original striking price, obviously placing the writer in great danger of being exercised against.

Rising Share Price

Naturally, if the share price rise is in line with your original expectations, you should stay with your original objectives when you wrote the put. If the price rise looks as if it will exceed these original expectations, both in the time for which the rise will endure and in its extent, then you could consider rolling up to a higher striking price.

Rolling Up

This strategy should only be used if you are convinced that the share price rise will continue for a considerable period of time and you wish to maximise your profit potential from the situation. The procedure is:

1. Close the position in your current option.
2. Write an option at a higher striking price.

By rolling up, you will be closing your original position at a profit, since the premium required to close the option will be less than it was when you wrote it. You will then in addition receive another premium for writing the option at a higher striking price, although this premium may well be less than the original due to the general fall-off in put premiums against the background of the share price rise. Note, though, that the penalty for this improved potential for profit is an increased risk, since the potential for loss is now the new, higher striking price.

11

Advanced Strategies 1. Spreads

So far our option strategies have involved taking a position in just one option, by either buying or writing call options or buying or writing put options. Advanced strategies require us to take positions in more than one series simultaneously. Most of these strategies involve two different series, although there are some that require three. The ability to calculate the overall profit and loss potential for an advanced strategy is vital if the strategy is to be successful, but the arithmetic used is simple, being just an extension of the methods we have used so far with simple strategies. Graphical representations are used wherever possible to illustrate the profit and loss potentials as the share price rises or falls.

Since we are taking a position in each of two option series, each of these "legs" of the strategy will have associated with it its own upside and downside potentials. Since the major aim of advanced strategies is to reduce risk, each leg will be chosen in such a way that its upside potential outweighs the downside potential of the other leg. By this approach we avoid the problems we saw with some simple strategies where the downside risk could be virtually unlimited. Note also that in the two-legged spreads discussed in this chapter, one leg is opened by buying an option while the other leg is opened by writing an option, and therefore the cost of buying one option is partly or wholly offset by receiving the premium from the opposite transaction.

Some examples of advanced strategies which will be discussed in detail are:

- **Bull spreads:** Buy a call with a low striking price and write a call with a high striking price; *or* buy a put with a low striking price and write a put with a high striking price.
- **Bear spreads:** Buy a call with a high striking price and write a call with a low striking price; *or* buy a put with a high striking price and write a put with a low striking price.

- **Calendar spreads:** Buy a put or call in a certain expiry month and take an opposing position (write a put or call at same striking price) in a later expiry month.
- **Butterfly spreads:** Buy a call with a low striking price and a call with a high striking price and write two calls with medium striking price; *or* the same transactions using puts.

Obviously the bull spreads and bear spreads reflect in their names the basic feeling of the investor as to the direction of the share price. On the other hand, calendar spreads can be designed to be bullish, bearish or neutral. A bullish calendar spread would use a striking price above the share price while a bearish spread would use a striking price below the share price. As you might expect, a neutral spread would use a striking price which is closest to the current share price, i.e. at-the-money.

BULL SPREADS

As we pointed out above, there are two ways of achieving a bull spread— bull call spreads and bull put spreads. The call spreads are achieved by buying a call with a low striking price and writing a call with a high striking price, while the put spreads are achieved by buying a put with a low striking price and writing a put with a high striking price. Bull spreads are the strategies for those investors who are moderately bullish. They limit the risk to such an investor, but also limit the upside potential. Obviously the very bullish investor does not wish to limit his profit potential, and should therefore look more closely at simple call strategies.

Costs and Margin Requirement

Note that, if we exclude the dealing costs of the spread, the overall cost will depend upon the difference between the two premiums. In the case of a call spread you will pay this difference, since the premium for buying the low striking price call will be higher than the premium received for writing the higher striking price. In the case of a put spread you will receive this difference, since the premium you pay for the put at a lower striking price will be less than the premium you receive for writing the put at the higher striking price. As long as the number of contracts for each leg of the call spread are the same, there will be no margin requirement, since you are not in a net exposure to being called. This is not true for put spreads, since you will be in a net exposure to having the shares put to you as your writing striking price is higher than your buying striking price. The margin requirement for put spread positions is easily calculated as the difference between the two striking prices multiplied by the number of shares for which you have written contracts.

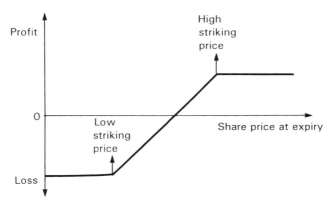

Figure 11.1　Profit and loss situation for a bull spread at expiry

Bull Call Spread

Gain/Loss Potential—Limited Gain, Limited Loss

The performance of the bull call spread for different share prices at expiry is shown in Figure 11.1. Ignoring the dealing costs, the maximum loss is simply the difference between the two premiums, i.e. your net initial outlay. This is incurred when the share price falls below the lower of the two striking prices. The maximum gain is obtained when the share price rises above the higher of the two striking prices. This profit is equal to the difference between the two striking prices less the initial capital outlay. The two changes in direction of the graph, from horizontal to upward sloping, and from upward sloping to horizontal, occur at each of the two striking prices.

Although of course all bull call spreads will follow the shape of the diagram, the actual profit and loss situation will depend on the premiums and the striking prices used. As an example an investor using channel analysis on the Cadbury-Schweppes share price would have been moderately bullish on 8th September 1995 (see the Cadbury-Schweppes chart, Figure 8.4, in Chapter 8), and would have had available the following data:

Share price: 494p
Call option premiums:　November 460s, 37p; 500s, 13p; 550s, 2p
　　　　　　　　　　　February 460s, 50p; 500s, 26p; 550s, 9p
　　　　　　　　　　　May 460s, 54p; 500s, 31p; 550s, 13p

From these data, it is possible to construct three November bull spreads, three February bull spreads and three May bull spreads:

1. Buy 460s, write 500s.
2. Buy 460s, write 550s.
3. Buy 500s, write 550s.

Table 11.1   Profit potentials (P) and loss potentials (L) for November, February and May Cadbury-Schweppes bull call spreads on 8th September 1995. The share price is 494p

Expiry date	Buy 460s/Sell 500s			Buy 460s/Sell 550s			Buy 500s/Sell 550s		
	P	L	P/L	P	L	P/L	P	L	P/L
November	16	24	0.67	55	35	1.57	39	11	3.5
February	16	24	0.67	49	41	1.20	33	17	1.9
May	17	23	0.74	49	41	1.20	32	18	1.8

As an example of the calculation for a Cadbury-Schweppes February bull call spread, buying 460s @ 50p and writing 500s @ 26p:

$$\text{Maximum loss} = \text{difference in premiums} = 50 - 26 = 24p$$
$$\text{Maximum profit} = \text{high striking price} - \text{low striking price}$$
$$- \text{overall premium paid}$$
$$= 500 - 460 - 24 = 16p$$

P/L ratio = 16/24 = 0.67

The P/L ratio is simply the ratio of the maximum profit to the maximum loss. The data on profit potential, loss potential and P/L ratio for each of these nine possible spreads are shown in Table 11.1.

The least bullish investor, not expecting much of a price rise, would be looking at the 460/500 spread, since with a share price of 494p, i.e. only just below the higher of the two striking prices, the profit potential is already almost at its maximum. A further share price rise will not increase the profit significantly. Note that there is very little difference in the potentials of the three different expiries for the 460/500 spreads. The investor would simply have to take a view about the rate of climb of the share price from its position on 8th September.

Both of the other two possibilities, the narrow 500/550 and the wider 460/550 spreads, are equally bullish in the sense that they both require a share price rise to 550p to achieve this maximum. Where they differ is that the narrower spread has lower potential for both profit and loss. The investor simply has to make up his mind as to whether he will accept greater risk for greater reward.

Bull Put Spread

Gain/loss Potential—Limited Gain, Limited Loss

The shape of the graph for a spread using puts rather than calls is exactly the same as that shown in Figure 11.1 for calls. The maximum loss occurs when the share price falls below the lower of the two striking prices, while the maximum profit occurs when the share price rises above the higher of the two striking prices. Of course the exact values for the maximum profit and loss positions will depend on the various premiums and the spread between the striking prices. As an example, taking the Cadbury-Schweppes data for put options on 8th September, we have the following data:

Share price: 494p
Put option premiums: November 460s, 5p; 500s, 20p; 550s, 62p
February 460s, 10p; 500s, 26p; 550s, 63p
May 460s, 15p; 500s, 33p; 550s, 67p

From these data it is possible to construct three November bull put spreads, three February bull put spreads and three May bull put spreads:

1. Buy 460s, write 500s.
2. Buy 460s, write 550s.
3. Buy 500s, write 550s.

As an example of the calculation for a Cadbury-Schweppes February bull put spread, buying 460s @ 10p and writing 500s @ 26p:

$$\text{Maximum loss} = \text{high striking price} - \text{low striking price}$$
$$- \text{net premium received} = 500 - 460 - 16 = 24\text{p}$$
$$\text{Maximum profit} = \text{difference in premiums} = 26 - 10 = 16\text{p}$$
$$= \text{overall premium received}$$

P/L ratio = 16/24 = 0.67

Taking all nine possible spreads, we get the values shown in Table 11.2. Broadly speaking, bull call spreads and bull put spreads are fairly similar in their risk/reward patterns. There are two aspects that make bull put spreads slightly more attractive. Firstly, the difference in premiums is actually pocketed at the time of the transaction, whereas with a call spread the investor has to pay this difference immediately. This is because the written side of the spread is always at the higher exercise price, and higher exercise prices command higher put premiums but lower call premiums. The second point is that the P/L ratios are higher than for the corresponding call spreads. This means that, in simple terms, the profit/loss situation is more favourable to the investor. Note that put spreads can be less attractive in another respect, and that is that they may be exercised against you at a point before you reach the maximum upside potential. This is particularly true if the written leg of the spread is well in-the-money.

Subsequent Action

If the Share Price Falls

The best action is simply to hold the position, since you already took into account this risk of the share price falling when you opened the position.

Table 11.2 Profit potentials (P) and loss potentials (L) for November, February and May Cadbury-Schweppes bull put spreads. The share price is 494p

Expiry date	Buy 460s/Sell 500s			Buy 460s/Sell 550s			Buy 500s/Sell 550s		
	P	L	P/L	P	L	P/L	P	L	P/L
November	15	25	0.60	57	33	1.73	42	8	5.25
February	16	24	0.67	53	37	1.43	37	13	2.85
May	18	22	0.82	52	38	1.36	34	16	2.13

Even if you are now totally convinced that the price will fall even further, any other action than holding will carry with it an even higher risk. For example, rolling down by closing out the original spread and opening a new spread with lower striking prices will simply lock in the loss that was made on the original spread. If you are not careful, you could end up initiating a new spread whose potential for profit is not enough to cover the loss made on the original spread. The circumstance where you could take action is if you are convinced that the share price fall is only temporary, and that the price will shortly move up so strongly that it will outperform your original expectations. If you held a bull call spread, then closing the position on the written call will now leave you holding a straightforward call at what was originally a low striking price, but now, as a result of the price fall, is a well out-of-the-money option. The share price must move considerably higher if you are to make a profit, since of course the original loss must be wiped out. Quite obviously, changing the strategy from a spread to a call option position unavoidably takes on board substantially higher risk.

If the Share Price Rises

If the price rises in line with your original expectations, then continue to hold the spread. Only if you become convinced that a much larger rise is in prospect should you consider changing the original strategy for a more bullish one. If you have a bull call spread, one move is to close the written call position, leaving you holding a simple call position which is now, as a result of the price rise, heavily in-the-money. The profit you made on the original spread is now locked into this new position, and therefore is put at risk. The downside potential for this call is higher than that of the original spread, because heavily in-the-money options will lose value virtually on a penny for penny basis if the share price starts to move downwards again. A much better approach than closing the written call postions is to roll the whole spread upwards.

Rolling Up

This is carried out by closing out the original bull spread and opening another one at higher striking prices. There is an additional risk involved, since the break-even point is now higher, necessitating a higher share price rise than was the case with the original spread. The point can be illustrated by reference to Bass call options on 28th September 1995. The investor opened a 650/700 bull call spread in the January options. The premiums were 73p and 40p respectively, so that the overall cost of the spread was 33p plus expenses. The share price at the time was 634p. The profit and loss potentials were:

Maximum loss = difference in premiums = 73 – 40 = 33p paid
Maximum profit = difference in striking prices – difference in premiums
= 700 – 650 – 33 = 17p

The maximum gain of this spread will be reached when the share price rises above the 700p striking price of the written option. By 6th December, with the share price at 695p, the spread was virtually at its maximum profit, and the investor became convinced that a further price rise was in the offing. He therefore closed the initial spread and opened the 700/750 spread. The premiums on 6th December were 110p, 62p and 27p for the January 650, 700 and 750 options respectively.

Thus, to close the initial spread:

- Write 650 option @ 110p
- Buy 700 option @ 62p
- Amount received = 48p, i.e. a profit of 15p over the original 33p paid

To open the new spread:

- Buy 700 option @ 62p
- Write 750 option @ 27p
- Net outlay = 62 – 27 = 35p

The new downside potential is this 35p paid, but since the previous profit was 15p, the overall downside potential is therefore 20p. The new maximum profit is 750 – 700 – 35 = 15p. Thus having pocketed the initial profit of 33p, there is now the potential to make a further 15p profit, making the overall profit 48p.

Note that additional risk has now been taken on board, since the share price has to rise above the highest striking price, i.e. higher than 750p from its current level of 695p before this maximum profit is made.

BEAR SPREADS

Bear spreads can be achieved by using the opposite transactions to those used in a bull spread. The two methods available are thus to buy a call with a high striking price and sell a call with a low striking price, or to buy a put with a high striking price and sell a put with a low striking price. Just as bull spreads are ideal for those investors who are moderately bullish, then bear spreads are ideal for those investors who are moderately bearish of the share price. Investors who are very bearish should use the simple strategies discussed in the earlier chapters.

Costs and Margin Requirement

If we ignore dealing costs, then the cost of a bear spread position is the difference between the two premiums. For a bear call spread, the higher striking price calls are of course less expensive than lower striking price calls, and therefore since the call spread is constructed by buying the higher striking price call and selling the lower striking price call, the investor will be credited with the difference. Conversely, for a bear put spread, the higher striking price puts are higher priced than the lower striking price puts, and therefore the investor will have to pay the difference. There will be a margin requirement for the bear call spread which is calculated as the difference between the two striking prices less the net premium which has been credited. There is no margin requirement for bear put spreads.

Bear Call Spreads

Gain/loss Potential—Limited Gain, Limited Loss

The profit and loss position for a bear call spread at expiry time is shown in Figure 11.2. The maximum profit is equal to the difference in the two premiums, i.e. the net premium credited or received. The maximum loss is equal to the difference between the two striking prices minus the net premium received. The maximum return is obtained when the share price is below the lower of the two share prices.

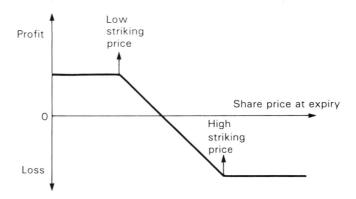

Figure 11.2 Profit and loss situation for a bear call spread at expiry

The values for profit and loss will, of course, depend on the premiums and striking prices of the particular options which make up the spread, but for any bear call spread the overall shape of the graph will remain the same. We can take the example of Cadbury-Schweppes which was used to illustrate bull spreads and carry out the appropriate calculation of upside and downside potentials for the bear call spread:

Share price: 494p
Call option premiums: November 460s, 37p; 500s, 13p; 550s, 2p
                       February 460s, 50p; 500s, 26p; 550s, 9p
                       May 460s, 54p; 500s, 31p; 550s, 13p

It is possible to construct three November call spreads, three February call spreads and three May call spreads out of these data:

1. Buy 550s, write 500s.
2. Buy 550s, write 460s.
3. Buy 500s, write 460s.

As an example of the calculation for a Cadbury-Schweppes February bear call spread, buying 550s @ 9p and writing 500s @ 26p:

Maximum loss = high striking price − low striking price − net premium received
= 550 − 500 − 17 = 33p

Maximum profit = difference in premiums

= 26 − 9 = 17p = overall premium received
P/L ratio = 17/33 = 0.52

Taking all nine possible put spreads, we get the values shown in Table 11.3.

The least bearish investor will be looking at the 500/550 call spreads, since with a share price of 494p, these are already at maximum profit. The other spreads, using the 460 option, require a 34p fall for maximum profit, although of course this profit is higher than that of the 500/550 spreads to compensate for the additional risk.

Table 11.3 Profit potentials (P) and loss potentials (L) for November, February and May Cadbury-Schweppes bear call spreads. The share price is 494p

Expiry date	Buy 460s/Sell 500s			Buy 460s/Sell 550s			Buy 500s/Sell 550s		
	P	L	P/L	P	L	P/L	P	L	P/L
November	24	16	1.5	35	55	0.64	11	39	0.28
February	24	16	1.5	41	49	0.84	17	33	0.52
May	23	17	1.35	41	49	0.84	18	32	0.56

Bear Put Spreads

Gain/loss Potential—Limited Gain, Limited Loss

The profit/loss graph for a bear put spread at expiry is very much the same shape as that for a bear call spread as shown in Figure 11.2. The maximum gain is equal to the difference in the striking prices less the net premium which has been paid for the spread. The maximum loss is equal to the net premium which has been paid, i.e. the difference between the premium received for writing the lower striking price put and the premium paid for the higher striking price put.

For the same Cadbury-Schweppes example, the put data are as follows:

Share price: 494p
Put option premiums: November 460s, 5p; 500s, 20p; 550s, 62p
                                         February 460s, 10p; 500s, 26p; 550s, 63p
                                         May 460s, 15p; 500s, 33p; 550s, 67p

It is possible to construct three November bear put spreads, three February bear put spreads and three May bear put spreads out of these data:

1. Buy 550s, write 500s.
2. Buy 550s, write 460s.
3. Buy 500s, write 460s.

As an example of the calculation for a Cadbury-Schweppes February bear put spread, buying 550s @ 63p and writing 500s @ 26p:

Maximum loss = difference in premiums = 63 − 26 = 37p
Maximum profit = high striking price − low striking price − net premium
received = 550 − 500 − 37 = 13p
P/L ratio = 13/37 = 0.35

Taking all nine possible put spreads, we get the values shown in Table 11.4.

Table 11.4 Profit potentials (P) and loss potentials (L) for November, February and May Cadbury-Schweppes bear put spreads. The share price is 494p

Expiry date	Buy 500s/Sell 460s			Buy 550s/Sell 460s			Buy 550s/Sell 500s		
	P	L	P/L	P	L	P/L	P	L	P/L
November	25	15	1.67	33	57	0.58	8	42	0.19
February	24	16	1.5	37	53	0.70	13	37	0.35
May	22	18	1.22	38	52	0.73	16	34	0.47

Subsequent Action

Share Price Rise

The best tactic in these circumstances is to continue to hold the existing position. The potential loss is already quantified and no further risk is being taken by staying put. Only if you feel that the price will continue to rise strongly should you contemplate any other course of action. One such course of action is to close out one leg of the spread to leave a bought call position in the case of a bear call spread, or a written put position in the case of a bear put spread. You will then be left holding either a high striking price call, or a written position in a low striking price put. Note that both of these may have moved into an in-the-money situation as a result of the share price rise. There is quite an amount of risk associated with deep in-the-money options, since subsequent price movement may be on a penny for penny basis with the share price itself, so that erosion of their value will be extremely rapid with an adverse share price trend.

Share Price Fall

A tactic other than continuing to hold the position should be employed only if you are totally convinced that the share price will continue to fall over the time remaining to expiry. If you are holding a bear put spread, one tactic is to close the position on the written put, leaving you holding a simple put option position, at a striking price that is now deeply in-the-money as a result of the share price fall. As with the position discussed above, subsequent adverse share price movement will rapidly diminish the value of this option, making it a high-risk holding. With a bear call spread, a corresponding tactic would be to close the position on the bought call, leaving a written call position, although this is not usually to be recommended in view of the low premiums associated with such calls, which give them a low profit potential for the degree of risk involved. A much better alternative is to roll down the entire spread.

Rolling Down

This is carried out by closing out the current spread and opening a new one at lower striking prices. There is an increased risk involved, since the break-even point is now lower, i.e. the share price has to fall much further than was the case with the original spread before the new position moves into profit. The possibilities are best illustrated by reference to Argyll options on 4th September 1995. The share price was 363p, and the premiums for January call options were: 330s, 42p; 360s, 24p; and 390s, 12p. An investor opened a 360/390 bear call spread by writing the 360s and buying the 390s, with the following potentials:

Maximum profit = net premium received = 24 − 12 = 12p
Maximum loss = 390 − 360 − 12 = 18p
P/L ratio = 0.67

By 14th September 1995, the share price had fallen to 346p, i.e., below the lower exercise price, and the investor, certain that a further fall was imminent, decided to stay on for the ride by aggressively rolling down to the 330/360 spread. The premiums for the January options were: 330s, 30p; 360s, 14p; and 390s, 6p.

To close the previous position, the steps are:

• Write the 390 option, premium received = 6p
• Buy the 360 option, premium paid = 14p
• Net outlay = 8p

Since an initial premium of 12p was received, the net profit is 4p, less of course dealing expenses.

To open the new position:

• Write the 330 option, premium received = 30p
• Buy the 360 option, premium paid = 14p
• Net premium received = 16p

Then

Maximum profit = net premium received = 16p
Maximum loss = 360 − 330 − 16 = 14p

The investor now has the potential to add a further 16p to the profit of 12p already received. Note that this maximum potential is only realised if the share price falls below 330p, and therefore the investor is operating at higher risk than in his initial position.

CALENDAR SPREADS

Although calendar spreads can be constructed so as to be bullish, bearish or neutral strategies, they are mostly used by investors who have neutral expectations for the share price. A neutral calendar spread will use options that are close to being at-the-money. In-the-money options should be avoided because of the risk that the written leg is exercised against the writer, thereby destroying the basis of the strategy.

The strategy involves the writing of a near-expiry option and the purchase of a further-expiry option. Although either puts or calls can be used, the time values of call options are usually somewhat higher than those of put options. Large time values for the written option makes the calendar spread particularly attractive, and so only call options are considered in this discussion. Before illustrating the profit/loss situation for calendar spreads by means of a diagram, it is useful to discuss the basic features that the investor should be looking for before taking his decision on the best calendar spread for the particular circumstances. Taking data already presented earlier, those given in Table 7.2 in Chapter 7 for LASMO, several calendar spreads could be constructed out of the 160 options on 12th January 1996. The share price was 176p, and the premiums for the three options were: February 180s, 6p; May 180s, 10p; and August 180s, 16p. The three calendar spreads possible from these options are:

1. Write February 180s, buy May 180s.
2. Write February 180s, buy August 180s.
3. Write May 180s, buy August 180s.

Ignoring the dealing costs and the spread of premiums between buying and writing the same options, the outlays for these three calendar spreads are:

- **Spread 1:** receive 6p for February 180s; pay 10p for May 180s; net outlay, i.e. maximum loss: 4p.
- **Spread 2:** receive 6p for February 180s; pay 16p for August 180s; net outlay, i.e. maximum loss: 10p.
- **Spread 3:** receive 10p for May 180s; pay 16p for August 180s; net outlay, i.e. maximum loss: 6p.

The simplest way of deciding between these three possibilities is to look at each leg of the spread independently, i.e. the best approach to the written leg and the best approach to the purchased leg.

As discussed in Chapter 8, time is to the disadvantage of the option writer, since a trend that initially is moving in the right direction may well reverse this direction within the timescale of a longer expiry option. Although there are sometimes good reasons to ignore this fact, for example the discovery that an option has an anomalously high premium, these should not be allowed to influence the situation with a calendar spread. Applying this principle to the three possibilities above, we would rule out strategy 3. For the near-expiry option, the objective is to find options with high time values, i.e. high CPP values, since these will reduce the overall cost of the spread. Since we are also looking for these to deteriorate as rapidly as possible, the ideal time is when there are about six weeks left to expiry, and the option has just started on its downward decay, as illustrated for example by Figure 5.4 in Chapter 5.

Out of the remaining two spreads we are faced with a simple choice: 4p downside potential for the medium expiry May option or 10p downside potential for the longer expiry August option. This time, the advantage lies with the longer expiry option, since as has been pointed out, there is more time for an adverse trend to rectify itself before expiry of the option. The only question is whether this advantage is worth the additional 6p per spread. Aspects such as CPP values, etc., as discussed in Chapter 7, should be taken into account before making the final decision. As always, the investor should be fairly clear as to the future direction of the share price from techniques such as channel analysis.

Loss/gain Potential—Limited Loss, Limited Gain

The potential for gain and loss has to be evaluated for the complete spread prior to the expiration of the written leg of the spread, since after this point the investor is left simply with a call option position. Because of this, the ideal combination to use, but one which may be difficult to find, will be options where the CPPs are high for the near expiry and low for the further expiry, and where the projected share price movement is sideways until the written option expires, and then sharply upwards in order to maximise the profit from the remaining leg.

The profit/loss potential for a calendar call spread is shown in Figure 11.3. The maximum loss occurs when the share price falls or rises below or above a share price band whose limits unfortunately cannot be calculated in advance. This is because these limits depend upon time values which of course cannot be predicted. However, the extent of the maximum loss is known, and this is the net outlay which has been made for the spread. As far as the maximum profit is concerned, again this cannot be quantified since we cannot predict the time values which might apply to the far option at the time of expiry of the near option. However, we can say at which share price the profit will be at its maximum, and that price is the striking price of the furthest option of the spread. This is because, as has been stated previously, time values are at their highest for at-the-money options, so that for maximum profit the furthest option should be standing at-the-money.

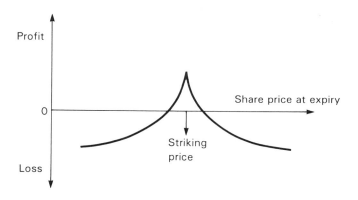

Figure 11.3 Profit and loss situation for a calendar spread at expiry

Subsequent Action

Naturally, if the share price behaviour you anticipated when you opened the spread is maintained, then you need do nothing more than leave the position as it is until expiry. Unlike the previous spreads in which the options all expired at the same time, with a calendar spread the first leg expires ahead of the second leg. At expiry of the first leg, therefore, you are left holding a call option with at least three months to go until expiry. This follow-on position would require you to have bullish expectations for the share price as opposed to the neutral expectations that you had when you opened the spread. You may of course have changed your view to a more bullish one, and if so should maintain your position of holding this call option. If your further expectations are for a continuing neutral share price, i.e. you have not changed your original stance, or if you now think the share price will fall, then you should close this second leg of the calendar spread, since otherwise your investment is not making further profit.

If the Share Price Falls

The action you should take following a share price fall depends upon whether you think the price fall will continue, the share price will stay neutral at its lower level, or the price will reverse direction and rise. If you think the fall will continue, then probably the best tactic is to liquidate the position, especially if this gives you a small profit. If you can see a fall to a lower level which you expect to remain stable, then you can roll down the option.

If you think the share price is now stable at a lower level, then the best tactic is to roll down.

If you think the share price will reverse direction and start to rise, then either you can close out the entire spread, hopefully still making a profit, or you can increase your profit potential by closing out the nearby written call, leaving yourself holding a further expiry call option, which of course is then the stance for a bullish investor, as discussed in Chapter 7. This will give you an unlimited profit potential, although of course since you will almost certainly be standing at a loss on the original position, because of the costs of closing the written call, the share price will have to rise a reasonable amount before you move into profit.

Rolling Down

This is the tactic to pursue if the price has fallen and you think the price will stabilise at this level, or you can anticipate a lower level at which the price will stabilise. Since we stated earlier that the maximum profit will be achieved if the spread expires in an at-the-money situation, then the striking prices for the rolled-down spread should be close to the price level at which you think the position will stabilise.

If an investor had initiated spread 1 of the three possible spreads, and he thinks the LASMO share price will fall from 176p to about 160p and then stabilise, then the steps required to close the original position and roll down are:

- Buy the near-expiry February 180 option
- Sell the further-expiry May 180 option
- Write the February 160 option
- Buy the May 160 option

The investor may be in the fortunate position of making at least a small profit on the original spread after all expenses, and will then have the opportunity of making a further profit on the rolled-down spread.

If the Share Price Rises

Action here depends upon whether you think the share price will continue to rise, will stay stable at a higher level, or will reverse direction and fall.

If you think the share price will continue to rise, then either you can close out the entire position, hopefully with a profit, or alternatively you can close the written leg of the spread, leaving yourself with a further expiry call option, which of course is the stance that a bullish investor would have adopted in any case.

If you think the share price will fall back, then it is probably sensible to continue to hold the position, so that it will move back towards the maximum profit position. An alternative if you now become more bearish is to adopt the stance which the bears would have had, i.e. to hold a written call position. This is of course achieved by closing the further expiry bought leg of the option, leaving you with the shorter expiry written option.

If you think the share price will stabilise at a higher level, then the best tactic is to roll up the spread.

Rolling Up

This is the tactic to pursue if the price has risen and you think the price will stabilise at this level, or you can anticipate a higher level at which the price will stabilise. Since we stated earlier that the maximum profit will be achieved if the spread expires in an at-the-money situation, then the striking prices for the rolled-up spread should be close to the price level at which you think the position will stabilise.

Using the LASMO case as an example, if we assume that an investor thinks the LASMO share price will rise from 176p to about 200p and then stabilise, then the steps required to close the original position and roll up are:

- Buy the near-expiry February 180 option
- Sell the further-expiry May 180 option
- Write the February 200 option
- Buy the May 200 option

The investor is now in the position of having the potential for further profit from this new spread, and may also have made a small profit on the original spread, depending on how far the price rise had gone before the decision to roll up was taken.

BUTTERFLY SPREADS

Butterfly spreads are strategies for those investors who have neutral expectation for the share price. Unlike the previous spreads which used only two legs, the butterfly spread has three components to it. Although puts can be used, calls have an advantage, and the butterfly is initiated by buying a call with a low striking price, writing two calls with middle striking prices and buying a call with a high striking price. The striking prices are normally chosen so as to be equally spaced, and for a neutral strategy, the middle striking price should be as close as possible to the share price. Naturally, one consequence of having so many legs to the strategy is that the dealing expenses will be higher than those for bull, bear or calendar spreads. The newcomer to traded options should avoid butterfly spreads until he has become experienced in all other traded option strategies, because it is often easy to open a butterfly where the chance of profit is extremely low.

Costs and Margin Requirements

If the butterfly is looked at as a combination of a bull call spread and a bear call spread, then the margin required by the butterfly is the margin that would be required by the bear spread half of the strategy, i.e. the difference between the two striking prices involved in this bear spread part.

Gain/loss Potential—Limited Gain, Limited Loss

The maximum loss which can be sustained in a butterfly is the difference (a net debit) between the premiums paid for the bought options and the premiums received for the two written contracts, plus of course the expenses involved in the overall transaction. The maximum gain is obtained when the share price is at the middle striking price, and the profit is equal to the difference between two adjacent striking prices and the original outlay. The situation is shown graphically in Figure 11.4. Since the profit is

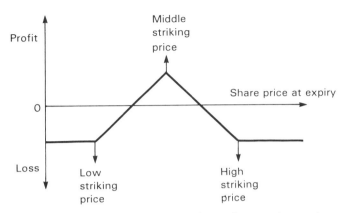

Figure 11.4   Profit and loss situation for a butterfly spread at expiry

dependent upon the spacing of the striking prices, obviously this profit is maximised if the striking prices can be chosen so as to be as far apart as possible. In the early life of options this is not possible due to the restricted number of striking prices available. The profit is also crucially dependent on the costs of the transactions, since the spread consists of three such transactions. The procedures used in identifying underpriced options by means of CPP values should be employed for the bought options, while the same procedures should be used to identify overpriced options for the written leg of the strategy. By this means the overall cost of the spread will be minimised. Adopting any other policy than this will make it a difficult strategy out of which to make any considerable profit.

Subsequent Action

Obviously if the share price stays more or less static at a similar level to the middle striking price, then the spread is achieving its objective, and no action needs to be taken. If the share price is falling or rising then action does need to be taken. This action of course will depend upon how you see the share price behaving after the current movement, i.e. whether it will reverse direction or continue in the same trend. One tactic that is usually not applicable to a butterfly is to roll down or roll up. This is because of the higher costs of closing and reopening the new positions in so many option series. It is possible that where you expect the share price to stabilise at a new lower or a new higher position, there may just be a glimmer of a profit in such a tactic, but it has to be looked at very closely before taking such action. A key to understanding how to deal with an adverse share price movement when holding a butterfly spread is to consider that the spread is simply composed of two other spreads—a bear call spread made from the bought high striking price option and one of the written medium striking price options, and a bull spread made from the bought low striking price option and the other written medium striking price option. Thus by closing out the appropriate half of the butterfly, the investor can be left holding either a bull call spread or a bear call spread, depending upon whether he thinks the share price will continue to rise if it is currently rising or will continue to fall if it is currently falling. If you think the present adverse trend will stabilise into a static share price which is higher or lower than you first anticipated, then provided this static share price is within the profit band for the spread, the best tactic is to continue to hold the position.

If the Share Price Rises

As we have mentioned, one tactic is to close out half of the spread, leaving a bull call spread in existence. To do this, the steps are:

- Write the high striking price option
- Buy one medium striking price option

This approach is the best if you have now changed to being moderately bullish for the share price. If you have become even more bullish of the share price, then you have another route available. This is to close out three of the four options, leaving you simply holding either the low striking price call option, which is now even further in-the-money, or the high striking price call, which may or may not have moved to an in-the-money position as a result of the share price rise.

If the Share Price Falls

As mentioned earlier, one tactic is to close out half of the spread, leaving a bear call spread in existence. The steps are:

- Write the low striking price option
- Buy one medium striking price option

This approach is best if you have now changed to being moderately bearish for the share price. If you feel even more bearish, then an alternative route available is to close out the bought high and low striking price options and perhaps one of the medium striking price options, leaving either one or two of the written calls in place.

Advanced Strategies 2. Straddles and Combinations

The advanced strategies discussed in the last chapter had one aspect in common—they involved either all call options or all put options, even though these may have had different striking prices or even different expiry dates. There is another way in which an option strategy can be built up, and that is by the use of both a call and a put at the same time. These strategies fall into two categories—straddles and combinations. Straddles are a restricted version of combinations in which the investor buys a put and a call option (buying a straddle) or writes a put and a call option (writing a straddle) with identical expiry dates and striking prices. In combinations, anything goes—it is possible to mix both expiry dates and striking prices, although the investor is still in the position of either buying the appropriate put and call or writing the appropriate put and call.

STRADDLES

Buying a Straddle

Here the investor buys a put and a call option on the same share, with both options having the same expiry date and the same exercise price. The straddle buyer is expecting the share price to move and not stay neutral, but the unusual aspect of the strategy is that the direction of the share price movement is immaterial. The straddle buyer will profit if the share price moves either upwards or downwards. This price movement has to be of a reasonable extent since the two option premiums will have been paid.

Profit/loss Potential—Unlimited Profit, Limited Loss

The graphical representation of the profit and loss situation is shown in Figure 12.1. The maximum loss which can be incurred is the sum of the

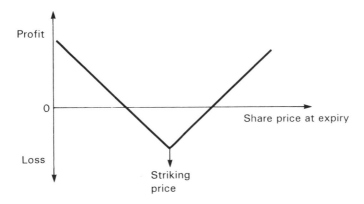

Figure 12.1   Profit and loss situation for a bought straddle at expiry

two premiums paid, plus of course the expenses involved in the transactions. The point of maximum loss is where the share price expires at the striking price of the straddle, i.e. where there has been no movement in the share price since the straddle was opened. The maximum profit is virtually unlimited, since the share price can either drop to zero, or rise indefinitely, although of course the original total premium paid and expenses have to be taken into consideration.

As an example we can take the investor interested in FTSE Index options. The Index had a rapid rise through the early part of April 1996, and on 19th April was standing at 3857.1, an all-time high. The investor was convinced that the least likely outcome was that the Index would stay at this level over the next month or two, but was unable to decide whether the FTSE would rise or fall from this position. The premiums for the June 3850 options were: calls, 80; puts, 69. Thus the combined cost of buying one contract in each would be 149 points (at £10 per point), plus expenses. The Index has to rise sufficiently from this position of 3857.1 to offset the initial cost of the put, which during such a rise will be falling in value. In the case of a fall, this must offset the initial cost of the call.

Action if the Share Price Rises

This is one of the outcomes that makes the straddle profitable, and therefore if you consider that the price rise will continue, then the only sensible course is to continue to hold the straddle. If you think the share price rise may reverse, so bringing you back below the break-even point into a potential loss situation, then the best tactic is to close the position, taking the existing profit, even though it may be smaller than you originally expected.

Action if the Share Price Falls

The same comment applies here as for a price rise. The strategy is working, so stay with it unless you feel the price fall may reverse, so eroding the profit that has accrued so far. The sensible course in this situation is to close the position, taking the existing profit.

Taking the investor who took out the straddle in the Index as an example, by 8th May the Index had fallen to 3707, and the premiums then were: calls, 13; puts, 160. The combined position was therefore worth 173 points, an increase of 16% over the initial cost (less expenses). It is obvious that the profitability of the position will grow rapidly if the Index continues to fall from the position on 8th May. Note, however, that it took a considerable fall in the Index to bring the position into a meaningful profit.

Action if the Share Price Remains Static

This, of course, is exactly the outcome that you do not want, since the profit in a straddle depends on price movement away from the original striking price at which the straddle was initiated. You can grin and bear it in the hope that a price movement will occur before the rapidly nearing expiry date, but of course the premiums of both the put and the call will be falling as a result of the disappearing time values. It is best to close out the position if you become convinced that no further movement will occur, so that you retrieve at least some of the premium still remaining in both options.

Writing a Straddle   NO NO NO ???

This is the opposite strategy to that employed by the straddle purchaser, and therefore the writer expects the opposite outcome, i.e. expects that the share price will remain static.

Price/loss Potential—Limited Profit, Unlimited Loss

The profit and loss situation for a written straddle is shown in Figure 12.2. Since the straddle writer has written both a put and a call option, he will receive a premium from both these transactions. This premium, less of course the expenses of the transactions, is the maximum profit that the straddle writer receives, and he will keep this if the share price stays within a short distance either side of the option striking price. Since the share price rise is unlimited, he may have the written call option exercised against him and have to pay this unlimited price to deliver the shares. Conversely, if the share price falls virtually to zero, he will have to buy the shares from the buyer of the put who will be exercising against him.

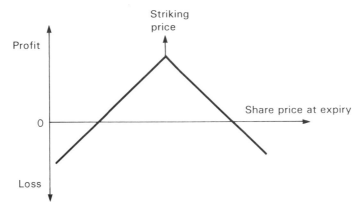

Figure 12.2   Profit and loss situation for a written straddle at expiry

Margin Requirements for Written Straddle

In this case, the writer will have to deposit a margin equivalent to 25% of the share price, plus an adjustment for the degree to which the put and call lies in-the-money. Naturally, since the share price will be constantly changing, then with a continually rising or falling share price, there will be constant calls to increase the margin. Because of the unlimited nature of the risk in a written straddle position, it should not be considered unless the writer is covered by holding the underlying shares.

Action if the Share Price Remains Static

As a writer you should continue to hold the position, since everything is proceeding according to plan. Only if you develop a feeling that this situation cannot last any longer should you take action. You then have the possibility of closing the position, which as a result of the static price so far should have seen premiums lose time value and thus give you a small profit on closing. If you feel you know in which direction the share price will start to move, then you can close one half of the straddle, leaving a written call if you think prices will fall, or a written put if you think prices will rise.

Action if the Share Price Rises

If and only if you are convinced that the rise is temporary and that the share price will fall back again, then continue to hold the position, since it will move back into profit. If you feel the rise will continue, then there are two courses of action—close out the whole position, taking either a small profit or a small loss, or close out the written call position, leaving you with a written put. This will reduce the risk of loss, although the profit potential will also be small.

Action if the Share Price Falls

As with a rising share price, you should maintain the position only if you are very convinced that the price fall is only temporary, and that the position will soon move back into profit. In any other circumstance you have two possibilities—either close out the whole straddle, possibly still with a small profit, or close out the written put position, leaving you with a written call. Again, this reduces the risk of loss, although the profit potential is small.

COMBINATIONS

Because of the variety of combinations possible, a book of this nature can cover only the fundamentals of such strategies. The best way of looking at combinations where a put and a call with the same expiries are either bought or written is that they are straddles which are biased one way or another as far as expected future movements of the underlying security are involved. The more usual combinations used are where the put and the call are both out-of-the-money and both are either bought or written.

Buying a Combination

Profit/loss Potential—Unlimited Profit, Limited Loss

The profit and loss situation for this strategy is shown in Figure 12.3. The maximum loss is the total premium paid, and the loss does not start to decrease until the share price moves outside either of the two share prices.

For the more usual case, the bought and written out-of-the-money combinations would have the striking price of the call above the current share price and the striking price of the put below the current share price. Thus, taking FTSE Index options as an example, the June premiums for 3900 calls and 3800 puts were 56 and 49 points respectively on 19th April. The position would therefore cost 105 points.

By 8th May, the 3900 calls were down to 2 and the 3800 puts up to 120, making the position worth 122 points, an increase of 16% from the initial cost.

If the investor is still convinced that the Index will not stay close to the current value, but is more inclined to think the Index will fall rather than rise, then the initial position can be biased so as to give a better profit in the event of a fall by using puts which are less out-of-the-money and calls which are more out-of-the-money.

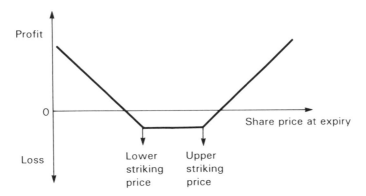

Figure 12.3   Profit and loss situation for a bought out-of-the-money combination at expiry

Thus, rather than 3900 calls and 3800 puts, the investor could go for 3950 calls and 3850 puts. On 19th April, the premiums for the June options were: 3950 calls, 37; 3850 puts, 69. Thus the total cost of the position is 106 points.

By 8th May the premiums were: 3950 calls, 1; 3850 puts, 160, making the position worth 161 points, a gain of 51%, compared with the 16% obtained when 3900s and 3800s were used.

Thus, in general, if you think the odds are say 60:40 in favour of a fall compared with a rise, then choose higher exercise prices. If you feel that a rise is more likely than a fall, choose lower exercise prices.

Subsequent Action

It is best to follow the same tactics as for a bought straddle, since the general principles are the same. If the share price is falling or rising, then leave the position as it is, since everything is then going to plan.

Writing a Combination

A written out-of-the-money combination is the strategy for the investor who expects the share price to remain more or less static between the two striking prices.

Profit/loss Potential—Limited Profit, Unlimited Loss

The profit and loss situation for this strategy is shown in Figure 12.4. The maximum profit is the sum of the two premiums received for writing each of the two options, less of course the expenses of the transactions. The profit does not start to decrease until the share price moves outside the upper or lower striking price.

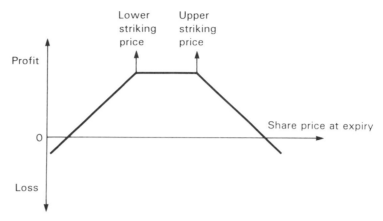

Figure 12.4 Profit and loss situation for a written out-of-the-money combination at expiry

Subsequent Action

Because of the unlimited nature of the loss with a written combination, it is important that action is taken at the first sign that the share price is moving away from the band between the two striking prices. The general tactics in such a situation are the same as those discussed above for written straddles.

In general, the risk involved with written straddles and combinations is not worth taking for the level of premiums which will be received from a typical transaction.

Finally, it is worth noting that a number of software packages are now available to test numerous strategies (see the Appendix). These will give the user an extremely valuable insight into the relationships between exercise prices, share price and premiums for the advanced strategies which have been discussed in the last two chapters.

Appendix

Addresses

For information, newsletters, expiry calendars, etc.

LIFFE Administration and Management
Cannon Bridge, London EC4R 3XX
Tel: 0171 623 0444
Fax: 0171 588 3624
Internet: http://www.liffe.com/

For microcomputer software (as used in this book) Microvest 5.0, Options Genius, Sigma-p, historical data on shares and options, investment course:

Qudos Publications Ltd
PO Box 27, Bramhall, Stockport, Cheshire SK7 1JH
Tel: 0161 439 3926
Fax: 0161 439 2327

Previous Editions by the Author

Stocks and Shares Simplified (3rd edn), ISBN 0-471-92131-9, published by John Wiley & Sons Ltd, Chichester.

Traded Options Simplified (1st edn), ISBN 1-871857-00-7, published by Qudos Publications, distributed by John Wiley & Sons Ltd, Chichester.

Channel Analysis (1st edn), ISBN 1-871857-02-3, published by Qudos Publications, distributed by John Wiley & Sons Ltd, Chichester.

Winning on the Stock Market (1st edn), ISBN 0-471-93881-5, published by John Wiley & Sons Ltd, Chichester.

Profitable Charting Techniques (1st edn), ISBN 1-871857-03-1, published by Qudos Publications, distributed by John Wiley & Sons Ltd, Chichester.

Index